T0215750

Communications
in Computer and Information Science   1550

More information about this series at https://link.springer.com/bookseries/7899

A. K. M. Muzahidul Islam · Jia Uddin ·
Nafees Mansoor · Shahriar Rahman ·
Shah Murtaza Rashid Al Masud (Eds.)

Bangabandhu and Digital Bangladesh

First International Conference, ICBBDB 2021
Dhaka, Bangladesh, December 30, 2021
Revised Selected Papers

 Springer

Editors
A. K. M. Muzahidul Islam 🆔
United International University
Dhaka, Bangladesh

Jia Uddin 🆔
Woosong University
Daejeon, Korea (Republic of)

Nafees Mansoor 🆔
University of Liberal Arts Bangladesh
Dhaka, Bangladesh

Shahriar Rahman 🆔
United International University
Dhaka, Bangladesh

Shah Murtaza Rashid Al Masud 🆔
University of Asia Pacific
Dhaka, Bangladesh

ISSN 1865-0929   ISSN 1865-0937 (electronic)
Communications in Computer and Information Science
ISBN 978-3-031-17180-2   ISBN 978-3-031-17181-9 (eBook)
https://doi.org/10.1007/978-3-031-17181-9

This Springer imprint is published by the registered company Springer Nature Switzerland AG
The registered company address is: Gewerbestrasse 11, 6330 Cham, Switzerland

Preface

It is my great pleasure to witness that the first International Conference on Bangabandhu and Digital Bangladesh (ICBBDB 2021) took place on the 100th anniversary of the birth of the Father of the Nation, Bangabandhu Sheikh Mujibur Rahman. This year Bangladesh also celebrated the 50th anniversary of Victory Day and the achievement of "Digital Bangladesh - Vision 2021".

Prime Minister Sheikh Hasina set her vision of transforming Bangladesh into a country of the digital economy by 2021 and a knowledge-based economy by 2041. Human Resource Development, Connecting Citizens, Digital Government, and Promotion of ICT Industry are among the four pillars of Digital Bangladesh. There is much need to cultivate research and innovation, and nurture young talent, in the area of ICT. Thus, to achieve Bangabandhu's Sonar Bangla and to transform Digital Bangladesh into Innovative Bangladesh it is important that we prioritize technology innovation, and focus research on the four pillars of Digital Bangladesh and the various development goals set by Bangabandhu to achieve Sonar Bangla. The aim of ICBBDB is to establish a platform to bring researchers from around the world together, encourage young home-grown talent to share their innovative and state-of-the-art ideas, and facilitate networking for further collaborations.

ICBBDB 2021 was organized by the Department of Computer Science and Engineering (CSE), United International University (UIU), Bangladesh. It was technically sponsored by Springer and financially supported by the ICT Division, Government of the People's Republic of Bangladesh. All accepted papers are included in this proceedings of ICBBDB 2021 published in Springer's CCIS series. The conference received 90 research papers from authors around the world, including Bangladesh, France, India, and China. The papers were submitted through Springer's OCS System. All submissions went through a careful anonymous review process (with three or more reviews per submission). Finally, only 18 papers were selected for regular oral presentation at the conference. The acceptance rate was thus only 20%, representing authors from 11 universities. Other than technical sessions, there were two keynote talks and two hands-on workshops on NLP and cybersecurity. ICBBDB 2021 also featured five technical sessions on scientific research of various topics.

N M Zeaul Alam, Honorable Senior Secretary, ICT Division, Government of the People's Republic of Bangladesh, was the Chief Guest while Khandoker Azizul Islam, Honorable Additional Secretary (ICT Promotion and Research Wing), ICT Division, Government of the People's Republic of Bangladesh was present as the Special Guest. The inauguration ceremony was chaired by Chowdhury Mofizur Rahman, Vice-chancellor of UIU. The welcome address was delivered by A.K.M. Muzahidul Islam, General Chair of ICBBDB 2021 and Professor, Department of CSE, UIU, and technical details were presented by Shahriar Rahman, Technical Program Committee Chair for ICBBDB 2021 and Associate Professor, Department of CSE,

UIU. We are grateful to everyone involved in ICBBDB 2021 for helping to make the conference a success.

Jia Uddin
Shahriar Rahman
Din M. Sumon Rahman
M. Mahfuzur Rahman

Organization

Patrons

Chowdhury Mofizur Rahman	UIU, Bangladesh
Mohammad Mahfuzul Islam	Canadian University of Bangladesh, Bangladesh
Habibullah N. Karim	Technohaven Company Ltd., Bangladesh

General Chair

A. K. M. Muzahidul Islam	UIU, Bangladesh

General Co-chairs

Alamgir Hossain	Teesside University, UK
Samiran Chattopadhyay	Jadavpur University, India
Khondaker Mizanur Rahman	Nanzan University, Japan
Vladimir Hahanov	Kharkiv National University of Radioelectronics, Ukraine
Rezaul Karim Milon	King Saud University, Saudi Arabia

Technical Program Committee Chairs

Jia Uddin	Woosong University, South Korea
Shahriar Rahman	JUST, Bangladesh
Din M. Sumon Rahman	ULAB, Bangladesh
M. Mahfuzur Rahman	JUST, Bangladesh

Publication Chair

Saddam Hossain	UIU, Bangladesh

Secretariat

Nafees Mansoor	ULAB, Bangladesh
Shah Murtaza Masud	GUB, Bangladesh
Ishtiak Al Mamoon	Presidency University, Bangladesh
Jebunnahar	Shanto-Mariam University of Creative Technology, Bangladesh

Publicity Chairs

Md. Hasibur Rahaman	JUST, Bangladesh
Atiqur Rahman	CIU, Bangladesh
Farzana Sultana	NICVD, Bangladesh

Information Technology Support

Mohammad Akter Hossain	UIU, Bangladesh
A. M. Fahad Hassan	UIU, Bangladesh

Technical Program Committee

M. Moshiul Hoque	CUET, Bangladesh
Salekul Islam	UIU, Bangladesh
Dewan Farid	UIU, Bangladesh
Swakkhar Shatabda	UIU, Bangladesh
Tariqul Islam	UKM, Malaysia
Md Zia Ullah	IRIT, France
Nabeel Mohammed	NSU, Bangladesh
Sifat Momen	NSU, Bangladesh
Motaharul Islam	UIU, Bangladesh
Muhammad Golam Kibria	ULAB, Bangladesh
Muhammad Nazrul Islam	MIST, Bangladesh
Shamim Ahmed	Rajshahi University, Bangladesh
Amitabha Chakrabarty	Brac University, Bangladesh
Moh A. Razzaque	Teesside University, UK
Mollah Md Zubaer	MIST, Bangladesh
Nurul Huda	UIU, Bangladesh
Aloke Kumar Shaha	UAP, Bangladesh
Kamruddin Nur	AIUB, Bangladesh
M. Zareei	Tecnológico de Monterrey, Mexico
Asim Zeb	Abbottabad University of Science and Technology, Pakistan
Mojtaba Alizadeh	Lorestan University, Iran
N. Syazwani	UiTM, Malaysia
Muhammad Firoz Mridha	AIUB, Bangladesh
Sadiq Iqbal	Bangladesh University, Bangladesh
Obaidur Rahman	EUB, Bangladesh
Bijan Paul	ULAB, Bangladesh
Sabrina Sworna	UIU, Bangladesh
Tama Fouzder	ULAB, Bangladesh
Asaduzzaman Asad	CUET, Bangladesh

Jannatun Naeem Muna	EUB, Bangladesh
Mobarak Hossain	Asian University of Bangladesh, Bangladesh
S. M. Shovan	RUET, Bangladesh
Md. Rakibul Haque	RUET, Bangladesh
Shahrum Shah Abdullah	UTM, Malaysia
M. Alam	UAP, Bangladesh
Nejib Moalla	DISP, Université Lumière Lyon 2, France
M. Nazim Uddin	East Delta University, Bangladesh
M. Moinul Islam	East Delta University, Bangladesh
Rudra Pratap Deb Nath	University of Chittagong, Bangladesh
Md. Nawab Yousuf Ali	East West University, Bangladesh
Adnan Quaium	AUST, Bangladesh
Syed Mustafizur	Standard University, Bangladesh
Ohidujjaman	Daffodil International University, Bangladesh
Hasan Tinmaz	Woosong University, South Korea
Md. N. Hoque	Bangabandhu Sheikh Mujibur Rahman Science and Technology University, Bangladesh
Md. Shajalal Hossain	Hajee Mohammad Danesh Science and Technology University, Bangladesh
Emranul Haque	IUB, Bangladesh

Contents

Dengue Outbreak Prediction from Weather Aware Data

Mazharul Islam Leon🆔, Md Ifraham Iqbal$^{(\boxtimes)}$🆔, Sadaf Meem🆔,
Furkan Alahi🆔, Morshed Ahmed🆔, Swakkhar Shatabda🆔,
and Md Saddam Hossain Mukta$^{(\boxtimes)}$🆔

Department of Computer Science and Engineering, United International University
(UIU), Madani Avenue, Badda, Dhaka, Bangladesh
{mleon153031,miqbal161282,smeem153048,falahi161212,
mahmed162036}@bscse.uiu.ac.bd, {swakkhar,saddam}@cse.uiu.ac.bd

Abstract. Vector-borne disease-carrying insects like the female Aedes Aegypti mosquitoes are the most active when the temperature is between 16–40 °C. The weather in Bangladesh is always in the range mentioned. In addition to that, Bangladesh has high humidity, which is a striking factor. Therefore, the country has a higher threat of being acutely affected by dengue outbreaks. In the previous studies conducted, researchers found that dengue has a strong association with weather attributes. In this study, we predict the degree of dengue outbreak for a specific area using the Directorate General of Health Services (DGHS) data. We build a hybrid dataset from 2 different sources: the Directorate General of Health Services (DGHS) and the Weather API (Darksky). To determine the degree of dengue outbreak (namely- *high, medium,* and *low*) in a region, we use a Convolutional Neural Network (CNN) based on the SuperTML approach. Alongside this method, we also apply the traditional classifiers. We find that the CNN using SuperTML achieves excellent performance with an accuracy of 0.74, which is significantly higher than the results achieved by the traditional classifiers.

Keywords: Dengue · Outbreak · Weather · CNN · Classification

1 Introduction

Dengue is a vector-borne (blood-feeding anthropoids, i.e., *Aedes Aegypti, Aedes albopictus*) disease that is transmitted by an infected mosquito. The mosquito's bite transmits the infectious dengue disease in other living beings. Dengue is most prone to the warm tropical belt of the globe [8]. As the tropical belt of the globe includes Bangladesh, dengue outbreaks may occur at a more severe degree there. The tropical weather, dense population and rapidly changing environment in Bangladesh work like a catalyst in dengue outbreaks. Therefore, we propose an automated system that can predict the degree of dengue outbreak from relevant weather attributes.

A. K. M. M. Islam et al. (Eds.): ICBBDB 2021, CCIS 1550, pp. 1–11, 2022.
https://doi.org/10.1007/978-3-031-17181-9_1

Previous studies [11] report that the Dhaka division is among the most affected region with a peak transmission of dengue outbreaks during the monsoon and post-monsoon season [21]. Hu et al. [11] find that weather has a strong correlation in propagating dengue among human communities. From May to August 2019, 49.73% of the dengue cases occurred during the monsoon season, while 49.22% of the dengue cases occurred during the post-monsoon season.

The disease is considered deadly and can cause health damages like plasma leakage, respiratory distress and organ impairment in affected patients [19]. Dengue is now a global epidemic. Research by Shepard et al. [20] demonstrates how the dengue disease burdens the economy around the globe. They find that in 2013, there was a total of 54 million symptomatic dengue virus infections, of which more than 13 Million fatal cases have been reported. The total annual global cost of dengue illness was US$8.9 billion with global distribution of 18% hospitalized, 48% ambulatory and 34% non-medical. The authors of [19] emphasize predicting dengue outbreak that could save billions of dollars, hence serving a need for policymakers, donors, developers, and researchers for economic assessment.

In recent times, studies have been conducted all over the world [4,7] to determine how the weather attributes affect dengue outbreaks. We observe that the same method and attributes used in [4,7] cannot be applicable for South Asia demographics (that includes Bangladesh). Studies [13,15] show the correlation between the degree of dengue outbreak and the weather in the context of Bangladesh. However, this research is not comprehensive because authors use a limited number of weather attributes, i.e., wind, temperature, etc. In our paper, we first build a new data set where we cross-link the dengue data taken from Directorate General of Health Services (DGHS)[1] and weather data (i.e., at least with 36 varied attributes) from a popular weather forecasting API, DarkSky[2]. Then, we use a CNN-based SuperTML model [22] to predict dengue outbreak for a specific region using tabular data successfully.

In summary, the objectives of this study are as follows:

– Building a hybrid dataset using DGHS dengue data and weather data from Dark Sky API.
– Performing Area Based Classification to predict the degree of infected dengue patients (i.e., high, medium, and low) based on weather features.

2   Literature Review

Researchers conduct different studies [23,24] to understand the correlation between weather and dengue outbreak. Wang et al. [23] conducted a study in China where they used weather attributes to predict dengue outbreak using

---

[1] https://dghs.gov.bd/index.php/en/mis-docs/epi/81-english-root/5200-daily-dengue-status-report.
[2] https://darksky.net/dev.

data from 2002 to 2018. However, the method required home-to-home inspection, which is practically not feasible. Wu et al. [24] meanwhile use Wavelet Transformation to find the correlation between actual and predicted data in Singapore. Weather data play a huge factor and assist the prediction. Choi et al. [5] also conducted a similar study but used weather data to create a negative binomial model and successfully predicted the degree of dengue outbreak for up to 90 days.

Despite the global study of dengue worldwide, none of these methods are applicable for Bangladesh demographics due to the differences in the weather. For Bangladesh, Karim et al. [15] and Islam et al. [13] conduct studies using data from the DGHS and weather data from the Meteorological Department at Dhaka. Both the studies associated climatic factors like rainfall, humidity, and temperature in the post-monsoon region to significantly impact the number of dengue patients. However, due to the unreliability of the data, the prediction models perform poorly.

However, previous studies show how effective they can be. Ibrahim et al. [12] use clustering to generate heat maps that display the infected regions and the severity of the infections. Nejal et al. [18] use several ML models on their dengue datasets which consist of weather and dengue patients data. Altogether the conclusion stands that the weather has a close correlation to the number of dengue cases. However, research for Bangladesh demographics could not use extended weather attributes and adequate ML model successfully, and hence the results were not satisfactory.

3   Methodology

For identifying the degree of dengue outbreak in the context of Bangladesh, we first build a new dataset as shown in Fig. 1. DarkSky has more than 36 weather features: cloud, dew point, moon phase, sunrise, UV-index, wind direction, etc. On the other hand, the medical information in the DGHS website contains the daily admitted patients affected by Dengue. The data from these two sources are combined to build the dengue dataset. Finally, we build an ML model to predict the degree of dengue outbreak for Dhaka city.

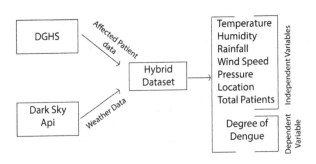

Fig. 1. Process of building our hybrid dataset.

4   Data Collection

We use both weather attributes and affected patients of different locations to create our hybrid dataset. The DGHS records the number of people affected and hospitalized due to dengue fever. The entry of the number of patients is recorded daily. We recorded the number of patients admitted from 27th August 2019 to 31st January 2020 from 27 hospitals. From this data, we find the number of people hospitalized and died that occur due to dengue. Note that due to the COVID-19 pandemic, we find less data on who is infected with dengue from March 2020 to June 2021.

For accessing weather attributes, we use the Dark Sky API. The API has 36 weather features like - *humidity, liquid precipitation rate, sunrise/sunset, temperature, UV index, wind speed, etc.* Dark Sky API returns a JSON object, which contains daily forecasting weather attributes. These weather attributes might have an immense relationship with the outbreak of dengue. Table 1 shows the statistics of our dataset. From the given data, we find that the weather data tends to be very similar due to the hospitals being in the same area. To avoid having identical weather data, we cluster the 27 hospitals into seven regions. The Table 2 below discusses which hospital situates in which region.

Table 1. Statistics of our dataset.

Total # of instances	1,401
Total # of weather attributes	36
Total # of selected features	14
# of admitted patients/day	60.3
Total # of days for data collection	230 days

5   Feature Engineering

In this paper, we use *Pearson Correlation* and *Multi Collinearity* for dimensionality reduction of the dataset. Afterward, we convert the dataset trainable for a classification problem. We use three classes for the range of values for the number of infected patients for each area.

Temperature Attributes: Temperature plays a significant role in shifting the conditions of the weather. Correlation between the temperature and dengue outbreak helps to measure how strongly associated these variables are. Increasing temperature increases the available habitat for the dengue fever vector- the Aedes aegypti mosquito. When the temperature increases, their breeding period shortens, leading to increased growth of population. Rising temperature increases the transmission rate of dengue fever as they grow faster [14]. From previous studies [10], it is evident that temperature is considered a vital attribute in the outbreak of dengue. Table 3 presents *P-value* (<0.05) and R (correlation) values of the temperature attributes.

Table 2. Clustering the Hospitals into zones

Zone	Hospital	Admt. Patients
DMC	Dhaka Medical College, Sir Salimullah Medical College	4,785
Shahabag	Bangabandhu Sheikh Mujib Medical University, Holy Family Red Crescent Medical college, Birdem Hospital Square Hospital, Samorita Hospital	1,315
Mohammodpur	Dhaka shishu Hospital, shahid suhrawardy medical college, Bangladesh, Specialized Hospital	1,501
Dhanmondi	Ibn Sina Hospital, Labaid Hospital, Central Hospital, Green Life Medical College Hospital, Popular Medical College Hospital, Anwer Khan Modern Medical College Hospital	945
Mirpur	Delta Hospital	151
Mohakhali	Universal hospital	72
Motijeel	police hospital. Islami Bank Central Hospital, Asgar Ali Hospital	200
Uttara	Hi-Care General Hospital, Shaheed Monsur Ali Medical College and Hospital	272
Gulshan	United Hospital, Apollo Hospital	142

Wind and Precipitation Attributes: Precipitation occurs when a portion of the atmosphere becomes saturated with water vapor so that the water condenses and eventually precipitates. The precipitation creates abundant outdoor breeding sources for Aedes aegypti, and the water storage containers can also serve as breeding habitats. Regarding the importance of correlations between the weather attributes and dengue outbreak, a study [10] shows that Wind and Precipitation are highly correlated with the dengue outbreak. Intense thunderstorms and winds can start a dust storm that can drastically reduce visibility. This measurement is known as the Wind Dust attribute. Wind directly affects the evaporation rates of vector breeding sites. Strong winds reduce mosquito density and make it difficult to find a host. Table 3 presents the correlation between wind and precipitation attributes with dengue incidence correlation.

Other Attributes. Dew point is the temperature in the air that needs to hold moisture in order to achieve humidity. Thus, the higher the dew point, the greater the moisture in the air. The breeding factor for the vector increases [10] due to dew point. From Table 3 above, we can say that the R-values from the Pearson correlation is 0.343, which represents a moderate correlation with a dengue outbreak.

Collinearity is the condition where independent variables are highly correlated. These variables have a perfect linear combination of one another in the model [6]. Collinearity becomes a concern in analysis when there is a high correlation or an association between two potential predictor variables when there is a dramatic increase in the P-value (i.e., reduction in the significance level). The variance inflation factor (VIF) provides a measure of the degree of collinearity. VIF can be found using Eq. 1.

Table 3. Correlation between the # of patients and weather attributes

Weather attributes	Correlation with the patients admitted	
	p-values	r-values
Moon phase	0.311	−0.027
Precipitation intensity	0.000	0.137
Precipitation intensity max	0.000	0.152
Precipitation probability	0.000	0.203
Temperature high	0.000	0.329
Temperature low	0.000	0.359
App. temperature high	0.000	0.392
App. temperature low	0.386	0.000
Dew point	0.000	0.343
Humidity	0.000	0.184
Pressure	0.000	−0.420
Wind speed	0.241	0.000
Wind dust	0.191	0.000
Wind bearing	0.000	−0.158
Cloud cover	0.000	0.265
UV index	0.000	0.146
Visibility	0.150	−0.038
Ozone	0.000	0.093
Temperature min	0.000	0.357
Temperature max	0.331	0.000
App. temperature min	0.000	0.383
App. temperature max	0.000	0.393

$$VIF = \frac{1}{1 - R_i^2} \tag{1}$$

Generally, VIF values greater than 100 are problematic, VIF greater than 5 is cause for concern, and VIF is greater than 10 indicates a serious collinearity problem [1]. VIF greater or equal to 2.5 indicates considerable collinearity. We remove variables with a VIF score greater than or equal to 2.5. Therefore we conclude that among all the weather variables we discard *ApparentTempMin*, *ApparentTempMax*, *ApparentTempHigh*, *ApparentTempLow*, *Dewpoint*, *and Humidity* due to values exceeding 100. Finally, Table 4 shows the following 14 attributes are the correlated features that we use while building our classification model.

Table 4. Final correlated features.

pressure	tempMin	tempLow	temp.Max	prepInten
precipProb.	windGust	windBearing	uvIndex	ozone
temp.High	cloudCover	windSpeed	prepInt.Max	

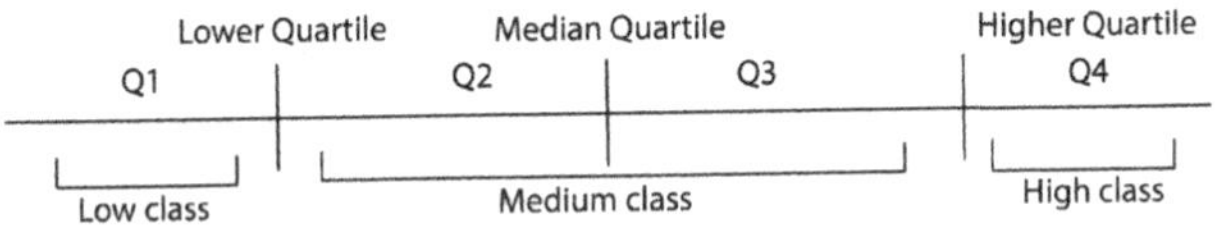

Fig. 2. Class level discretization from the number of affected patients

5.1   Class Level Discretization for Affected Patients

The dataset is divided into three different quartiles. A quartile divides data into three points—a lower quartile, median, and upper quartile—to form four dataset groups. Since two standard deviations inside the mean have the highest number of values in the normal distribution, we also take a medium-class by merging both Q2 and Q3 quartiles. In our research, we considered 0 to the lower quartile to be Q1, from lower quartile to median as Q2, from median to upper quartile as Q3 and from upper quartile to 100 is considered Q4. Hence, the instances that lie between the 0 to lower quartile range are classified as class 0 and represent a low number of dengue patients. The data points between the upper quartile to the 100th quartile are considered Class 2 and represent a high number of dengue patients. Lastly, the data points between the lower quartile to the median and from median to the upper quartile, that is, Q2 and Q3, are considered to be class 1 and represent a medium number of dengue patients. Now from the previous section, as shown in Table 4.2, Finally, we classify the number of patients into three classes- *Low, Medium,* and *High*. Figure 2 shows the class level discretization for the dataset. *Low* class represents instances where the number of patients is eight or less, *Medium* represents instances where the number of infected patients is between 9 and 20, and *High* represents instances with infected patients that are greater than 21.

Table 5. Performance comparison of our experiments on the dengue dataset

Model name	Accuracy	Precision	Recall	F1-Score
Ada Boost Classifier	59.46%	0.59	0.59	0.59
k-Nearest Neighbour	63.74%	0.58	0.58	0.57
Random Forest	60.53%	0.58	0.58	0.58
Light Gradient Boost	60.89%	0.61	0.61	0.60
Logistic Regression	65.16%	0.65	0.65	0.65
Gradient Boost	60.88%	0.61	0.61	0.61
SuperTML + Resnet-18	74%	0.75	0.74	0.74

6   Results and Discussion

This section presents the results achieved from our dataset by using ML and DL models to predict dengue outbreaks. Then we discuss the impacts of our study and the challenges we face while conducting the research.

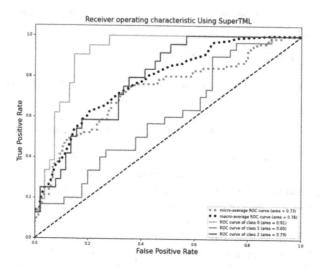

Fig. 3. ROC Curve for SuperTML on dengue test dataset.

We split our training and testing datasets as 70% and 30%, respectively. Then, we train several traditional ML models with 10-fold cross-validation with ten iterations to classify the degree of dengue outbreak in a specific area. We use Python and the scikit-learn[3] library for implementing the traditional classifiers and predicting dengue outbreak. Additionally, we also apply the SuperTML [22] which uses two-dimensional embeddings to create images for each instance, thus creating an image dataset for dengue outbreak prediction. We use the open-source library OpenCV to create the images for each instance[4]. As a result, this enables us to use DL models on the dataset. The results from our experiments are displayed in Table 5. We use the pretrained Resnet-18 [9] model on the image dataset created by using SuperTML. For training the Resnet-18 model, we use the Cross-Entropy loss function alongside the Stochastic Gradient Descent optimizer with a learning rate of 0.001. We also use an exponential learning rate decay with the optimizer. We use the open-source machine learning framework Pytorch[5] for classification on the dengue image dataset with Resnet-18. From the results in Table 5 we observe that the Resnet-18 model using SuperTML obtains an accuracy of 74%, which outperforms most traditional ML classifiers

---

[3] https://scikit-learn.org/stable/.

[4] https://opencv.org/.

[5] https://pytorch.org/.

like KNN, RF, Logistic Regression. In this study, we find that the DL model can perform better than traditional ML models. We observe that the traditional classifiers produces subpar results in predicting dengue outbreak. The KNN is a lazy classifier and hence cannot produce high precision scores. On the other hand, tree-based techniques like Random Forest produce poor results, most likely due to the coincidental selection of a subset of weakly correlated features.

The SuperTML [22] performs outstanding while learning tasks on tabular data. We adopt this strategy in our research to compare the performance of deep learning models to that of classic machine learning classifiers. Amongst the traditional classifiers, the K Nearest Neighbor and Logistic Regression perform much better than the tree-based classifiers [3]. However, the SuperTML+Resnet-18 model performs significantly better than all traditional classifiers due to its ability to extract information from images. The results are much better for the *low* and *high* classes which suggest this model can be used in other datasets for predicting the degree of impact of other epidemic diseases. Figure 3 shows that the ROC curve for our test dataset. The ROC curve using SuperTML shows that the classifier can provide excellent discrimination amongst the three classes (i.e., AUC = 0.73).

We observe that the advent of dengue has an extremely close relationship with the weather factors like- temperature attributes, rainfall precipitation, humidity. An increase in humidity and temperature raises the breeding of the Aedes Agypytie mosquito (vector-borne disease-carrying insect). It also increases the transmission of dengue. Our model can predict the tentative time frame of prolonging dengue outbreaks that can be helpful to make an economic decision that can save time, money, lives, and capital.

In this study, we provide a methodology to predict dengue outbreaks for Bangladesh demographics. However, there are many issues associated with this study. Firstly, due to the hospitals being located very close to one another, the changes in weather attributes are sometimes identical for a group of hospitals. Hence, we cluster the hospitals into various regions. Secondly, we use the Darksky API for collecting historical weather data [17]. However, Darksky only allows us 1000 API calls per week, and hence it takes us a long time to collect the weather data. Lastly, due to the COVID-19 pandemic, the patient number and dengue victims are less than usual [2]. Hence, it becomes impossible to forecast dengue outbreaks for the year of 2021 by using our methodology due to temporal nature of the outbreak [16].

7   Conclusion

In this paper, we have created a dengue dataset by merging the daily dengue incidence notification from the DGHS and daily weather data from the Dark Sky API. The existing dataset used in the previous studies contained missing or incorrect values, leading to a less favorable outcome. In order to solve this issue, we have built a hybrid dataset for better dengue outbreak prediction. More transparent statistical information on the data can help future researchers to select the ML models. In the future, we plan to make the dataset more enriched by adding more demographic features.

CRediT Author Statement. Mazharul Islam Leon: Methodology, Software **Md Ifraham Iqbal:** Writing - Original Draft, Investigation, Methodology, Data Curation, Software, Visualization, Formal Analysis, Project Administration **Sadaf Meem:** Writing - Original Draft, Investigation, Formal Analysis **Furkan Alahi:** Software, Investigation, Visualization **Morshed Ahmed:** Investigation, Data Curation **Swakkhar Shatabda:** Writing - Review and Editing, Supervision, Validation, Resources **Md. Saddam Hossain Mukta:** Writing - Review and Editing, Conceptualization, Supervision, Validation, Resources, Project Administration.

References

1. Ahmad, M.H., Adnan, R., Adnan, N.: A comparative study on some methods for handling multicollinearity problems. MATEMATIKA Malays. J. Ind. Appl. Math. 109–119 (2006)
2. Ahmed, A., Mukta, M.S.H., Muntasir, F., Rahman, S., Islam, A.N., Ali, M.E.: Can COVID-19 change the Big5 personality traits of healthcare workers? In: 7th International Conference on Networking, Systems and Security, pp. 12–17 (2020)
3. Al Rafi, A.S., Rahman, T., Al Abir, A.R., Rajib, T.A., Islam, M., Mukta, M.S.H.: A new classification technique: random weighted LSTM (RWL). In: 2020 IEEE Region 10 Symposium (TENSYMP), pp. 262–265. IEEE (2020)
4. Cheong, Y.L., Burkart, K., Leitão, P.J.: Assessing weather effects on dengue disease in Malaysia. IJERPH **10**(12), 6319–6334 (2013)
5. Choi, Y., et al.: Effects of weather factors on dengue fever incidence and implications for interventions in Cambodia. BMC Public Health **16**(1), 241 (2016)
6. Daoud, J.I.: Multicollinearity and regression analysis. In: Journal of Physics: Conference Series, vol. 949, p. 012009. IOP Publishing (2017)
7. Estallo, E.L., et al.: A decade of arbovirus emergence in the temperate southern cone of South America: dengue, Aedes aegypti and climate dynamics in Córdoba, Argentina. bioRxiv (2020)
8. Gubler, D.J.: Epidemic dengue/dengue hemorrhagic fever as a public health, social and economic problem in the 21st century. Trends Microbiol. **10**(2), 100–103 (2002)
9. He, K., Zhang, X., Ren, S., Sun, J.: Deep residual learning for image recognition. In: Proceedings of the IEEE Conference on Computer Vision and Pattern Recognition, pp. 770–778 (2016)
10. Hii, Y.L., Zhu, H., Ng, N., Ng, L.C., Rocklöv, J.: Forecast of dengue incidence using temperature and rainfall. PLoS Negl. Trop. Dis. **6**(11), e1908 (2012)
11. Hu, W., et al.: Forecasting climate change impacts on locally-transmitted dengue fever. Environ. Epidemiol. **3**, 166 (2019)
12. Ibrahim, N., Akhir, N.S.M., Hassan, F.H.: Using clustering and predictive analysis of infected area on dengue outbreaks in Malaysia. J. Telecommun. Electron. Comput. Eng. (JTEC) **9**(2–12), 51–58 (2017)
13. Islam, M.Z., et al.: Correlates of climate variability and dengue fever in two metropolitan cities in Bangladesh. Cureus **10**(10) (2018)
14. Kakarla, S.G., et al.: Lag effect of climatic variables on dengue burden in India. Epidemiol. Infect. **147** (2019)

15. Karim, M.N., Munshi, S.U., Anwar, N., Alam, M.S.: Climatic factors influencing dengue cases in Dhaka city: a model for dengue prediction. Indian J. Med. Res. **136**(1), 32 (2012)
16. Mukta, M.S.H., Ali, M.E., Mahmud, J.: Temporal modeling of basic human values from social network usage. J. Am. Soc. Inf. Sci. **70**(2), 151–163 (2019)
17. Nawshin, S., Mukta, M.S.H., Ali, M.E., Islam, A.N.: Modeling weather-aware prediction of user activities and future visits. IEEE Access **8**, 105127–105138 (2020)
18. Nejad, F.Y., Varathan, K.D.: Identification of significant climatic risk factors and machine learning models in dengue outbreak prediction. BMC Med. Inform. Decis. Mak. **21**(1), 1–12 (2021)
19. World Health Organization: Dengue and severe dengue. Technical report, WHO, Regional Office for the Eastern Mediterranean (2014)
20. Shepard, D.S., Undurraga, E.A., Halasa, Y.A., Stanaway, J.D.: The global economic burden of dengue: a systematic analysis. Lancet. Infect. Dis **16**(8), 935–941 (2016)
21. Singh, P., et al.: The first dominant co-circulation of both dengue and chikungunya viruses during the post-monsoon period of 2010 in Delhi, India. Epidemiol. Infect. **140**(7), 1337–1342 (2012)
22. Sun, B., et al.: SuperTML: two-dimensional word embedding for the precognition on structured tabular data. In: Proceedings of the IEEE Conference on Computer Vision and Pattern Recognition Workshops (2019)
23. Wang, X., et al.: A combination of climatic conditions determines major within-season dengue outbreaks in Guangdong Province, China. Parasit. Vectors **12**(1), 45 (2019)
24. Wu, Y., Lee, G., Fu, X., Hung, T.: Detect climatic factors contributing to dengue outbreak based on wavelet, support vector machines and genetic algorithm (2008)

A Dynamic Approach to Identify the Most Significant Biomarkers for Heart Disease Risk Prediction Utilizing Machine Learning Techniques

Faria Rahman$^{(\boxtimes)}$ (iD) and Md. Ashiq Mahmood (iD)

Institute of Information and Communication Technology (IICT), Khulna University of Engineering and Technology, Khulna, Bangladesh
fariarahman337@gmail.com, ashiqmahmoodbipu@gmail.com

Abstract. Coronary artery disease is a well-known term among us, since the number of persons affected is steadily growing. Low- and middle-income nations bear the burden of the consequences. This is the leading cause of mortality on a global scale. Cardiovascular disease should be detected as soon as possible. It cannot be cured, but can be stabilized by controlling symptoms and reducing the risk of complications. We can extract the potential explanation for it by analyzing biological data; therefore we put the data into our suggested model and try to highlight the most significant possible result of early heart disease. We have utilized three strategies for concentrating on features in our suggested model: Lasso, Mutual Information, and Recursive Feature Elimination approaches, as well as three classification algorithms: K-Nearest Neighbors, Random Forest and Naive Bayes. These are done by using 10-fold cross validation procedure in this study. We have also employed the Bagging ensemble approach with Random Forest to improve the result. Our suggested model has given 85.18% accuracy through Recursive Feature Elimination with Bagging (Random Forest).

Keywords: Random Forest · K-Nearest Neighbors · Naive Bayes · Bagging · Heart disease

1 Introduction

Heart disease is such a major public health issue because when the heart experiences problems, the entire body suffers. The heart is a fist-sized muscle. It circulates blood throughout body at a rate of 70 beats per minute. Blood flows to the lungs to pick up oxygen after leaving the heart's right side. The blood returns to heart by carrying full of oxygen, where it is pushed to the body's organs via a network of arteries. Blood returns to the heart via veins before being sent back to the lungs. Every year, 17 million people worldwide are affected by cardiovascular illnesses such as heart attacks and strokes [1]. CVDs include rheumatic heart disease and various cardiovascular diseases, four out of every five CVD deaths are caused by heart strokes and attacks, with one-third of these deaths happening before the age of 70 [2]. Small blood arteries are crucial for delivering oxygen and blood to the heart, and as these channels narrow, coronary heart disease develops, as the arteries constrict, blood flow begins to slow, this can cause a chest pain, heart attack, and shortness of breath [3]. Finding out what's causing the problems, as well as the risk factors and conditions that come with heart disease, is more essential. Computer-assisted diagnostics for coronary heart disease has grown in popularity alongside the advancement of information technology. Data analysis is a strategy for dealing with massive amounts of data. In the medical field, machine learning helps to analyze data for uncovering hidden patterns in medical datasets [4].

Cardiovascular disease is a broad phrase that refers to a range of heart-related illnesses. This is linked to, chest pain, blood vessel difficulties, irregular heartbeats, cardiac muscle disorders and so on. Shortness of breath, exhaustion, lightheadedness, pressure or chest pain, and numb or cold extremities are only a few of the well-known worrisome indications. The heart's perfect functioning ensures the existence of any creature because the other organs are completely reliant on it [5]. Heart performs a critical role in maintaining our required essential nutrition and oxygen in bodily components [6].

In our experiment, we have used three feature selection methods to recognize the features that are most closely related and have a good impact on the Statlog heart disease dataset, and then we have used these three classifier techniques for each of the feature selection methods. We also have employed the Bagging ensemble technique with Random Forest to improve the outcome. Six retrieved features through Recursive Feature Elimination with Bagging (Random Forest) have explored higher efficiency result.

2 Related Works

Bendi Venkata Ramana et al. [7] On medical datasets, this research investigates a few categorization techniques. Bagging, JRip, IBK, Naive Bayes (NB), Multilayer Perceptron (MP), and J48 classifiers are among the classification techniques explored in this work. Where, the accuracy of Naive Bayes classifiers for Statlog (Heart) datasets has given 83.7%.

M. Haider Abu Yazid et al. [8] this research has proposed ann parameter tuning for the datasets from the UCI machine learning data collection. The impact of the proposed system has analyzed using two different heart datasets. Where, the dataset has been separated into three sections: 80% training, 10% testing and 10% validation.

Jan Bohacik et al. [9] the study has used the Statlog Heart Database to investigate a probabilistic method to heart disease identification using Naive Bayes and provides a numerical attribute discretization strategy that takes individual heart disease patients' characteristics into considerations. Experiments utilizing Age, Serum Cholesterol Level, Resting Blood Pressure, Maximum Achieved Heart Rate, Colored Vessels, and ST Segment Depression attributes using 10-fold cross-validation indicate enhancements in accuracy as assessed by sensitivity, specificity, and their sum.

Kemal Akyol et al. [10] First, using feature selection methods such as RFECV and Stability Selection, the best characteristics set for SPECT and Statlog Heart Disease datasets has identified. Second, RFECV and SS techniques have used to develop Gradient Boosted Machines, Naive Bayes, and Random Forest algorithms on original datasets as well as datasets with specified attributes. Using twelve attributes of the STATLOG dataset provided by the SS technique yielded the best accuracy.

Randa El-Bialy et al. [11] the objective of this research is to merge machine learning findings, analyses performed on several datasets to target the CAD disease. According to the findings, the acquired dataset's classification accuracy is 78.06% higher than the 75.48% classification accuracy of all independent datasets.

Chaitrali S. Dangare et al. [12] this study has examined at prediction algorithms for heart disease that have a larger number of input features. To estimate the chance of a patient developing heart disease, the algorithm employs 13 variables. Obesity and smoking were added as new features in this study. The effects of classification algorithms such as Naive Bayes, Neural Networks and Decision Trees on dataset are investigated.

Ramalingaswamy Cheruku et al. [13] they have proposed 2-level ensemble architecture in this paper that combines RBFN, logistic regression, PNN, and SVM. The suggested model is tested against the heart disease dataset.

Safial Islam Ayon et al. [14] they have used seven computational intelligence approaches in this study, including Decision Tree, Deep Neural Network, K-Nearest Neighbor, Support Vector Machine, Nave Bayes, Random Forest, and Logistic Regression.

Hidayet TAKCI [15] they have employed a combination of machine learning and attribute selection methods. The better accuracy was 82.59% without any feature selection. SVM-linear has given model accuracy of 84.81% with relief features selection method.

Md. Razu Ahmed et al. [16] for early identification of cardiac disease, they have applied five common supervised learning techniques. The findings of the investigation have shown the Artificial Neural Network has provided best result of all the classification models, with an accuracy of 84.00%.

2.1 Justification

In the previous work [7], the authors utilized Bagging, JRip, IBK, Naive Bayes (NB), Multilayer Perceptron (MP), and J48 classifiers over Statlog (Heart) dataset that contain 270 cases. The accuracy of Naive Bayes classifiers for Statlog (Heart) datasets has provided 83.7%. We have employed three approaches for marking features in our experiment to discover the most related characteristics that have a major effect on the Statlog Heart disease dataset; Recursive Feature Elimination with Bagging (Random Forest) has provided the best accuracy of 85.18%. On the other side in previous paper [9] there study has given specificity 84.2%. Where, our model has explored specificity of 91.73% by applying RFE with Bagging (Random Forest).

3   Proposed Work

Machine learning permits computers to find out and develop consistent with their own without explicitly programmed. The field of machine learning cares with the making of computer programs which can approach data and acquire on their own. The process of training begins with survey or data, like samples, instruction or real experience, in order that we can explore the natures of data and mark better choices within the future supported the examples we supply. The main goal is for computers to figure things out on their own, without the necessity for human contribution, and to regulate their ways accordingly. To get desire outcome machine learning goes through some steps like data preprocessing, handling the data with some algorithms and feature selection methods etc.

In our proposed work at first we have preprocessed our data. Preprocessing of data has some steps in any Machine Learning technique, in which the data is categorized, or encoded, to make it easier for the machine to digest it. In other words, the algorithm can now effectively analyze the data's features. We come across a number of features in the dataset while creating a machine learning model for a real-life dataset, and not all of these features are useful most of the time. When, we add unneeded characteristics to the model while training it, the model's overall accuracy drops. So, we have applied three types of feature selection method. It helps to select those features that contribute the most to the decision boundary or output that are interested in, either automatically or manually. The three types of feature selection we have used here are Lasso from embedded methods, Mutual information from filter methods and Recursive Feature Elimination from wrapper methods. Classification is the process for organizing data into a series of categories. The main purpose of the classification challenge is to determine which category or class the new data belongs to. In our proposed work we have run Naive Bayes, K-Nearest Neighbors and Random Forest these three classifier techniques. For better output we have also used Bagging ensemble technique with Random Forest. Ensemble methods are ways for enhancing the accuracy of model findings by aggregating numerous models rather than utilizing just one. The integrated models considerably improve the accuracy of the outcomes. Total procedure have done using 10 fold cross validation and the result have taken as mean value. We have measured accuracy, sensitivity, precision, specificity, f1 and roc_auc (Fig. 1).

3.1 Dataset

In our approach, we employ Statlog (Heart) datasets to predict early heart disease. The UCI Machine Learning Repository has made available the original dataset of cardiac disease. There are 270 examples in all, with 14 attributes, including the target attribute. Patients who do not have heart disease have a target attribute of 0, while those who do have heart disease have a target attribute of 1. In the Statlog (Heart) dataset, 150 samples are classified as class 0 and 120 as class 1. This information assists in the early detection of heart disease. The features present in the dataset are given in the Table 1.

3.2 Experimental Design

To find the most relevant features, we have employed the Lasso, Mutual Information, and Recursive Feature Elimination approaches. This improves the efficiency of our disease prediction model. We have used Mutual Information to obtain nine features, six features from Recursive Feature Elimination, and seven features using Lasso. Table 2 shown all experimental schemas,

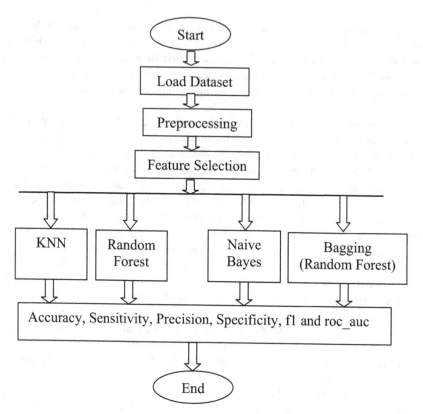

Fig. 1. Flowchart of proposed model

Table 1. Features from statlog (heart) datasets

Features	Description
1. age	In years
2. sex:	Male = 1 and Female = 0
3. cp	Value = 1, 2, 3, 4
4. trestbps	Resting blood pressure
5. chol	Serum cholestoral in mg/dl
6. fbs	Blood sugar (fasting)
7. restecg	Electrocardiographic results (Resting) value = 0, 1, 2
8. thalach	Achieved maximum heart rate
9. exang	Angina caused by exercise
10. oldpeak	ST depression induced by exercise relative to rest

(*continued*)

Table 1. (*continued*)

Features	Description
11. slope	The slope of the ST portion of the peak exercise
12. ca	The number of large vessels colored by flourosopy
13. thal	Value = 3, 6, 7
14. num	Heart disease (Absent) = 0 Heart disease (Present) = 1

Table 2. Experimental design

Schema number	Feature selection	Schema initial	Number of features
1.	Lasso	KNN-7	7
2.	Lasso	Random Forest-7	7
3.	Lasso	Naive Bayes-7	7
4.	Lasso	Bagging (RF)-7	7
5.	Mutual Information	KNN-9	9
6.	Mutual Information	Random Forest-9	9
7.	Mutual Information	Naive Bayes-9	9
8.	Mutual Information	Bagging (RF)-9	9
9.	RFE	KNN-6	6
10.	RFE	Random Forest-6	6
11.	RFE	Naive Bayes-6	6
12.	RFE	Bagging (RF)-6	6

4 Outcome

The computer language 'Python 3' and the Scikit library have utilized in this work for implementation. We preprocessed our data before applying three types of feature selection approaches in our suggested model. For identifying features, we have applied Lasso from embedded methods, Mutual information from filter methods and Recursive Feature Elimination from wrapper methods. After that, we have used three different classifying methods. For Further improving the model efficiency we have run bagging ensemble technique with Random Forest learner. After preprocessing we have used three feature selection approaches: Lasso, Mutual Information, and Recursive Feature Elimination. The dataset yielded seven features using Lasso, nine features from Mutual Information, and six features from RFE. Table 3 displays the obtained features.

Table 3. Selected features from statlog dataset

Lasso	Mutual information	Recursive feature elimination
1. sex	1. sex	1. sex
2. cp	2. cp	2. cp
3. restecg	3. chol	3. exang
4. exang	4. thalach	4. oldpeak
5. oldpeak	5. exang	5. slope
6. ca	6. oldpeak	6. ca
7. thal	7. slope	
	8. ca	
	9. thal	

We have run extracted features through three classifiers and the bagging ensemble approach after using the Lasso selection method. Where, the accuracies are 77.80% (K-Nearest Neighbor), 79.60% (Random Forest), 84.81% (Naive Bayes), and 80.74% (Bagging with Random Forest). Naive Bayes produced the better results, with accuracy 84.81%, precision of 83.82%, specificity of 87.68%, sensitivity of 81.57%, f1 value of 82.13%, and roc_auc of 89.92% (Fig. 2).

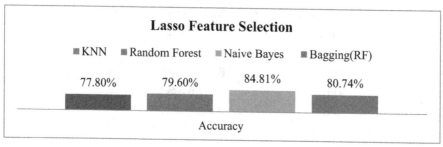

Fig. 2. Accuracy for the lasso feature selection

From Mutual Information we have chosen nine features from the dataset based on the top rank. Next, in the same way we have run selected features over three classifiers and Bagging(RF) ensemble technique, where the accuracies are 63.70% (K-Nearest Neighbor), 83.33% (Random Forest), 84.07% (Naive Bayes) and 83.70% (Bagging with Random Forest). Using this feature selection methods Naive Bayes generated best output and the accuracy 84.07%, precision 83.30%, specificity 86.89%, sensitivity 80.92%, f1_value 81.42% and roc_auc 90.12% (Fig. 3).

After that, we have run six extracted features through three classifiers and the bagging ensemble approach after using the Recursive Feature Elimination method. Where, the accuracies are 77.04% (K-Nearest Neighbor), 84.07% (Random Forest), 81.11% (Naive

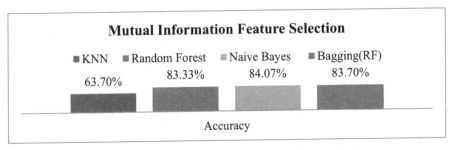

Fig. 3. Accuracy for the mutual information feature selection

Bayes), and 85.18% (Bagging with Random Forest). Bagging (Random Forest) produced the better results, with 85.18% accuracy, precision of 88.39%, specificity of 91.73%, sensitivity of 77.83%, f1 value of 82.07%, and roc_auc of 89.07%.

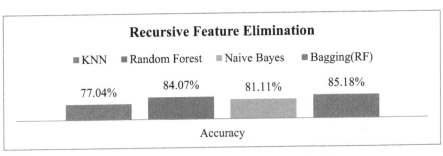

Fig. 4. Accuracy for recursive feature elimination

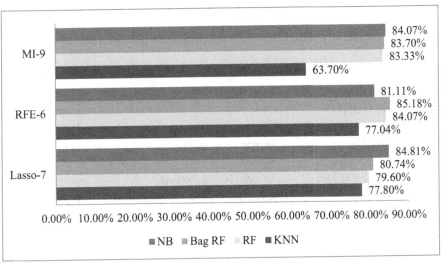

Fig. 5. Performances (accuracy) of three feature selection methods.

In Fig. 4 where we can identify that Recursive Feature Elimination with Random forest has given accuracy 85.18%. We have observed other sections like Precision, Sensitivity and Specificity also reacted well (Fig. 5 and 6).

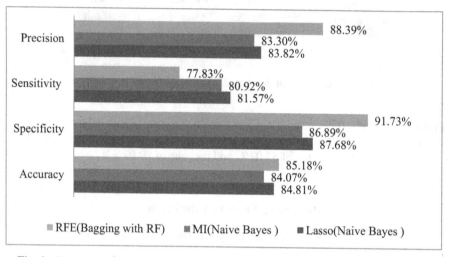

Fig. 6. Compare performances among all top outcomes in each feature selection method.

From above all results we can define easily that using Recursive Feature Elimination with Bagging (Random Forest) has given overall better result where the accuracy of 85.18%, precision of 88.39%, specificity of 91.73%, sensitivity of 77.83%, f1 value of 82.07%, and roc_auc of 89.07%. Table 4 shows a comparison between existing work and our proposed work.

Table 4. Comparison of proposed method with previous work

Author's name	Methods	Accuracy (%)
Bendi Venkata Ramana et al. [7]	Naive Bayes	83.7%
Randa El-Bialy et al. [11]	C4.5 Fast Decision Tree	76.6% 76.6%
Hidayet TAKCI [15]	Support vector machine and relief method	84.81%
Md. Razu Ahmed et al. [16]	Artificial Neural Network	84.00%
Proposed work	**Recursive Feature Elimination with Bagging (Random Forest)**	**85.18%**

5 Conclusions

We have used three methods for selecting features to identify the far more common characteristics that are traced with a decent sign over the output in the model we have proposed here. The model has three phases: at first, we have gathered relevant data; second, we have used three methods for selecting features to identify the far more common characteristics those are traced with a decent sign over the output. And the third stage includes Naive Bayes, Random Forest, K-Nearest Neighbors, and Bagging (Random Forest), all of which have done by 10-fold cross validation. The accuracies are 77.80% (K-Nearest Neighbor), 79.60% (Random Forest), 84.81% (Naive Bayes), and 80.74% (Bagging with Random Forest), while using Lasso. The accuracies are 63.70% (K-Nearest Neighbor), 83.33% (Random Forest), 84.07% (Naive Bayes) and 83.70% (Bagging with Random Forest), using Mutual Information. When we have applied Recursive Feature Elimination with Bagging (Random Forest), our model has performed better, with an accuracy of 85.18%. We have selected machine learning algorithms because it has the capacity to make recommendations based on input data, but it has certain limitations, such as taking longer to create results due to the enormous amount of data. Whereas, noisy value reduces output accuracy, processing the raw data is equally crucial. Every model has some limits. In order to categorize how our model works so effectively with such vast quantities of data, we need to train more data samples in our work, and running several algorithms for training the dataset is more challenging. In the future, we'd like to use our model to run other clinical datasets for early disease prediction.

References

1. Krishnaiah, V., Srinivas, M., Narsimha, G., Chandra, N.: Diagnosis of heart disease patients using fuzzy classification technique. Int. Conf. Comput. Commun. Technol. (2014). https://doi.org/10.1109/iccct2.2014.7066746
2. Cardiovascular diseases (2021). https://www.who.int/health-topics/cardiovascular-diseases/#tab=tab_1
3. Chauhan, A., Jain, A., Sharma, P., Deep, V.: Heart disease prediction using evolutionary rule learning. In: Proceedings of the 2018 4th International Conference on Computational Intelligence & Communication Technology (CICT) (2018). https://doi.org/10.1109/ciact.2018.8480271
4. Normawati, D., Winarti, S.: Feature selection with combination classifier use rules-based data mining for diagnosis of coronary heart disease. In: Proceedings of the 2018 12th International Conference on Telecommunication Systems, Services, and Applications (TSSA) (2018). https://doi.org/10.1109/tssa.2018.8708849
5. Sonawane, J., Patil, D.: Prediction of heart disease using multilayer perceptron neural network. In: Proceedings of the International Conference on Information Communication and Embedded Systems (ICICES2014) (2014). https://doi.org/10.1109/icices.2014.7033860
6. Junaid, M., Kumar, R.: Data science and its application in heart disease prediction. In: Proceedings of the 2020 International Conference on Intelligent Engineering and Management (ICIEM) (2020). https://doi.org/10.1109/iciem48762.2020.9160056
7. Ramana, B., Kumar Boddu, R.: Performance comparison of classification algorithms on medical datasets. In: Proceedings of the 2019 IEEE 9th Annual Computing and Communication Workshop and Conference (CCWC) (2019). https://doi.org/10.1109/ccwc.2019.8666497

8. Abu Yazid, M., Haikal Satria, M., Talib, S., Azman, N.: Artificial neural network parameter tuning framework for heart disease classification. In: Proceedings of the 2018 5th International Conference on Electrical Engineering, Computer Science and Informatics (EECSI) (2018). https://doi.org/10.1109/eecsi.2018.8752821
9. Bohacik, J., Zabovsky, M.: Naive bayes for statlog heart database with consideration of data specifics. In: Proceedings of the 2017 IEEE 14th International Scientific Conference on Informatics (2017). https://doi.org/10.1109/informatics.2017.8327218
10. Akyol, K., Atila, Ü.: A study on performance improvement of heart disease prediction by attribute selection methods. Acad. Platform J. Eng. Sci. 7(2), 174–179 (2019)
11. El-Bialy, R., Salamay, M.A., Karam, O.H., Khalifa, M.E.: Feature analysis of coronary artery heart disease data sets. Procedia Comput. Sci. 65, 459–468 (2015)
12. Dangare, C.S., Apte, S.S.: Improved study of heart disease prediction system using data mining classification techniques. Int. J. Comput. Appl. 47(10), 44–48 (2012)
13. Cheruku, R., Nalluri, P.K., Gopi, K.Y.G., Charan, J.B.S., Sanketh, V.N., Beechu, N.R.: A bi-level cascaded ensemble framework for effective disease diagnosis. In: Proceedings of the TENCON 2019–2019 IEEE Region 10 Conference (TENCON), pp. 2059–2062. IEEE (2019)
14. Ayon, S.I., Islam, M.M., Hossain, M.R.: Coronary artery heart disease prediction: a comparative study of computational intelligence techniques. IETE J. Res. 68(4), 1–20 (2020)
15. Takci, H.: Improvement of heart attack prediction by the feature selection methods. Turk. J. Electr. Eng. Comput. Sci. 26(1), 1–10 (2018)
16. Ahmed, M.R., Mahmud, S.H., Hossin, M.A., Jahan, H., Noori, S.R.H.: A cloud based four-tier architecture for early detection of heart disease with machine learning algorithms. In: Proceedings of the 2018 IEEE 4th International Conference on Computer and Communications (ICCC), pp. 1951–1955. IEEE (2018)

A Feasible Approach to Predict Survival Rates Post Lung Surgery Utilizing Machine Learning Techniques

Faria Rahman[(✉)] [iD], Shanjida Khan Maliha[iD], and Md. Ashiq Mahmood[iD]

Institute of Information and Communication Technology (IICT),
Khulna University of Engineering and Technology, Khulna, Bangladesh
fariarahman337@gmail.com

Abstract. Lung cancer starts in the lungs' tissues, most commonly in the cells that line the airways. Cancer-affected cells, unlike healthy cells may develop without order or control in the process of destroying other normal lung tissue. The volumes of clinical data are increasing day by day. Systems can learn from the input data, discover patterns and make decisions based on that information using machine learning techniques. Monitoring for high-risk individuals has the potential to greatly improve lung cancer survival rates by finding lung cancer at an earlier stage, when it is more likely to be cured. By analyzing the data, we have tried to explore the relevant causes of lung cancer for decreasing lung cancer deaths in this research. In our proposed model, we have used three methods for focusing on features: Decision Tree, ANOVA and Recursive Feature Elimination. Three classification algorithms are Decision Tree, K-Nearest Neighbors, and Gaussian Naïve Bayes. By using Recursive Feature Elimination run over Decision tree classifier, our proposed model has given 89.00% accuracy on it.

Keywords: Lung disease · Naïve Bayes · K-Nearest Neighbor · Decision Tree

1 Introduction

Cancer causes death but among all types of cancer, lung cancer is the main cause of death [1]. Over 10 million people died because of cancer in 1.80 million died in lung cancer. Worldwide the number of active lungs cancer cases is 2.21 million [2]. Old chest pain and emphysema have probably created the chance of lung cancer. Cigarettes, tobacco are noted as the main reason of affected with lung cancer [3]. Other identified symptoms are air pollution, harmful chemicals which polluted the lungs. In the initial stage, cancer is situated in the lung then it started to spread to other organs. Identifying lung cancer and treatment procedure of lung cancer is so complicated, time-consuming, and also platform-dependent operation [4]. As it is a platform-dependent disease, patients do the operation for the sake of being alive and leading a healthy life. Our paper is based on identifying the rate of death and life after surgery.

Feature Selection is a technique that helps to reduce unnecessary features and it causes the dataset will be robust. In our paper used three types of feature selection algorithm decision tree, analysis of variance (ANOVA), and recursive feature elimination (RFE). Data mining is nowadays the most important topic that helps in early prediction. In the medical field, the machine learning algorithm technique is used to predict early anything it helps in cost reduction and also time complexity. Using a machine-learning algorithm the result will more accurate, robust [5]. For identifying the rate of death and life after surgery of lung cancer three types of classifier algorithms are used like decision tree, k-nearest neighbors, and Gaussian Naïve Bayes.

Post-lung surgery condition prediction is such sensitive work. For this purpose, many types of analysis are required to get an accurate result. In our paper, the Thoracic Surgery Patients dataset from UCI Machine Learning Repository is used here which contains lung disease surgery patient data. The feature selection algorithm is used to reduce irrelevant data. Dataset is trained by splitting it into training and testing it. Applying machine learning algorithms the best accuracy comes from extracting five features from the recursive feature elimination (RFE) algorithm used decision tree classifier algorithm.

2　Related Works

S. Roshan et al. [6] the focus of this study is to compare and contrast several data mining methods for estimating the survival of lung cancer patients after thoracic surgery. This research also offers a novel methodology for prediction that combines data mining methods. The factors that cause individuals to die following thoracic surgery are also discussed in this paper. The results show that the combine of Naïve Bayes and J48 outperforms the other data mining techniques, with an accuracy of 88.73%. They have also learned from this study that the features of dyspnea, hemoptysis, diagnosis and pain prior to thoracic surgery are primarily relevant for lung cancer patients' survival for a year following surgery.

Pradeep Singh et al. [7] they have used seven machine learning methods to analyze the performance of feature selection methods in their study, including Naïve Bayes, SMO, MLP, Linear SVM, RBF Network, CART and KNN. With correlation-based feature selection employing five features, a maximum accuracy of 85.11% was achieved.

Nachev et al. [8] they have explored support vector, Naïve Bayes and decision trees machines models, as well as the viability of each algorithm for use on thoracic surgery data. The SVM provided a better result with 79.40% accuracy.

Abeer S. Desuky et al. [9] they have provided three attribute approaches to improve algorithm efficiency for health outcomes research on the dataset with five machine learning algorithms before and after implementing the feature ranking and selection methods.

Kwetishe Joro Danjuma et al. [10] in their work, they have applied Naïve Bayes, multilayer perceptron and J48 classifiers where The multilayer perceptron scored best, with 82.3% classification accuracy.

Md. Ahasan Uddin Harun et al. [11] in their paper they have used Boosted simple logistic regression, Simple logistic, Multilayer Perceptron, Boosted Multilayer Perceptron, Naïve Bayes, J48, Boosted Naïve Bayes and Boosted J48. Where, according accuracy J48, logistic regression & boosted simple logistic regression performed well than the others.

Jo Hanna Lindsey Serato et al. [12] an anonymous patient's lung sounds have recorded using a mobile app and digital stethoscopes, and a library of digital lung sounds has established. K-Nearest Neighbors and Support Vector Machine are the most effective of the six classification algorithms used in this dataset.

Abdulhamid et al. [13] used feature selection. The selected feature was AGE, PRE5, PRE6, PRE8, PRE10, PRE11, PRE14, PRE19, PRE25, PRE30, and PRE32. They also used three machine-learning algorithms.

Steve Iduye BN et al. [14] used the Weka tool for predicting the survival rate of surgery patients after one year. For removing irrelevant data they have used weka.filters.unsupervised.attribute.Remove and eliminated Diagnosis, FVC, FEV1, Z scale, and Pain attributes. 70% training and 30% testing data are used in their work. Three Machine learning algorithm is used Logistic Regression, Naïve Bayes and j48 algorithm. All those three algorithms Logistic Regression performed better and the accuracy is 84%.

Sindhu et al. [15] in their paper they work with many types of classification algorithms. They used surgical information of body sections. All those algorithms j48 performs best than others.

2.1 Justification

Pradeep Singh et al. [7] have acquired a better accuracy of 85.11% using correlation-based feature selection with five features in their article. In our experiment, we have used three methods for marking features to identify the highlighted features that have a strong relationship with the thoracic surgery dataset. Then, for each of the feature selection approaches, we have used Decision Tree, K-Nearest Neighbors, and Gaussian Naïve Bayes. The RFE with five extracted features using Naïve Bayes has given a better outcome, with an accuracy of 89.00%.

3 Proposed Work

3.1 Data Sources

For performing the experiments we used the UCI machine learning repository which is named the thoracic surgery dataset. The dataset has 17 attributes. The dataset is consists of biomedical data. There are 470 instances this data is divided into two sections like the number of patients who died after surgery within one year and the one is survival. Dataset has no missing values. Here 400 patients survive after one year and the other 70 patients have died. Table 1 shows the attributes name which is used in the dataset.

Table 1. Attribute from dataset

Serial no.	Attribute name
01	Diagnosis (DNG)
02	Forced vital capacity - FVC (PRE4)
03	Volume that has been exhaled at the end of the first second of forced expiration - FEV1 (PRE5)
04	Performance status - Zubrod scale (PRE6)
05	Pain before surgery (PRE7)
06	Haemoptysis before surgery (PRE8)
07	Dyspnoea before surgery (PRE9)
08	Cough before surgery (PRE10)
09	Weakness before surgery (PRE11)
10	T in clinical TNM - size of the original tumor (PRE14)
11	Type 2 DM - diabetes mellitus (PRE17)
12	MI up to 6 months (PRE19)
13	Peripheral arterial diseases-PAD (PRE25)
14	Smoking (PRE30)
15	Asthma (PRE32)
16	Age at surgery (AGE)
17	1 year survival period (Risk1Y)

Table 1 shows all attributes of the dataset and also the elaboration of that keyword. This data help to find the accuracy rate of death and survival rate after one year of surgery.

3.2 Feature Selection

The dataset contains many types of data both relevant and irrelevant data. It is important to identify which data is effective for the dataset. Feature selection is a process which is helped in that purpose. Another name of feature selection is an attribute or variable selection [16]. Automatically, the feature selection method chooses and attempts to delete irrelevant characteristics. It also removes noise without changing the dataset value. There are two types of feature selection model supervised model and unsupervised model. Supervised model increased model efficiency by using target attribute. On the other side, an unsupervised model is used in unlabeled data. In feature selection output level data is not needed. Supervised methods have three classes named intrinsic model, wrapper model, and filter model [17] (Fig. 1).

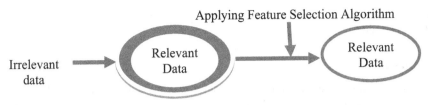

Fig. 1. Feature selection

There are many types of feature selection algorithm in our paper we use three types of feature selection algorithm. Three feature selection algorithm is used here Decision tree, ANOVA, Recursive Feature Elimination (RFE). Windows 10 operating system is used and python 3 programming language is used here for implementation purposes.

3.3 Decision Tree

Feature selection's main problem is to maintain its quality and importance. A huge amount of data creates a complex model which made difficulties for feature selection and also creates complication in prediction. The easy way to understand the process is to split the data into nodes. All the nodes are divided based on their weight. It also considers the standby splitter value while counting. Though the variable is not able to split any kinds of nodes but it also gets much importance [18]. In the feature selection procedure decision tree model create a locally optimal solution to extend it up to maximum [19]. Finally, the decision is deciding on features' importance.

3.3.1 Analysis of Variance (ANOVA)

Identifying the difference between double and multiple groups that are different. This approach describes a statistical approach. It calculates Hypothesis as 0 and 1.0 is for equal groups and 1 is for the minimum group have different mean. F-tet is used to check whether any important changes happened between the groups in Analysis of Variance. If any changes are not found between the groups then the result will be near to 1 [20]. There are two types of ANOVA one way and two way. One-way ANOVA works only for one predictor vs response. Then they identify the relationship between them. Two-way ANOVA is working for multi features.

3.3.2 Recursive Feature Elimination (RFE)

RFE is a well-known and famous algorithm. In feature selection, it is most important to identify useful and relevant features RFE plays a vital role in this purpose. RFE considers two important things numbers of attributes to choose from and an algorithm that helps to select those features. Recursive Feature Elimination is known as the wrapper based but it also used filter style. Predictors are backwardly chosen in recursive feature elimination. The first model is built on the basis of all incubate predictors. Then less effective predictors will be reduced. The diagram is built again and calculation will resume that helps to find an effective result. Subset size is as important as it is denoted as a tuning guideline. It also enhances the working criteria. The final structure is trained and is enhanced by subset.

3.4 Classifiers

Data mining is one of the trending topics that a massive amount of researchers work with. For classification purposes, classifiers are also important. A clear dataset helps in the classification. Binary and multi-class is the two form of a classification type. These two types of classifiers' main targets are to identify and level the dataset. Prediction is one of the most important tasks that help us find anything before it arrives based on circumstance [21]. Prediction of any circumstance before time can reduce the loss rate. The decision tree, Gaussian Naïve Bayes, and K-nearest neighbor algorithm are used in this work.

3.4.1 Decision Tree

A Decision Tree is a binary method that is used in both categorization and regression. Here we used it as a classification algorithm and structured it as a tree that has nodes. Two nodes are Decision Node and Leaf Node. The decision tree has a duple subdivision and the final decision is made by the Decision Node and Leaf Node denote as output. Decision trees think like humans while they made decisions and it structures like trees so it is easy to catch them. The first step is the root branch which is full of all data. By Attribute Selection Measure (ASM) best feature will be selected. Then the root branch is divided into sub-branch considering the best features. After that, the decision tree is decided based on the best feature.

3.4.2 K-Nearest Neighbors

K-Nearest Neighbors is a protean algorithm. K-Nearest Neighbors is also a binary method that is used in both categorization and regression. It is the most simple but effective algorithm. Implementation of K-Nearest Neighbors is easy. First, the data is loaded then a number for K is selected from neighbors. Suspicion and regular data distance are measured and add in a periodic order. K is picked from the ascendant set they got labels. Classification will also return the K label.

3.4.3 Gaussian Naïve Bayes

Bayes Theorem is the basic of Naïve Bayes. Attributes are self-reliantly classified from each other. Gaussian distribution enhances the absolute value of Naïve Bayes. Gaussian is an accessible approach that helps to identify meaningfully and also ideal aberrations from the guidance data. It pursues Gaussian ordinary distribution and bolsters stable data. The performance of this algorithm is appreciable it is applicable when input is immense.

3.5 Experimental Design

Data mining is a process that extracts effective material from the dataset. The procedure is done by following some steps (Fig. 2).

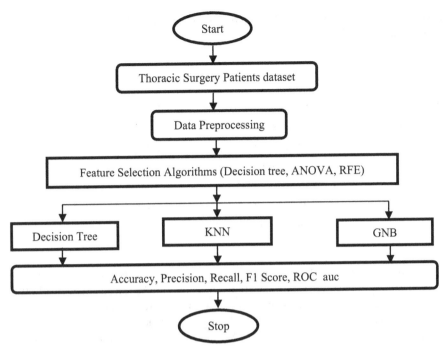

Fig. 2. Flow chart of working procedure

Thoracic Surgery Patient's dataset is used here which contains lung disease surgery patient data. Data prepossessing is the first step. This step eliminates unnecessary data and also manages handling the data. For data analyze we have used data splitting 80%. For selecting feature three algorithms is used Decision tree, Analysis of Variance and Recursive Feature Elimination. In the Decision tree algorithm, five features are used, Analysis of variance used six features and Recursive Feature Elimination also has used five features. Applying three feature selections the resulted data is ready for the classifier algorithm. Three classifier algorithms is used to predict the data named Decision tree, K-Nearest Neighbors and Gaussian Naïve Bayes. These classifiers help to find out Accuracy, Precision, Recall, F1 Score, ROC_auc.

4   Outcome

This paper is implemented using Python 3 programming language and Scikit library. We use the standard value as the "Gini" in the decision tree algorithm. In our suggested model, we first pre-process our data before determining features using three methods: Decision Tree, ANOVA, and Recursive Feature Elimination. After that, we have used the Decision Tree, Gaussian Naïve Bayes and K-Nearest Neighbors classification algorithms. We have exploited three feature selection approaches after preprocessing the thoracic surgery dataset in our model: Decision Tree, ANOVA, and Recursive Feature Elimination. From the dataset, the Decision Tree retrieves five features, the ANOVA marks six features, and the RFE extracts five features. The properties that were extracted are listed below (Table 2):

Table 2. Selected features from thoracic surgery dataset

Decision Tree	ANOVA	RFE
1. Smoking	1. Weakness	1. Pain
2. FVC	2. Performance	2. Dyspnoea
3. FVC1	3. Dyspnoea	3. Tumor_size
4. Tumor_size	4. Cough	4. Diabetes_mellitus
5. Age	5. Tumor_size	5. Smoking
	6. Diabetes_mellitus	

We have passed top values directed features over three classifiers after using the Decision Tree approach for feature selection. Decision Tree has an accuracy of 84.00%, Gaussian Naïve Bayes has an accuracy of 87.00%, and K-Nearest Neighbor has an accuracy of 86.00%. Gaussian Naïve Bayes have provided the best results, with accuracy of 87.00%, precision of 82.00%, recall of 87.00%, f1 value of 83.00%, and roc auc of 53.00% (Fig. 3).

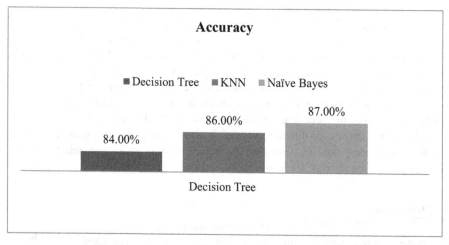

Fig. 3. Accuracy for the decision tree feature selection

Next, ANOVA we selected six features from dataset based on the top rank. In the same way we have run selected features over three classifiers. Where Decision Tree accuracy is 88.00%, Gaussian Naïve Bayes accuracy is 81.00%, and K-Nearest Neighbor accuracy is 86.00%. On it Decision Tree generated best output and the accuracy 88.00%, precision 84.00%, recall 88.00%, f1_value 84.00% and roc_auc 54.00% (Fig. 4).

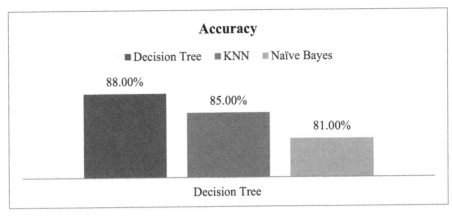

Fig. 4. Accuracy for the ANOVA

RFE has now chosen five features from the dataset. Similarly, we have tested selected features across three classifiers. Decision Tree, Gaussian Naïve Bayes and K-Nearest Neighbor accuracy is 89.00%, 78.00%, and 88.00% respectively. Using these feature selection approaches, Decision Tree has produced the best results, with accuracy of 89.00%, precision of 90.00%, recall of 89.00%, f1 value of 85.00%, and roc auc of 55.00% (Fig. 5).

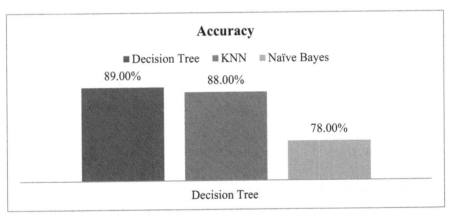

Fig. 5. Accuracy for the RFE

We can simply determine from the above results that employing RFE with Decision Tree yielded a better outcome, with an accuracy of 89.00% (Fig. 6 and 7) (Table 3).

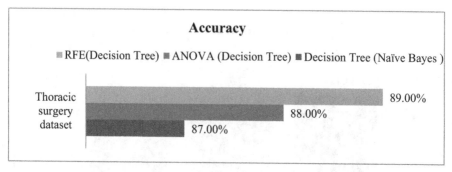

Fig. 6. Top accuracies of classifier from three feature selection methods.

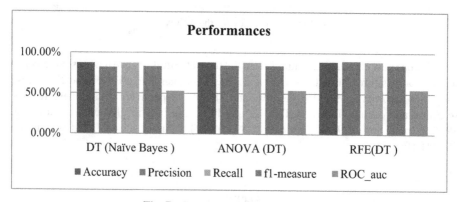

Fig. 7. Compare best performances.

Table 3. Comparison of proposed method with previous work

Author's name	Method	Accuracy (%)
S. Roshanet al. [6]	J48 and Naïve Bayes	88.73%
Pradeep Singh et al. [7]	Correlation with CART	85.11%
Nachev et al. [8]	SVM	79.40%
Kwetishe Joro Danjumaet al. [10]	Multilayer perceptron	82.3%
Proposed work	**Recursive feature elimination with decision tree**	**89.00%**

5 Conclusions

The work which is discussed in this paper is done in four parts. First is collecting data and then used a feature selection algorithm which helps to reduce irrelevant data. By splitting the dataset, it is trained properly. Applying a decision tree, the accuracy of the respective algorithms decision tree is 84.00%, Gaussian Naïve Bayes is 87.00%, and k-nearest neighbor is 86.00%. By applying the ANOVA feature selection method, the accuracy of the decision tree is 88.00%, Gaussian Naïve Bayes is 81.00%, and k-nearest neighbor is 85.00%. By applying the RFE feature selection method, the accuracy of the decision tree is 89.00%, Gaussian Naïve Bayes is 78%, and k-nearest neighbor is 88.00%.Our preferred work performed better for RFE feature selection and decision tree algorithm that is 89% accurate. Machine learning algorithms are easy to understand and help to predict disease early with medical data. It is just not a machine learning algorithm approach is a toolkit. If the amount of data is large, the machine learning algorithm will work slowly. It creates time complexity. In the future, we will add more functionality to get more performance. More datasets will use to identify other diseases in the future.

References

1. Chen, Y.C., Ke, W.C., Chiu, H.W.: Risk classification of cancer survival using ANN with gene expression data from multiple laboratories. Comput. Biol. Med. **48**, 1–7 (2014)
2. Cancer.Who.int. (2021). https://www.who.int/news-room/fact-sheets/detail/cancer
3. Radhika, P.R., Nair, R.A., Veena, G.: A comparative study of lung cancer detection using machine learning algorithms. In: Proceedings of the 2019 IEEE International Conference on Electrical, Computer and Communication Technologies (ICECCT), pp. 1–4. IEEE (2019)
4. Lee, H.K., et al.: A system-theoretic method for modeling, analysis, and improvement of lung cancer diagnosis-to-surgery process. IEEE Trans. Autom. Sci. Eng. **15**(2), 531–544 (2017)
5. Klement, W., et al.: Chest tube management after lung resection surgery using a classifier. In: Proceedings of the 2019 IEEE International Conference on Data Science and Advanced Analytics (DSAA), pp. 432–441. IEEE (2019)
6. Roshan, S., Rohini, V.: Prediction of post-surgical survival of lung cancer patients after thoracic surgery using data mining techniques. Int. J. Adv. Res. **5**(4), 596–600 (2017). https://doi.org/10.21474/IJAR01/3852
7. Singh, P., Singh, N.: Intelligent approaches for prognosticating post-operative life expectancy in the lung cancer patients. In: Proceedings of the 2017 International Conference on Inventive Computing and Informatics (ICICI), pp. 844–848. IEEE (2017)
8. Nachev, A., Reapy, T.: Predictive models for post-operative life expectancy after thoracic surgery. Mathematical and Software Engineering **1**(1), 1–5 (2015)
9. Desuky, A.S., El Bakrawy, L.M.: Improved prediction of post-operative life expectancy after thoracic surgery. Adv. Syst. Sci. Appl. **16**(2), 70–80 (2016)
10. Danjuma, K.J.: Performance evaluation of machine learning algorithms in post-operative life expectancy in the lung cancer patients (2015). arXiv preprint arXiv:1504.04646
11. Harun, A., Alam, N.: Predicting outcome of thoracic surgery by data mining techniques. Int. J. Adv. Res. Comput. Sci. Softw. Eng. **5**(1), 7–10 (2015)
12. Serato, J.H.L., Reyes, R.: Automated lung auscultation identification for mobile health systems using machine learning. In: Proceedings of the 2018 IEEE International Conference on Applied System Invention (ICASI), pp. 287–290. IEEE (2018)
13. Abdulhamid, A., Bahtchevanov, I., Jia, P.: Life expectancy post thoracic surgery. Stanford University-CS229 (2014)
14. Steve Iduye, B.N., Scotia, H.N.: Effectiveness of Data Mining Algorithm in Predicting Post Lung Resection Surgery Prognosis
15. Sindhu, V., Prabha, S.A.S., Veni, S., Hemalatha, M.: Thoracic surgery analysis using data mining techniques. Int. J. Comput. Technol. Appl. **5**, 578–586 (2014)
16. Brownlee, J.: An introduction to feature selection. Machine Learning Mastery (2021). https://machinelearningmastery.com/an-introduction-to-feature-selection/

17. Gopika, N., Meena Kowshalaya, A.: Correlation based feature selection algorithm for machine learning. In: Proceedings of the 2018 3rd International Conference on Communication and Electronics Systems (ICCES), pp. 692–695. IEEE (2018)
18. Feature selection using Decision Tree – Busigence. Busigence.com. (2021). http://busigence.com/blog/feature-selection-using-decision-tree
19. Euldji, R., Boumahdi, M., Bachene, M.: Decision-making based on decision tree for ball bearing monitoring. In: Proceedings of the 2020 2nd International Workshop on Human-Centric Smart Environments for Health and Well-being (IHSH), pp. 171–175. IEEE (2021)
20. Bohari, Z.H., Ghazali, R., Atira, N.N., Sulaima, M.F., Rahman, A.A., Nor, M.K.: Building energy management saving by considering lighting system optimization via ANOVA method. In: Proceedings of the 2018 4th International Conference on Computer and Technology Applications (ICCTA), pp. 216–220. IEEE (2018)
21. Maliha, S.K., Ema, R.R., Ghosh, S.K., Ahmed, H., Mollick, M.R.J., Islam, T.: Cancer disease prediction using naïve bayes, K-nearest neighbor and J48 algorithm. In: Proceedings of the 2019 10th International Conference on Computing, Communication and Networking Technologies (ICCCNT), pp. 1–7. IEEE (2019)

Cardiac Abnormality Prediction Using Multiple Machine Learning Approaches

Jahid Hasan Rana$^{(\boxtimes)}$ ⓘ, Moniara Farhin ⓘ, Saif Ahamed Turzo ⓘ,
Sagar Chandra Roy ⓘ, Rashidul Hasan Nabil ⓘ, and Aneem-Al-Ahsan Rupai ⓘ

Department of Computer Science, American International University-Bangladesh,
Dhaka, Bangladesh
xahidhasanrana07.5@gmail.com, {rashidul,aneem}@aiub.edu

Abstract. Heart disease is one of the deadliest diseases in the modern world. Consistently right around 26 million patients are being influenced by this sort of problem. From the heart consultant and specialist's perspective, it is intricate to foresee the cardiovascular breakdown correctly. This early detection, in addition, can help control the side effects of the illness just as the appropriate treatment of the Abnormality. Machine learning can play a vital role to predict heart disease using previous medical data. It's possible to predict heart disease using various data mining and machine learning algorithms, a faster, easier and cost-effective solution for medical science. The primary purpose of this paper is to predict Cardiac Abnormalities using various data mining techniques. 6 machine learning algorithms were used (Decision Tree, K-Nearest Neighbors, Logistic Regression, Naïve Bayes Classifier, Random Forest, Support Vector Machine) to predict whether a person has cardiovascular disease or not. We applied a raw dataset with 12 attributes and our engineered dataset with 16 attributes on these algorithms. In both dataset number of data points were 62500. After analyzing the accuracy, Logistic Regression provides better accuracy, and Decision Tree provides the lowest accuracy.

Keywords: Machine learning · Supervised learning · Algorithms · Heart disease · Cardiac abnormality detection

1 Introduction

Cardiac Abnormality is one of the common deadly diseases of death today. Unhealthy lifestyles, as well as unavoidable hereditary issues, are just contributing much more towards this dynamic. In our country majority of people are not aware of their heart condition. Most people died of heart disease, but they never know they have heart issues because people think they have gastrological problems. Heart disease and gastrological symptoms have significant similarities. So, in medical science, they need some advanced technology to predict patients' heart conditions soon, and our heart Disease prediction using data mining will play a significant role in medical science. Cardiac related Abnormality is the main reason for an excessive number of deaths within the world over the previous couple of decades and has emerged because of the most life-threatening disease in the whole world. Millions of people are getting some heart disease every year, and heart disease is the biggest threat to both men and women worldwide. The World Health Organization (WHO) analyzed that 17.9 million deaths occur worldwide due to Heart diseases. In almost every 34 s the heart disease kills one person all over the world. So, there is a requirement for a reliable, accurate and feasible system to diagnose such diseases in time for proper treatment. Medical diagnosis plays a vital role and yet complicated task that must be executed efficiently and accurately. The diagnosis of the heart disease is usually based on the signs, symptoms and physical examination of the patient, which is being tested and reported by a doctor. Statistical analysis has identified risk factors related to a heart condition: age, total cholesterol, diabetes, hypertension, case history of heart condition, obesity and lack of physical exercise, fasting blood sugar, etc. Data mining is the best approach to discover beforehand obscure examples dataset and utilize that data to assemble prescient models. These days, Data mining getting more well known in wellbeing areas since it produces an enormous number of complex information about clinic assets determination, patients, electronic patient records, clinical gadgets, and so forth [1]. Hospitals face issues providing the best quality services by detecting Accurate diagnoses, which lead to less effective treatment of Patients. Disasters can occur as a result of lower diagnosis results which are unacceptable. Data mining is the way toward extricating attractive information or fascinating patterns from existing data sets for explicit purposes. Most customary data mining calculations recognize the connections among exchanges utilizing paired. [2] Data mining, an incredible creating method that rotates around investigating and uncovering critical data from a huge assortment of data which can be further advantageous in examining and drawing out patterns for settling on business-related choices. Discussing the Medical area, usage of data mining in this field can yield finding and pulling out important patterns and data that can demonstrate useful in performing clinical conclusions. The exploration centres around coronary illness findings by considering past data and information. [2] We looked for other researches based on similar dataset and found out that we could improve the accuracy using different methods. We selected two research based on same dataset randomly and tried to improve the accuracy. In our research we applied 6 machine learning algorithms on our dataset to improve the accuracy.

2   Literature Review

Cardiac Abnormality includes heart stroke, strain, arterial sclerosis, and other circulatory diseases. CA is the only cardio cause of death worldwide, responsible for more than 45% of yearly death. On average of death caused to CA happens every 40 s in the World. [3] Poorly managed Cardiac Abnormality can lead to notable long-term disorders from the issue of angina pectoris, strokes, and end-stage nephritis. The death occurred costs enormously. Medical and disability cost for Cardiac Abnormality -related disorders amounts to billion of dollars each year. [4] Heart Research worldwide are ongoing and invented many systems to reduce Cardiac Abnormality. Cardiac Abnormality is a public health issue with the greatest observation to encourage the public's consciousness and care. [4] Hospitals facing issues providing the best quality services by detecting Accurate diagnoses, which lead to less effective treatment of Patients. Disasters can occur as a result of lower diagnosis results which are unacceptable. Data mining is the way toward extricating attractive information or fascinating patterns from existing data sets for explicit purposes. Most customary data mining calculations recognize the connections among exchanges utilizing paired. [5,8] Cardiac Abnormality prediction using data mining techniques has been performed effortlessly for the last few years. [6] Medical organizations worldwide have collected statistics on other health get on issues like-Cardiac Abnormalities, High Pressure, Blood Sugar etc. These statistics can utilize in many learning systems to achieve helpful comprehension. These statistics are collected in a massive and, most of the time can be rowdy. [7] By implementing Data Mining techniques and working some data mining on some Cardiac Abnormalities attributes, it can be skilful to foretell more accurate results, which the tranquil will be identified with Cardiac Abnormalities. [8] While supervised learning has been around for over a decade, its full prospective is only now being realized. Data mining is a technique for extracting valuable information from a wide collection of raw data. It involves using machine learning, statistics, and database systems to analyze data sets. Data mining is the method of searching massive datasets for secret and unknown trends, relationships, patterns and knowledge that are not so easy to detect. Unsupervised and supervised learning are two methods used in data mining. Unsupervised learning does not use a training set, whereas supervised learning uses one to learn model parameters [9]. Depending on the modelling target, each data mining technique serves a different purpose. Prediction and classification are two common model goals. Models of classification predict the categorical labels, and prediction models predict the continuous variable functions [10]. Prediction algorithms are used by Regression, Association Rules, and Clustering, while Decision Trees and Neural Networks use classification algorithms [7]. Data mining tools can be used to assist with health policy and disease prevention. Based on clinical data from heart patients, a heart disease prediction system will help predict heart disease. Many mining techniques like K nearest neighbor, Decision Tree, Naive Bayes, kernel density, random forest automatically defined classes, bagging algorithm, and support vector machine, were used in most of the papers to predict heart disease. We used some of them as reference [18,19] and tried to better the accuracy in our research. [6] The papers vary in terms of the criteria that the methods were applied. Many people have used various criteria and databases to assess the validity of their hypotheses.

3   Proposed Methodology

The use of machine learning is increasing in medical science. Researchers are achieving significant success using it. To predict heart disease in our dataset, we checked and removed outliers; then, after categorizing data, we took user input and fit the training dataset to our selected model. Here is our proposed model illustrated in Fig. 1.

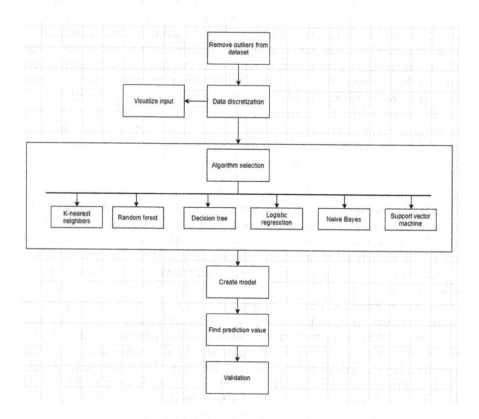

Fig. 1. Proposed model

3.1   Dataset

Data Dictionary. This dataset was collected from Kaggle which was published by Svetlana Ulianova as in the title of Cardiovascular Disease dataset. This dataset contains records of 70000 patients data and carries 11 features. As attributes of a dataset most often have dependencies on each other so it is important to find correlation between them in order to train them and set a model. For this purpose, study on full dataset was needed. Table 1 represents all the attributes in our dataset with possible values.

Table 1. Attributes table

Attributes	Description	Possible Values
Age	Age in years	int (days)
Gender	Male or Female	Male: 1 Female: 2
Height	Height of Patient	int (cm)
Weight	Weight of Patient	float (kg)
Ap_hi	Systolic blood pressure	int
Ap_lo	Diastolic blood pressure	int
Cholesterol	Cholesterol of Patient	1: normal: above normal: well above normal
Gluc	Blood Sugar Levels	1: normal: above normal: well above normal
Smoke	Smoking History	0: No: Yes
Alco	Alcohol intake	0: No: Yes
Active	Physical activity	0: No: Yes
Cardio	Presence/absence of cardiovascular disease	0: Absence: Presence

Correlation Between Attributes. In a dataset attributes have positive or negative relation between features. [11] To fit correct attributes in a machine learning models it is necessary to keep track of attributes which has positive or negative relation among them so that the attributes can be easily fitted in model. [12] Following figure shows the correlation of attributes between them (Fig. 2).

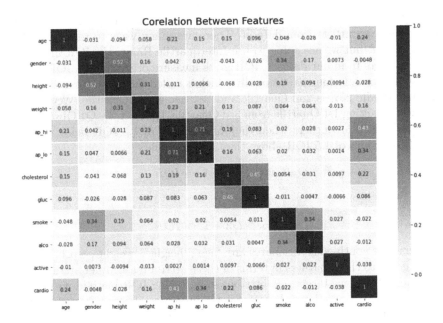

Fig. 2. Correlation between attributes

3.2   Dataset Preprocessing

Data preprocessing is a must to deal with real time data. In a dataset there might be lots of irregularities as real-world data is often incomplete or inconsistent and likely to contain many errors. This dataset contains 13 attributes with 70000 instances. Before fitting our dataset into a model, we have to check some criteria like whether there is missing values on our dataset or not, check whether all the values of attributes are within their range or not, check for negative values to make sure out dataset is completely ready. To meet these criteria, we used standard scaler form the sklearn library to process our data.

Missing Values. Missing Data occurs when no information is provided for one or more items or for a whole unit. If missing data are not handled properly it may lead us to draw an inaccurate inference about the data which will eventually lead us to inaccurate result. Here we used Pandas Data frame in order to check missing values in our dataset.

Removing Outliers Using IQR. From the upper figure we can see there are some errors in our dataset. Systolic and diastolic blood pressure can't be negative. Minimum weight listed here also impractical, same goes for age and height. So basically, this dataset contains outliers. Outliers indicate experimental error. If we don't remove outliers from our dataset it can affects the result seriously thus outliers cause problems in analysis and in data prediction. So, we have to remove outliers from dataset. There are many ways to remove outliers from a dataset but we are going to use Interquartile Range aka IQR method to remove outliers from our dataset. IQR gives measure of variability. IQR divides the distribution into four parts equally which is called quartiles. First 25% is 1st Quartile. Middle 25% is 2nd Quartile and last one is 3rd Quartile. We calculate IQR by subtracting 1st Quartile from 3rd Quartile. IQR = Q3 − Q1 Observations can be identified as outliers when they have values of 1.5 IQR below than 1st Quartile or values of 1.5 IQR above than 3rd Quartile.

$$Outliers < Q1 - 1.5 * IQR$$

or

$$Outliers > Q3 + 1.5 * IQR$$

In our dataset continuous attributes are: 'age', 'height', 'weight', 'ap_hi', 'ap_lo'. We are going to check outliers in terms of these attributes as other attributes are categorical. First, we target age attributes and using IQR method we removed outliers which is 'age' related. It costs us 4 datapoints. Then we removed outliers from 'height' attributes which cost us 519 datapoints. After that we removed outliers from 'ap_hi' attributes which cost us 1309 datapoints. Then we removed outliers from height attributes which cost us 3908 datapoints. Finally, we checked 'ap_hi' and 'ap_lo' and it costs us 2 datapoints and after removing all outliers from dataset we have 62500 datapoints with 12 attributes.

Adding New Attributes

BMI: We have height and weight in this dataset and out target attribute is cardio. We can use 'height' and 'weight' to determine BMI as it may give us better insights. [16] To determine BMI first we converted 'height' attributes in meter which was given in cm in dataset. BMI = Weight in Kilograms/height in Meter2.

Ap_hi_Group (Systolic Blood Pressure): The normal systolic blood pressure stage 1 level is below 120 where the elevated is 120–129. High blood pressure is 130–139 range and high blood pressure stage 2 level is 140 or higher. [13] We categorized data from attribute 'ap_hi' and added another attribute named 'Ap_hi_Group' in our dataset based on criteria stated above [13].

Ap_lo_Group (Diastolic Blood Pressure): The normal systolic blood pressure stage 1 level is below 80 where the elevated is also below 80. High blood pressure is 80–89 range and high blood pressure stage 2 level is 90 or higher [13] We categorized data from attribute 'ap_lo' and added another attribute named 'Ap_lo_Group' in our dataset based on criteria stated above [13].

BMI_class: We first added an attribute named 'BMI' in our dataset using attributes 'height' and 'weight'. Then we categoried data from attribute 'BMI' and added another attribute 'BMI_class' in our dataset. Here we divided data in 4 categories. BMI below 18.5 is Underweight which we put in category 1. BMI between 18.5–24.9 is Normal or Healthy Weight which we put in group 2. BMI 25.0–29.9 is Overweight which we put in group 3 and BMI 30.0 and above is Obese [17] which we put in group 4 in 'BMI_class'.

3.3 Modelling

The target of our entire project is to predict the heart disease with significant accuracy. For this purpose, we are going to use 6 algorithms. Before applying algorithms, we have to divide our dataset in training and test datapoints. We used 80% of our datapoints for training purpose and rest 20% for test purpose. After splitting training and test datapoints we are going to create a model and compare them to get the best result.

3.4 Visualize Data Prediction

The following bar diagrams are the predicted report visualization for given inputs. We are giving input for attributes 'cholesterol', 'ap_hi' (systolic blood pressure), 'ap_lo' (diastolic blood pressure), 'glucose' from out dataset. For 'cholesterol' there are three states. Normal, Above normal and High. Each state has their own range.

Cholesterol. Normal cholesterol range is less than 200. Above normal range is 200–239 and High range is 240 or higher [16]. In Fig. 3 green bar is showing normal range, yellow bar is for above normal range is red bar is for high range. Here we gave a random value 210 as input cholesterol level and in the diagram blue dot showing the value in yellow bar range which indicates that the cholesterol is in above normal range.

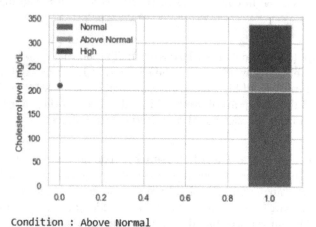

Condition : Above Normal

Fig. 3. Predicted report visualization for Cholesterol (Color figure online)

Systolic Blood Pressure. Normal range is less than 120. Above normal range is 120–129 and High range is 130 or higher [13]. In Fig. 5 green bar is showing normal range, yellow bar is for above normal range is red bar is for high range. Here we gave a random value 120 as input systolic blood pressure level and in the diagram blue dot showing the value in green bar range which indicates that the systolic blood pressure level is in normal range.

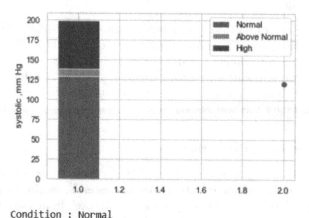

Condition : Normal

Fig. 4. Predicted report visualization for diastolic blood pressure (Color figure online)

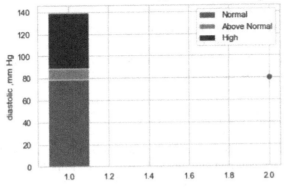

Condition : Above Normal

Fig. 5. Predicted report visualization for systolic blood pressure (Color figure online)

Diastolic Blood Pressure. Normal range is less than 80. Above normal range is 80–89 and High range is 90 or higher [13]. In Fig. 4 green bar is showing normal range, yellow bar is for above normal range is red bar is for high range. Here we gave a random value 80 as input diastolic blood pressure level and in the diagram blue dot showing the value in green bar range which indicates that the systolic blood pressure level is in above normal range.

Glucose. Normal range is when fasting plasma glucose is less than 100 mg/dL. Prediabetes range is when fasting plasma glucose is between 100–125 mg/dL and Well above normal Diabetes range is when fasting plasma glucose is 126 mg/dL or higher [14,15]. In Fig. 6 green bar is showing Normal range, yellow bar is for Prediabetes range is red bar is for Diabetes range. Here we gave a random value 80 as input glucose level and in the diagram blue dot showing the value in green bar range which indicates that the glucose level is in normal range.

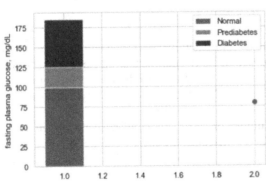

Condition : Normal

Fig. 6. Predicted report visualization glucose (Color figure online)

Cardio Vascular Disease Prediction. Out of 12 attributes 'cardio' is out target output. In our model we gave rest 11 attributes values as input and our model will predict output based on given value whether that particular parson has cardio vascular disease or not.

4   Result Analysis

In previous section we discussed about data processing, algorithms, creating models and how we conduct out project. We successfully fitted out data in our models. Now in this section we are going to discuss results and analyzes them.

4.1   Accuracy of Models

We got this results my applying different algorithms. First, we used our training dataset(raw) with 12 attributes to obtain this result then we engineered our dataset and used our engineered dataset which had 16 attributes to obtain result. Here Table 2 contains the accuracy in % of different algorithms we applied using our raw dataset and engineered dataset and Fig. 7 is a graph representation of the accuracy of our applied algorithms.

Table 2. Attributes table

Attributes	Description	Possible Values
Classifiers	Accuracy for raw dataset (%)	Accuracy for engineered dataset (%)
Decision Tree	63.38%	63.14%
K-Nearest Neighbors	68.86%	66.58%
Logistic Regression	73.11%	73.06%
Naïve Bayes Classifier	71.44%	72.27%
Random Forest	71.11%	70.46%
Support Vector Machine	73.08%	72.76%

Confusion Matrix. Confusion matrix is the summary of the prediction results on a classification problem. It summarizes the numbers of correct and wrong predictions with count values. There are four outcomes of the confusion matrix. In our case True Positive: Number of cases predicted with cardio vascular disease and actually had cardio vascular disease

True Negative: Number of cases predicted with no cardio vascular disease and actually had no cardio vascular disease

False Positive: Number of cases predicted with cardio vascular disease and actually had no cardio vascular disease

False Negative: Number of cases predicted with no cardio vascular disease and actually had cardio vascular disease

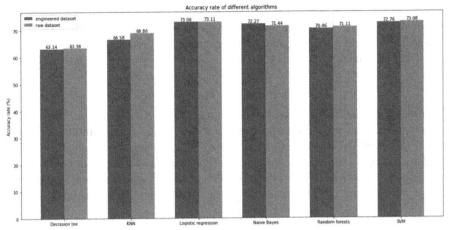

Fig. 7. Accuracy bar chart of applied algorithms

Evaluation of Decision Tree. For engineered dataset Decision tree gives an average accuracy of 62.06% with minimum of 61.94% and maximum of 63.86% accuracy. It gives us 3876 true positive cases, 4017 true negative cases, 2341 false positive cases and 2266 false negative cases. For raw dataset Decision tree gives an average accuracy of 62.64% with minimum of 61.70% and maximum of 63.50% accuracy. It gives us 3890 true positive cases, 4032 true negative cases, 2326 false positive cases and 2252 false negative cases.

Evaluation of K-Nearest Neighbors. For engineered dataset K-Nearest Neighbors gives an average accuracy of 66.48% with minimum of 65.38% and maximum of 67.68% accuracy. It gives us 3978 true positive cases, 4345 true negative cases, 2013 false positive cases and 2164 false negative cases. For raw dataset K-Nearest Neighbors gives an average accuracy of 68.12% with minimum of 66.70% and maximum of 69.22% accuracy. It gives us 4051 true positive cases, 4557 true negative cases, 1801 false positive cases and 2091 false negative cases.

Evaluation of Logistic Regression. For engineered dataset Logistic Regression gives an average accuracy of 72.18% with minimum of 71.20% and maximum of 73.50% accuracy. It gives us 4036 true positive cases, 5097 true negative cases, 1261 false positive cases and 2106 false negative cases. For raw dataset Logistic Regression gives an average accuracy of 72.12% with minimum of 71.08% and maximum of 73.42% accuracy. It gives us 4100 true positive cases, 5040 true negative cases, 1318 false positive cases and 2042 false negative cases.

Evaluation of Naïve Bayes Classifier. For engineered dataset Naïve Bayes Classifier gives an average accuracy of 71.81% with minimum of 70.92% and maximum of 73.52 % accuracy. It gives us 3994 true positive cases, 5140 true negative cases, 1218 false positive cases and 2248 false negative cases. For raw dataset Naïve Bayes Classifier gives an average accuracy of 70.95% with minimum of 69.90% and maximum of 72.26 % accuracy. It gives us 3808 true positive cases, 5122 true negative cases, 1236 false positive cases and 2334 false negative cases.

Evaluation of Random Forest. For engineered dataset Random Forest gives an average accuracy of 70.33% with minimum of 69.30% and maximum of 71.36% accuracy. It gives us 4234 true positive cases, 4573 true negative cases, 1785 false positive cases and 1908 false negative cases. For raw dataset Random Forest gives an average accuracy of 70.35% with minimum of 69.82% and maximum of 71.40% accuracy. It gives us 4285 true positive cases, 4604 true negative cases, 1754 false positive cases and 1857 false negative cases.

Evaluation of Support Vector Machine. For engineered dataset Support Vector Machine gives an average accuracy of 71.95% with minimum of 70.74% and maximum of 73.44% accuracy. It gives us 3870 true positive cases, 5225 true negative cases, 1133 false positive cases and 2272 false negative cases. For raw dataset Support Vector Machine gives an average accuracy of 72.11% with minimum of 71.20% and maximum of 73.54% accuracy. It gives us 4074 true positive cases, 5077 true negative cases, 1281 false positive cases and 2068 false negative cases.

4.2 Analysis

We trained 6 different models with different penalty but for Logistic regression, Naïve Bayes and Support vector machine we got almost same result. In our project we are predicting a disease which has a major impact on human lives so we need our model to be accurate. In this case it is not life threatening if the model predicts a non-cardiovascular case as cardio vascular case (false positive) but we can't afford to predict cardio vascular case a non-cardio vascular case as it might cost someone's life. Considering false negative and accuracy as major factors we think Logistic Regression is more accurate than other models and only logical to select as the only model to predict cardio vascular disease for out project. We selected 2 research and tried to improve accuracy. In One of the research [18] highest accuracy was 72% and in another one [19] the highest accuracy was 72.9%. In our research the highest accuracy is 73%. We conducted this research and tried to improve the accuracy to predict cardiovascular abnormalities.

5   Conclusion and Future Work

5.1   Conclusion

In this project 6 machine learning algorithms were applied to predict whether a person has cardiovascular disease or not based on given history of a person. We applied six algorithms and after comparing the accuracy we selected one which gave us the most significant result. We used dataset from Kaggle which was published by Svetlana Ulianova as in the title of Cardiovascular Disease dataset. Our used dataset contains 62500 instances after removing outliers and we used cross validation to divide our data in test and training set. For our raw dataset out of 13 attributes we considered 12 attributes and for our engineered dataset we considered 16 attributes and applied 6 algorithms and then analyzed the accuracy after comparing all 6 algorithms. It was found that Logistic Regression gave the maximum accuracy level of 73% and Decision Tree gave us lowest level of accuracy of 63% for both raw and engineer dataset. Logistic Regression, SVM and Naïve bayes gave almost same level of accuracy but considering the lowest false positive rate we found out Logistic Regression is the most significant one.

5.2   Future Works

We implemented 6 algorithms in raw and engineered dataset and the maximum accuracy level was 73.11% which is not good enough. Better accuracy level can be achieved by implementing advanced algorithms like Convolution Neural network, Radial Basis Neural Network, Time Domain Neural Network with multi class and binary kernel. Techniques like Bayesian belief or Regression analysis can be used for data preprocessing.

References

1. Bhatla, N., Jyoti, K.: An analysis of heart disease prediction using different data mining techniques. Int. J. Eng. **1**(8), 1–4 (2012)
2. Hong, T.P., Kuo, C.S., Chi, S.C.: Mining association rules from quantitative data. Intell. Data Anal. **3**(5), 363–376 (1999)
3. Ara, S.: PharmD, is a clinical pharmacist, Health Net Inc, Woodland Hills, California. At the time of this study, Ara was a health outcomes research fellow, WellPoint Pharmacy Management, West Hills, California (1996–2001)
4. Ara, S.: PharmD, Clinical Pharmacist, Health Net Inc, 21281 Burbank Blvd., B5 Woodland Hills, CA 91367 (2004)
5. Obenshain, M.K.: Application of data mining techniques to healthcare data. Infect. Control Hosp. Epidemiol. **25**(8), 690–695 (2004)
6. Patel, J., TejalUpadhyay, D., Patel, S.: Heart disease prediction using machine learning and data mining technique. Heart Dis. **7**(1), 129–137 (2015)
7. Charly, K.: Data mining for the enterprise. In: 31st Annual Hawaii International Conference on System Sciences, vol. 7, pp. 295–304. IEEE Computer (1998)
8. Fayyad, U.: Data mining and knowledge discovery in databases: implications for scientific databases. In: Proceedings of the 9th International Conference on Scientific and Statistical Database Management, Olympia, Washington, USA, pp. 2–11 (1997)
9. Obenshain, M.K.: Application of data mining techniques to healthcare data. Infect. Control Hosp. Epidemiol. **25**(8), 690–695 (2004)
10. Han, J., Kamber, M.: Data Mining Concepts and Techniques. Morgan Kaufmann Publishers, Burlington (2006)

11. Kumar, S., Chong, I.: Correlation analysis to identify the effective data in machine learning: prediction of depressive disorder and emotion states. Int. J. Environ. Res. Public Health **15**(12), 2907 (2018)

12. Gupta, B.: Interview Questions Business Analytics. Springer, Heidelberg (2016). https://doi.org/10.1007/978-1-4842-0599-0

13. Sobieraj, P., Lewandowski, J., Siński, M., Gaciong, Z.: Determination of optimal on-treatment diastolic blood pressure range using automated measurements in subjects with cardiovascular disease-analysis of a SPRINT trial subpopulation. J. Clin. Hypertens. **21**(7), 911–918 (2019)

14. Luo, J., Chen, Y.J., Chang, L.J.: Fasting blood glucose level and prognosis in non-small cell lung cancer (NSCLC) patients. Lung Cancer **76**(2), 242–247 (2012)

15. Repaka, A.N., Ravikanti, S.D., Franklin, R.G.: Design and implementing heart disease prediction using Naives Bayesian (2019)

16. Kim, K.S., Owen, W.L., Williams, D., Adams-Campbell, L.L.: A comparison between BMI and Conicity index on predicting coronary heart disease: the Framingham Heart Study. Ann. Epidemiol. **10**(7), 424–431 (2000)

17. Freedman, D.S., Khan, L.K., Dietz, W.H., Srinivasan, S.R., Berenson, G.S.: Relationship of childhood obesity to coronary heart disease risk factors in adulthood: the Bogalusa Heart Study. Pediatrics **108**(3), 712–718 (2001)

18. Yue, W., Voronova, L.I., Voronov, V.I.: Comparison of several models for cardiovascular diseases prediction. Synchroinfo J. **6**(6), 24–28 (2020)

19. Marbaniang, I.A., Choudhury, N.A., Moulik, S.: Cardiovascular Disease (CVD) Prediction using Machine Learning Algorithms, December 2020

COVID-19 Detection from Lung CT Scan Using Transfer Learning Models

Nazmus Shakib Shadin$^{(\boxtimes)}$ ⓘ, Silvia Sanjana ⓘ, and Nusrat Jahan Lisa ⓘ

Department of Computer Science and Engineering, Ahsanullah University of Science and Technology, Dhaka, Bangladesh
shadhin.aust.cse@gmail.com, nusratlisa.cse@aust.edu

Abstract. Initial prognosis of the COVID-19 is vital for pandemic avoidance. Nowadays, The lung infection driven by SARS-CoV-2 has spread throughout the world, urged the World Health Organization (WHO) to proclaim it a pandemic disease for its rapid spread. The COVID-19 infection has detrimental effects on respiration, and the severity of the infection might be discovered using particular imaging techniques and lung CT scan is one of them. So, quick and precise coronavirus disease (COVID-19) testing is a possibility utilizing computed tomography (CT) scan images with the alliance of AI. The goal of this work is to use lung CT scans to recognize COVID-19 using transfer learning models and a comparative analysis among various transfer learning models using CT scans. The research was conducted using two standard datasets containing 2792 lung CT scan images. Xception, MobileNetV2, InceptionV3, DenseNet201, and InceptionResNetV2 were utilized to tag COVID-19 as negative or positive in case of the CT scan inputs. Our used transfer learning based Xception, MobileNetV2, InceptionV3, DenseNet201, and IncpetionResNetV2 achieved the highest validation accuracy of 92.19%, 97.40%, 85.42%, 86.98%, and 95.31% accordingly.

Keywords: COVID-19 · Lung CT scan · Transfer learning · Xception · MobileNetV2 · InceptionV3 · DenseNet201 · IncpetionResNetV2

1 Introduction

Coronavirus disease (COVID-19) is a coronavirus that was discovered recently and induces communicable diseases [1]. It was in the first instance discovered in Wuhan city, China in January 2020, and the effect has afterwards become widespread around the world. It was officially declared emergency of global significance on January 30th, 2020, by the World Health Organization (WHO). [2]. Essentially, COVID-19 is an infection of the respiratory tract caused by the SARS-CoV-2 virus, according to experts. Upper (throat, nose, and sinus) or lower part of respiratory system can be affected (lungs and windpipe) [3]. It spreads in just the same way that other coronaviruses do, primarily through

A. K. M. M. Islam et al. (Eds.): ICBBDB 2021, CCIS 1550, pp. 49–63, 2022.
https://doi.org/10.1007/978-3-031-17181-9_5

direct contact between people [4]. Animals can also potentially spread the virus while being infected themselves [5]. COVID-19 symptoms include a dry coughs, fatigue, moderate to mild respiratory disease, loss of appetite, and high feverish body [6]. Up to July 30, 2021, It has resulted in the deaths of 4,189,148 people, and the number of Covid cases were 195,886,929 [9].

A major technique for properly managing this pandemic is to identify patients early, isolate them, and treat them. The ability to quickly, easily, affordably, and reliably identify COVID-19 pathology in a person is critical for reducing advancement of COVID-19 virus. The standard of excellence for diagnosing COVID-19 is currently reverse transcriptase quantitative polymerase chain reaction (RT-qPCR) testing [10]. But it is a time consuming procedure and it has a excessive false-negative rate and poor sensitivity, therefore it might overlook a positive case, causing contaminated people to be classified as non infected [11]. Imaging technology based methods such as computed tomography (CT) imaging [12] and X-Ray [13] imaging, as well as Ultrasound imaging [14], are examples of other testing methods of COVID-19. Chest X-rays (CXRs) are less expensive than other radiological tests like CT scans, and they're available in practically every clinic, so they're a good way to find out if anyone has COVID-19. However, qualified clinicians may not always be available, especially in distant locations, making CXR-based detection of COVID-19 individuals difficult. Furthermore, the radiological indications of COVID-19 are new and foreign to many professionals, who have never seen COVID-19 positive patient CXRs before. Its sensitivity is also lower than computed tomography (CT) [15]. The high rate of false negatives in chest X-rays, as in PCR, is also a drawback. On the other hand, Lung ultrasound (LUS) is a rapidly evolving diagnostic tool that is commonly used in intensive care, nephrology, and cardiology. It can also be used to diagnose and monitor COVID-19 [16]. Whilst lung ultrasound offers various advantages, such as the lack of radiation, decreased danger of contamination, repeatability, and lower costs, one of the drawbacks is its lesser sensitivity when compared to a CT. Other drawback of ultrasonic imaging is that it is sometimes unable to distinguish lesions that are deeper and intrapulmonic [17]. Chest computed tomography (CT) imaging has been widely used to identify and evaluate COVID-19 sufferer with the novel coronavirus disease. CT imaging is widely recognized for its high sensitivity and negative predictive value (NPV). As a result, physicians are increasingly recommending chest computed tomography (CT) as a screening test [18]. Ai et al. [35] recently examined the diagnostic usefulness and consistency of CT scans. It was discovered that 59% of 1014 patients had positive RT-PCR results, whereas 88% had positive chest CT scans, indicating that chest CT scans have a high sensitivity for COVID-19 diagnosis. As a result, chest computed tomography may be used as the principal method for detecting COVID-19 in epidemic areas.

Computer-aided diagnostic (CAD) technologies are required to make an efficient, well-founded, and fast diagnosis of COVID-19. COVID-19 has been found throughout time utilizing a number of machine learning [19], transfer learning (TL) [20], and deep learning (DL) methods [21].

For image classification, different deep learning models have been utilized so far. For unique medical disorders like COVID-19, obtaining a sufficiently big, publically available archive of medical image data set is tough because of the resources and time needed to obtain and classify image data. By pre-weighting the system with the outcomes of a prior training cycle from another realm, transfer learning can be utilized to train DL models.

This paper targets to make a significant impact in mentioned areas: In this paper we proposed more efficient learning deep convolutional layers, on top of the pretrained transfer learning models we have applied the convolutional layer which has created a hybrid model. We have deployed five transfer learning models in this study. COVID-19 identification is particularly challenging in countries where competent doctors and equipment are scarce, therefore these Transfer Learning models will help doctors to identify COVID-19 more quickly and effectively. This study makes use of one of the most well-known datasets in COVID-19 detection for testing the efficiency of all of the Transfer Learning models that have been deployed.

The following is a synopsis of the layout of the paper. In Segment II, we reviewed earlier research on COVID-19 detection. In Segment III, the study is described in detail, and the outcomes are analyzed in Segment IV. In Segment V, research remark and important topics were addressed, additionally, a survey of the current research in construction for future endeavors.

2 Literature Review

Several studies and groundwork using DL and TL have been developed in the area of medical imaging such as CT scans. A newer dataset was introduced by Rahimzadeh et al. [22], the architecture uses a new feature pyramid network built for classification challenges to improve the ResNet50V2 model's ability while avoiding losing data from small objects, resulting in a 98.49% accuracy. A DenseNet201 focused deep transfer learning (DTL) is presented to classify patients as COVID affected or not. The proposed model achieves a 97% accuracy rate. The chest CT-scans are classified by a convolutional neural network and a pretrained DenseNet201 model with training, validation and, validation accuracy of 99.82%, 97.4%, and 96.25% in [23].

Using a combination of Mobilenetv2 and ResNet50 characteristics, an automatic solution for COVID-19 diagnosis is proposed in Kaur et al. [24]. Classification accuracy can be improved by combining features from the transfer learned Mobilenetv2 and the transfer learned ResNet50's final average pooling layer. To generate the output, an SVM classifier is trained using the fused feature vector and the related labels and has a testing accuracy of 98.35%, an 98.39% F1-score, 99.19% precision, and 97.60% recall. DenseNet, NASNet, Xception, MobileNet, ResNet, InceptionV3, VGGNet, ResNet, and InceptionResNetV2 were selected from a collection of deep CNNs in [25] to produce the most accurate feature. The collected attributes were then passed into a series of machine learning models to determine COVID-19 cases. The DenseNet121 feature extractor with Bagging tree classifier yielded the top results, which had a 99.5% accuracy, and the ResNet50 feature extractor trained using LightGBM, which had a 98% accuracy.

Alshazly et al. [26] utilized enhanced deep network architectures which implemented a TL technique that used custom sized input tailored for each deep architecture to perform accurate. In Serte et al. [27], COVID-19 and normal CT volumes were classified using an artificial intelligence (AI) technique and it predicts COVID-19 using the ResNet-50 then it merges image-level predictions, achieving an AUC value of 96%. Arora et al. [7] used a super-residual dense neural network to solve their problem. XceptionNet, InceptionV3, MobileNet, DenseNet, VGG, and ResNet50 were used to determine whether COVID-19 was positive or negative. MobileNet achieved a precision of 94.12% and 100% respectively.

Horry et al. [28] improved the chosen VGG19 architecture for the picture modalities to demonstrate how the models may be employed for the COVID-19 datasets. They also suggest an image pre-processing stage for constructing and testing deep learning models on a reliable image dataset. The new technology tries to eliminate superfluous noise from images, allowing deep learning models to focus on spotting diseases with distinct characteristics. The VGG19 model achieved X-Ray precision of up to 86%, Ultrasound precision of 100%, and CT scan precision of 84%.

3   Methodology

We will briefly outline our intended methodology in this section. For the identification of COVID-19, we will elaborate on the working technique of Transfer Learning (TL) based Xception, MobileNetV2, IncpetionV3, DenseNet201, and IncpetionResNetV2. The stages of data collection and data pre-processing will also be covered in this section of the paper.

3.1   Dataset Collection

COVID-19 detection from Lung CT scan was accomplished through the collection of a total of 2792 images from two separate datasets [31,32] that made publicly available on the internet. The balance data from COVID-19 affected lung CT scans and normal lung CT scans were included in this study. As a result, our models can learn both cases appropriately and precisely. Nearly 80% of the images in here in this dataset were utilized in the training phase, and the rest 20% were utilized in the testing phase. Figure 1 depicts a sample of the lung CT scan image data.

3.2   Data Pre-processing

In the transfer learning environment, it is widely acknowledged that all transfer learning models are data thirsty, and that transfer learning architectures perform

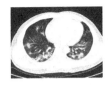

Fig. 1. Lung CT scan image data sample

better when given larger amounts of data. We've used the ImageData Generator Keras library to generate more data [30]. The characteristics are listed in Table 1 below.

Table 1. Augmentation parameters

Rescale_Size	Shear_Range	Zoom_Range	Horizontal_Flip
1/255	0.2	0.2	TRUE

The data images have been transformed into a new shpae of $256 \times 256 \times 3$. This research used Binary Crossentropy's model loss. NumPy arrays are used to aid in the calculation of images. The LabelBinarizer() method is responsible for image labeling. To hasten the computation, images are transformed into NumPy arrays. The images are labeled using the Binarizer() method.

3.3 Xception Model

The Xception model is pre-trained on the basis of ImageNet [29] with Keras as well as Tensorflow.

The Xception model employs depth-wise separable convolutions in a deep CNN architecture. Google researchers developed the Xception Model. It's essentially a more advanced version of the Inception Model. In the Xcepiton model, data first flows via the input flow, then eight times through the middle flow, and finally through the exit flow.

There are three flows in the Xception Architecture: entry, middle, and exit. There are numerous depth wise Separable Convolutions with Convolutional 2D (Conv2D) in the Entry flow, as well as 'MaxPooling' as the Pooling layer and the 'Relu' activation function as the Classification-Activation. In the middle flow (18,18,728), three depth-wise separable convolutions are used with the 'Relu' activation function, and three depth-wise separable convolutions were also used with the 'Relu' activation function. Eight times the middle flow is performed. There are additionally (18,18,728) features maps with several depth-wise separable convolutions and a Convolutional 2D map in the exit layer (Conv2D). The ClassifierActivation function is also used as the ClassifierActivation function, and the Pooling layer is 'GlobalAveragePooling.' There are 204-dimensional vectors in the exit layer. After that, logistic regression is used.

3.4   MobileNetV2 Model

28 Deep Convolutional Neural Network Layers have been used in MobileNetV2. Here, Bottleneck levels are connected by residual connections in an inverted residual structure.

Figure 2 illustrates the MobileNetV2 architectural module: 1. 1×1 Convolution 2. 3×3 Depthwise Convolution. Each block is made up of three layers: Convolution 1×1 with Relu6 activation function, Convolution Layer with Depthwise Convolution, and Convolution 1×1 with No Linearity Concept.

There are Stride 1 Blocks and Stride 2 Blocks, as may be seen in Fig. 2.

The first block has the following characteristics:

i. Input Layer, ii. 1×1 Convolution with Relu6 activation function, iii. Depthwise Convolution with Relu6 Activation, iv. Linearized 1×1 Convolution Layer, v. Adding the layers.

The following are the characteristics of the Stride 2 Block: i. Input Layer, ii. 1×1 Convolution with Relu6 activation function, iii. Depthwise Convolution with stride = 2 and Relu6 activation function, iv. 1×1 Convolution Layer without any linearity.

The Stride 2 Block has the following characteristics: it has an input layer, which is made up of a single 1×1 convolution with Relu6 activation function, followed by a depthwise convolution with stride 2 and Relu6 activation, and then it has a 1×1 convolution layer without linearity.

In our research, MobileNetV2 employed this architecture.

This is the architecture used by MobileNetV2 in our research.

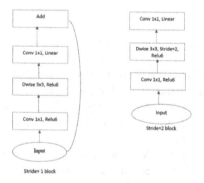

Fig. 2. Illustration of MobileNetV2

3.5   InceptionV3 Model

The addition of new techniques such as LabelSmoothing, Factorized 7×7 convolutions, and the incorporation of an auxiliary classifier for propagating label information down the network have significantly changed the InceptionV3 model.

Side-head batch normalization is also performed on the layers. Generally, the primary use of this technology is for image processing and object detection.

To begin, we've locked down the foundational structure of our InceptionV3 model in our testbed. We achieved this by including the top = false command in our trainable layer, and layered it on top of the base layer and made the same size as each other (225,225,3). The Adam stochastic gradient descent method was utilized along with the Relu activation function to learn how to optimize. This is the rate at which our InceptionV3 architecture learns backpropagation, and it's set at 0.01.

This is our study model as depicted in the InceptionV3 architecture diagram:

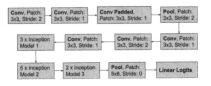

Fig. 3. Illustration of InceptionV3 [13]

The InceptionV3 model, which is based on transfer learning, has a basic architecture depicted in Fig. 3. In order to use multiple smaller convolutional filters, an inception model that combines multiple smaller filters into a single larger filter has been proposed. This type of design reduces the number of parameters that must be trained, which in turn cuts down on the difficulty of the calculation.

3.6   DenseNet201 Model

The DenseNet-201 neural network is made up of a total of 201 layers. A similar pre-training of DenseNet201 is performed on the ImageNet Dataset [30]. The trained network is able to categorize images into 1,000 object categories, such as pencil, keyboard, mouse, and a variety of animal species. Due to this process, the network has learned a wide range of image features. To be equivalent to a network with DenseNet101 input nodes of the DenseNet201 is (224,224,3).

In the Fig. 4 we can observe that, In contrast to the more conventional CNN, DenseNet (also known as Dense Convolutional Network) uses a much smaller number of parameters since redundant feature maps were not learnt here. As the levels in DenseNet are quite thin, that is, there are only twelve filters on top of one another, the new feature-maps that are created are a smaller subset of the whole feature-map space. DenseNet is accessible in four various varieties: DenseNet121, DenseNet201, DenseNet169 and DenseNet264. DenseNet201 has

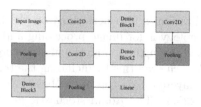

Fig. 4. Illustration of DenseNet201

been adopted in this paper for the COVID-19 detection. DenseNet's layers all have immediate access to the source images as well as its gradients, as seen in Fig. 4. As a result, the computational cost has been greatly decreased, which enables DenseNet a more attractive option for image classification applications.

3.7 InceptionResNetV2 Model

InceptionResNetV2 was also trained using over a million images from the Im ageNet Database [30], which contain large numbers of concept classes. It is a convolutional neural network, which means it has many depth layers. It had a total depth of 164 layers in the past. However, the Keras library now claims that the depth is 572 layers deep. Figure 5 illustrates the architectural module, called InceptionResNetV2.

Figure 4 below presents the InceptionResNetV2 architecture module:

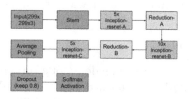

Fig. 5. Illustration of InceptionResNetV2

These are shown in Fig. 5, the input layer contains $299 \times 299 \times 3$-pixel im ages. The $35 \times 35 \times 256$-pixel output data from the Stem appears in the results. After applying 5x Inception-resnet-A, a $35 \times 35 \times 256$ output image is gener- ated. Reduction-A was then used to reduce the image to $17 \times 17 \times 896$ pixels. After that, 10x Inception-resnet-B ($17 \times 17 \times 896$) is added. With the help of the Reduction-B technique, the image is then reduced to $8 \times 8 \times 1792$ pixels. The pooling layer is 'average pooling' in this instance. The dropout rate of 0.8 is also used in the In ception Res-NetV2 model, as well as Classifier Activation is being used, which is 'Softmax'.

3.8 Hyperparameters for All the CNN Based Transfer Learning Models

This study used five CNN (Convolutional Neural Network) based transfer learning models, which we described in the previous sub-sections. In all the five CNN-based transfer learning models, we used the same hyper-parameters. The hyper-parameters for these CNN-based transfer learning models are shown below in Table 2.

Table 2. Hyperparameters

Batch_Size	Epoch	Loss_Function	Optimizer	Learning_Rate
32	30	Binary_Crossentropy	Adam	0.01

4 Results Analysis

4.1 Performance Examination Using the Confusion Matrix

Following the completion of the training and testing stage, the performance of the models are evaluated on the basis of TP, FP, TN, and FN which are the parameters for Confusion Matrix. To measure the five transfer learning models performance, the calculation of their accuracy, recall, along with precision and F1-score has been done. The total number of true-positives, true-negatives, false-positives, and false-negatives is represented by the letters TP, TN, FP, and FN correspondingly [28]. Furthermore, the equations for accuracy, sensitivity/recall, precision, along with f1-score are stated here:

$$Accuracy = \frac{TP + TN}{TP + TN + FP + FN} \tag{1}$$

$$Precision = \frac{TP}{TP + FP} \tag{2}$$

$$Recall = \frac{TP}{TP + FN} \tag{3}$$

$$F1 - Score = \frac{2 * Precision * Recall}{Precision + Recall} \tag{4}$$

TP, TN, FP, and FN were employed to generate a confusion matrix for each of the five deep learning techniques.

4.2 Xception Model Results Analysis

Accuracy Diagram: Following the implementation of the Xception Architecture, the following accuracy and loss was achieved in the duo training and validation sets:

Figure 6 shows that in training phase in epochs 18, 24, and 20, we have achieved the highest accuracy of 91.70%, and in the validation phase in epoch 20, we have got the top accuracy of 92.19%.

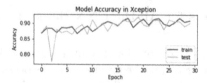

Fig. 6. Training and testing accuracy for the Xception model in each epochs

4.3   MobileNetV2 Model Results Analysis

Accuracy Diagram: Following the implementation of the MobileNetV2 Architecture, the following accuracy and loss was achieved in the both training and validation phases:

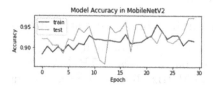

Fig. 7. Training and testing accuracy for the MobileNetV2 model in each epochs

Figure 7 shows that in the training phase in epoch 23, we have achieved the highest accuracy of 95.85%, and in the validation phase in epochs 29, and 30, we have got the maximum accuracy of 97.40%.

4.4   InceptionV3 Model Results Analysis

Accuracy Diagram: Following the implementation of the InceptionV3 Architecture, the model was able to attain the following accuracy and loss in the both training and validation phases:

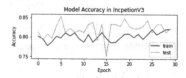

Fig. 8. Training and testing accuracy for the InceptionV3 model in each epochs

Figure 8 shows that in the training phase in epochs 26, and 29, we have achieved the highest accuracy of 82.06%, and in the validation phase in epoch 6, the model has accomplished the highest accuracy of 85.42%.

4.5   DenseNet201 Model Results Analysis

Accuracy Diagram: Following the implementation of the DenseNet201 Architecture, the model has the ability to attain the following accuracy and loss in the both training and validation phases:

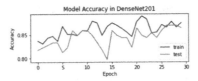

Fig. 9. Training and testing accuracy for the DenseNet121 architecture in each epochs

Figure 9 shows that in the training phase in epoch 22, we have achieved the highest accuracy of 89.02%, and in the validation phase in epochs 27, 28, and 29, we have achieved the highest accuracy of 86.98%.

4.6   InceptionResNetV2 Model Results Analysis

Accuracy Diagram: Following the implementation of the InceptionResNetV2 Architecture, the model performed the following accuracy and loss in the both training and validation phases:

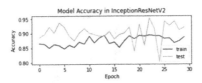

Fig. 10. Training and testing accuracy for the InceptionResNetV2 Architecture in each epochs

Figure 10 shows that in the training phase in epoch 23, the model performed the highest accuracy of 89.42%, and in the testing phase in epoch 23, the model attained the highest accuracy of 95.31%.

4.7   Performance Analysis of Transfer Learning Models

Table 3 compares the accuracy, precision, recall, F1-score, and area under the Receiver Operating Characteristic curve (ROC) or AUC of the TL Models. Here, the Transfer learning models are assessed on the basis of the Confusion Matrix parameters.

Table 3. Results comparison among the transfer models

Model	Accuracy	Precision	Recall	F1-Score	AUC
Xception	90.10%	92.13%	87.23%	89.61%	0.9418
MobileNetV2	97.40%	95.88%	98.94%	97.38%	0.9964
InceptionV3	82.29%	84.09%	78.72%	81.31%	0.9162
DenseNet201	86.46%	84.00%	89.36%	86.59%	0.9603
InceptionResNetV2	92.19%	96.47%	87.23%	91.62%	0.9688

From Table 3 we can see that this is the case here for **Accuracy:** MobileNetV2 achieved the maximum accuracy of 97.40% among all the transfer learning models, for **Precision:** InceptionResNetV2 achieved the highest precision of 96.47% among all the transfer learning models, for **Recall:** MobileNetV2 achieved the maximum recall of 98.94% among all the transfer learning models, for **F1-Score:** MobileNetV2 achieved the highest F1-Score of 97.38% among all the transfer learning models as well, and finally for **AUC:** MobileNetV2 achieved the maximum AUC value of 0.9964 too.

Though, this is apparent, it's possible to draw the conclusion that MobileNetV2 performs significantly better than other transfer learning models in this situation.

As illustrated in Fig. 11, the model is able to identify the primary class for a single image.

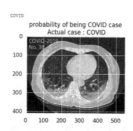

Fig. 11. Actual detection of COVID-19.

4.8   Outperforming Existing Models

Table 4. Our models outperforming existing models

Methods	[34]	[33]	[8]	[7]	Our result
MobileNetV2	95.00% (A)	–	–	94.12% (P)	95.88% (P)/97.40% (A)
InceptionV3	–	–	53.40% (A)	–	82.29% (A)
DenseNet	–	84.70% (A)	–	–	86.46% (A)

Table 4 shows that our techniques have excelled the current models that were employed in this study. In Table 4, (A) indicates performance was assessed in terms of 'Accuracy' and (P) indicates 'Precision'. Using roughly the same dataset, our model surpasses the others in accuracy and precision.

5 Conclusion

Medical practitioner in both developing and developed countries can benefit from this study's perceptible analysis of COVID-19 detection, which can assist them in detecting COVID-19 at an earlier stage. Some models presented here outperform their counterparts in terms of performance when compared to existing models. It has proposed architectures based on Transfer Learning, including the Xception, MobileNetV2, InceptionV3, DenseNet201, and InceptionResNetV2 networks. In future research, we will attempt to demonstrate a comparison between various more Transfer Learning models using a larger number of images. This research has the drawback of using radioactive CT scans on youngsters and pregnant women. In addition, it is costly, time-consuming, and not accessible in disadvantaged regions. Our model will be built on a larger dataset in the next. We'll explore if these models can be applied to different COVID-19 Lung CT Scan datasets. In addition, we will also strive to improve the models' accuracy.

References

1. Coronavirus.   Who.int.   www.who.int/health-topics/coronavirus#tab=tab_1. Accessed 31 July 2021
2. Archived: WHO Timeline - COVID-19. Who.int. https://www.who.int/news/item/27-04-2020-who-timeline-covid-19. Accessed 31 July 2021
3. Coronavirus (COVID-19) Overview. WebMD. https://www.webmd.com/lung/coronavirus. Accessed 31 July 2021
4. Transmission of SARS-CoV-2: implications for infection prevention precautions. Who.int. https://www.who.int/news-room/commentaries/detail/transmission-of-sars-cov-2-implications-for-infection-prevention-precautions. Accessed 31 July 2021
5. Mallapaty, S.: What's the risk that animals will spread the coronavirus? Nature.com (2020). https://www.nature.com/articles/d41586-020-01574-4. Accessed 31 July 2021
6. Symptoms of Coronavirus (COVID-19). WebMD. https://www.webmd.com/lung/covid-19-symptoms#1. Accessed 31 July 2021
7. Arora, V., Ng, E., Leekha, R., Darshan, M., Singh, A.: Transfer learning-based approach for detecting COVID-19 ailment in lung CT scan. Comput. Biol. Med. **135**, 104575 (2021). https://doi.org/10.1016/j.compbiomed.2021.104575
8. Shah, V., Keniya, R., Shridharani, A., Punjabi, M., Shah, J., Mehendale, N.: Diagnosis of COVID-19 using CT scan images and deep learning techniques. Emerg. Radiol. (2021). https://doi.org/10.1007/s10140-020-01886-y
9. WHO Coronavirus (COVID-19) Dashboard. Covid19.who.int. https://covid19.who.int/. Accessed 31 July 2021

10. Staff A Why qPCR is the gold standard for COVID-19 testing - Ask a Scientist. Ask a Scientist. https://cutt.ly/AQGqmhj. Accessed 12 Aug 2021
11. Asai, T.: COVID-19: accurate interpretation of diagnostic tests-a statistical point of view. J. Anesth. **35**, 328–332 (2020). https://doi.org/10.1007/s00540-020-02875-8
12. Shah, V., Keniya, R., Shridharani, A., Punjabi, M., Shah, J., Mehendale, N.: Diagnosis of COVID-19 using CT scan images and deep learning techniques. Emerg. Radiol. **28**, 497–505 (2021). https://doi.org/10.1007/s10140-020-01886-y
13. Shadin, N., Sanjana, S., Lisa, N.: COVID-19 diagnosis from chest X-ray images using convolutional neural network (CNN) and InceptionV3. In: 2021 International Conference on Information Technology (ICIT) (2021). https://doi.org/10.1109/ICIT52682.2021.9491752
14. Born, J., et al.: Accelerating detection of lung pathologies with explainable ultrasound image analysis. Appl. Sci. **11**, 672 (2021). https://doi.org/10.3390/app11020672
15. Martínez Chamorro, E., Díez Tascón, A., Ibáñez Sanz, L., Ossaba Vélez, S., Borruel Nacenta, S.: Radiologic diagnosis of patients with COVID-19. Radiología (English Edition) **63**, 56–73 (2021). https://doi.org/10.1016/j.rxeng.2020.11.001
16. Buda, N., Segura-Grau, E., Cylwik, J., Wełnicki, M.: Lung ultrasound in the diagnosis of COVID-19 infection - a case series and review of the literature. Adv. Med. Sci. **65**, 378–385 (2020). https://doi.org/10.1016/j.advms.2020.06.005
17. Khalili, N., Haseli, S., Iranpour, P.: Lung ultrasound in COVID-19 pneumonia: prospects and limitations. Acad. Radiol. **27**, 1044–1045 (2020). https://doi.org/10.1016/j.acra.2020.04.032
18. Bernheim, A., et al.: Chest CT findings in coronavirus disease-19 (COVID-19): relationship to duration of infection. Radiology **295**, 200463 (2020). https://doi.org/10.1148/radiol.2020200463
19. Mohammad-Rahimi, H., Nadimi, M., Ghalyanchi-Langeroudi, A., Taheri, M., Ghafouri-Fard, S.: Application of machine learning in diagnosis of COVID-19 through X-ray and CT images: a scoping review. Front. Cardiovasc. Med. (2021). https://doi.org/10.3389/fcvm.2021.638011
20. Maghdi, H., Asaad, A., Ghafoor, K., Sadiq, A., Khan, M.: Diagnosing COVID-19 Pneumonia from X-Ray and CT Images using Deep Learning and Transfer Learning Algorithms (2020). arXiv:2004.00038
21. Rohila, V., Gupta, N., Kaul, A., Sharma, D.: Deep learning assisted COVID-19 detection using full CT-scans. Internet Things **14**, 100377 (2021). https://doi.org/10.1016/j.iot.2021.100377
22. Rahimzadeh, M., Attar, A., Sakhaei, S.: A fully automated deep learning-based network for detecting COVID-19 from a new and large lung CT scan dataset. Biomed. Signal Process. Control **68**, 102588 (2021). https://doi.org/10.1016/j.bspc.2021.102588
23. Jaiswal, A., Gianchandani, N., Singh, D., Kumar, V., Kaur, M.: Classification of the COVID-19 infected patients using DenseNet201 based deep transfer learning. J. Biomol. Struct. Dyn. **39**(15), 5682–5689 (2020). https://doi.org/10.1080/07391102.2020.1788642
24. Kaur, T., Gandhi, T.K.: Automated diagnosis of COVID-19 from CT scans based on concatenation of Mobilenetv2 and ResNet50 features. In: Singh, S.K., Roy, P., Raman, B., Nagabhushan, P. (eds.) CVIP 2020. CCIS, vol. 1376, pp. 149–160. Springer, Singapore (2021). https://doi.org/10.1007/978-981-16-1086-8_14

25. Kassania, S., Kassanib, P., Wesolowskic, M., Schneidera, K., Detersa, R.: Automatic detection of coronavirus disease (COVID-19) in X-ray and CT images: a machine learning based approach. Biocybern. Biomed. Eng. **41**, 867–879 (2021). https://doi.org/10.1016/j.bbe.2021.05.013

26. Alshazly, H., Linse, C., Barth, E., Martinetz, T.: Explainable COVID-19 detection using chest CT scans and deep learning. Sensors **21**, 455 (2021). https://doi.org/10.3390/s21020455

27. Serte, S., Demirel, H.: Deep learning for diagnosis of COVID-19 using 3D CT scans. Comput. Biol. Med. **132**, 104306 (2021). https://doi.org/10.1016/j.compbiomed.2021.104306

28. Horry, M., et al.: COVID-19 detection through transfer learning using multimodal imaging data. IEEE Access **8**, 149808–149824 (2020). https://doi.org/10.1109/access.2020.3016780

29. ImageNet. https://www.image-net.org/. Accessed 12 Aug 2021

30. Shadin, N., Sanjana, S., Farzana, M.: Automated detection of COVID-19 pneumonia and non COVID-19 pneumonia from chest X-ray images using convolutional neural network (CNN). In: 2021 2nd International Conference on Innovative and Creative Information Technology (ICITech) (2021). https://doi.org/10.1109/icitech50181.2021.9590174

31. COVID-19 Lung CT Scans. Kaggle.com. https://www.kaggle.com/luisblanche/covidct. Accessed 12 Aug 2021

32. COVID-19 Lung CT Scans. Kaggle.com. https://www.kaggle.com/mehradaria/covid19-lung-ct-scans. Accessed 12 Aug 2021

33. Yang, X., He, X., Zhao, J., Zhang, Y., Zhang, S., Xie, P.: COVID-CT-Dataset: A CT Scan Dataset about COVID-19 (2021). arXiv: 2003.13865. Accessed 31 July 2021

34. Ahsan, M., Nazim, R., Siddique, Z., Huebner, P.: Detection of COVID-19 patients from CT scan and chest X-ray data using modified MobileNetV2 and LIME. Healthcare **9**, 1099 (2021). https://doi.org/10.3390/healthcare9091099

35. Ai, T., et al.: Correlation of chest CT and RT-PCR testing for coronavirus disease 2019 (COVID-19) in China: a report of 1014 cases. Radiology **296**, E32–E40 (2020). https://doi.org/10.1148/radiol.2020200642

Statistical Analysis and Clustering of Dengue Incidents and Weather Data of Bangladesh Using K-Means Clustering

Md. Monirul Islam[1] ⓘ, Fazly Rabbi[2] ⓘ, Javed Meandad[3] ⓘ, K. M. Rafiqul Alam[2] ⓘ,
and Jia Uddin[4(✉)] ⓘ

[1] Department of Computer Science and Engineering,
University of Information Technology and Sciences, Dhaka 1212, Bangladesh
monirul.islam@uits.edu.bd
[2] Department of Statistics, Jahangirnagar University, Savar, Dhaka 1342, Bangladesh
[3] Department of Meteorology, University of Dhaka, Dhaka 1000, Bangladesh
[4] AI and Big Data Department, Endicott College, Woosong University, Daejeon, South Korea
jia.uddin@wsu.ac.kr

Abstract. In recent years, Dengue incidents have become a big issue in the public health sector in Bangladesh. This study mainly attempts to investigate the association among different weather parameters and the number of Dengue incidents in monthly frequency. The weather data has been collected from Bangladesh Meteorological Department and several Dengue incidents have been collected from the Institute of Epidemiology, Disease Control and Research (IEDCR), finally, the merged dataset has been used in this study. We found the Rainfall, Minimum Air Temperature, and Month have the highest association with Dengue incidents. Increasing the value of these variables increases the chance of Dengue incidents. After performing K-Means Clustering, we found 4 number of weather clusters with different numbers of Dengue incidents. Dengue incidents perform 431.23 on an average with 7.96 on an average value of Month, 32.22 on an average value of Maximum Temperature, 25.04 on an average value of Minimum Temperature, 84.84 on an average value of Humidity, and 49.94 on an average value of Rainfall.

Keywords: Dengue incident · K-means clustering · Weather data of Bangladesh · EDA · Anova test

1 Introduction

Dengue fever is the most widespread, lethal, and symbol mosquito-borne viral disease in Bangladesh [1]. It is a climate-sensitive disease spread by the bite of female Aedes mosquitos infected with Flaviviridae dengue virus serotypes [2–4]. According to a recent study, approximately 390 million dengue cases are reported globally each year. Dengue virus distribution and burden are primarily concentrated in tropical as well as subtropical regions [5, 6]. The triggering factors for dengue dynamics are said to be influenced by 3 central risk factors including biological, sociological, along environmental [7]. The environmental aspect, specifically meteorological variables, was examined in this

A. K. M. M. Islam et al. (Eds.): ICBBDB 2021, CCIS 1550, pp. 64–75, 2022.
https://doi.org/10.1007/978-3-031-17181-9_6

study to better understand the association with dengue epidemics. Aedesalbopictus and Aedesaegypti transmit the five-dengue virus serotypes, which are highly sensitive to environmental factors. Temperature, rainfall, as well as humidity, can all have an impact on dengue epidemiology by increasing mosquito development, population growth rate, and virus reproduction [8, 9]. Infestation usually starts during the monsoon season, when the humidity along with temperature conditions are ideal for the development of the mosquito embryo.

Bangladesh appears to be a suitable habitat for the primary dengue vector and its increased spread. The primary cause of this disease in Bangladesh has been identified as environmental effects (average rainfall, humidity, and temperature) as well as inappropriate urbanization [10]. In recent years, the country's rising atmospheric temperature has likely contributed to the development of mosquito larvae and pupa habitats, particularly in the cities of Dhaka and Chattogram, leading to an increase in the frequency of dengue contagion.

Although the association between dengue incidence as well as weather patterns has been extensively considered, little attention has been paid to determining the threshold properties of weather variability on dengue spread. To reduce dengue risk effectively, a suitable alert system for dengue incidents based on the threshold effect of weather variables is required. The goal of this study is to investigate the nonlinear relationships between weather variables as well as dengue incidence in Bangladesh. To meet the research objectives, the study's specific objectives have been defined as follows:

- To investigate the relationship between meteorological variables as well as the number of dengue cases atmonthly scale; and
- To develop an algorithm for predicting dengue incidence based on meteorological parameters.

The rest of the paper is structured as follows. Section 2 states the literation review. The proposed methodology is discussed in Sect. 3. Section 4 dictates the experimental setup and result. Finally, we conclude the paper in Sect. 5.

2 Literature Review

A lot of research has been done on the relation between dengue and meteorological data in China. In [11], The authors investigated the relationship between dengue occurrence and potential risk factors to progress a predicting model for dengue control along with prevention in Guangzhou, China. The authors [12] predicted that a time series analysis of Mosquito Density and Meteorological Factors on Dengue Fever Epidemics would be conducted. In Zhongshan, a time-series regression tree model was used to estimate the hierarchical relationship between reported autochthonous DF cases and potential risk factors such as DF surveillance system timeliness like median time interval between symptom onset date and diagnosis date, mosquito density, imported cases, and meteorological factors, China from 2001 to 2013 in [13]. The authors proposed in [14] to investigate individual risk factors for dengue virus infection in Guangdong Province and to provide a scientific foundation for future DF prevention and control. The authors [15] used boosted regression trees (BRT) to investigate the delayed effect of meteorological factors, as well as the relationships between five climatic variables and the risk for DF, from 2005 to 2011, to control the best timing as well as a strategy for familiarizing such protective actions.

In Bangladesh, the impact of meteorological factors on dengue mosquitoes is not researched. That is why; we tried to explore the relationship between the dengue and meteorological data of Bangladesh.

3   Methodology

Figure 1 demonstrates the detailed block diagram of the proposed methodology. We utilized two datasets including the dengue and weather datasets in the merge. Then we did the preprocessing, EDA, standardization, and k-means clustering part.

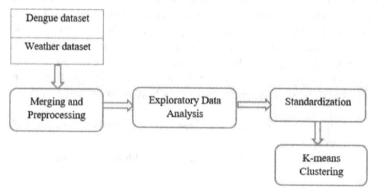

Fig. 1. Block diagram of proposed methodology.

3.1   Data Description

The dataset was collected from the Bangladesh Meteorological Department and Institute of Epidemiology, Disease Control and Research (IEDCR). The dataset is grouped into two parts containing the dengue dataset from IEDCR and the weather dataset from Bangladesh Meteorological Department. There are 7 columns including year, month, minimum average air temperature, maximum average air temperature, humidity, rainfall, and several dengue patients and 135 rows. The dataset contains the record from 2008 to 2019.

3.2   Merging and Preprocessing

We merged both datasets for analyzing our experiment. The first step is the data preprocessing. For the experimental setup, we used the python programming language. In this step, we import all necessary libraries and the proposed dataset.

3.3 Exploratory Data Analysis (EDA)

Exploratory Data Analysis (EDA) is a process to explore the unseen insights from the data. Through EDA, we can extract various information from the data set including null values, outliers, the relation among the dataset, etc. which helps make various decisions as well as in selecting the machine-learning model. EDA is done through various types of statistical methods, data visualization, etc.

Descriptive Statistics

Table 1 displays the descriptive statistics of the variables. We found RAINFALL and DENGUE have the highest Standard Deviations that means the most variability of these variables. On the other hand, MAX has the lowest variability that means the Tropical weather condition of Bangladesh.

Table 1. Descriptive statistics of dataset

	Year	Month	Min	Max	Humidity	Rainfall	Dengue
Count	13	134	134	134	134	134	134
Mean	2013	6.42	20.94	30.84	80.11	27.84	211.58
Std	3.23	3.49	4.83	2.85	5.25	98.39	451.21
Min	2008	1	10.59	23.52	67.54	0	0
25%	2010	3	16.40	29.27	77.18	0.547	0
50%	2013	6	22.93	31.98	80.09	6.00	36
75%	2016	9	25.27	32.67	84.77	12.77	187
Max	2019	12	26.48	35.76	88.38	689.16	3087

Range and Outliers of the Variables

Figure 2 shows the visualizing of the Box Plot. We found DENGUE has the largest range among other variables. At the same time, DENGUE and RAINFALL show some outliers. Especially DENGUE contains most of the extreme values. MIN, MAX, and HUMIDITY variables have the lowest range without any outliers.

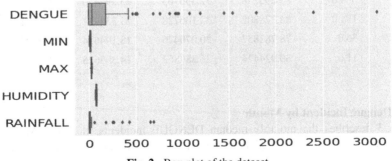

Fig. 2. Box plot of the dataset

Correlation Checking

Table 2 shows the weak correlation with DENGUE incidents and weather parameter variables, but performing the Hypothesis test for association checking using Pearson's correlation shows the statistically significant relationship with the given variables. This result shows DENGUE incidents have the highest relationship with RAINFALL.

Table 2. Pearson's correlation

Variable 1	Variable 2	Pearson's correlation	Result	Decision
MIN	Dengue	0.3013	stat = 0.301, p = 0.000403	Dependent
MAX	Dengue	0.1778	stat = 0.178, p = 0.039837	Dependent
Humidity	Dengue	0.2753	stat = 0.275, p = 0.001281	Dependent
Rainfall	Dengue	0.3686	stat = 0.369, p = 0.000012	Dependent

Monthly Dengue & Weather Parameter Pivot Table

Table 3 shows the MONTH-wise Median value of MAX, MIN, RAINFALL, HUMIDITY, and DENGUE.

Table 3. The month-wise median value of dengue and weather parameters

Month	Median value				
	Dengue	Humidity	Max	Min	Rainfall
1	3.0	78.743318	24.944470	12.248925	0.030415
2	1.5	71.853008	28.915002	14.943736	0.438776
3	2.0	70.321659	32.391073	19.581158	0.771429
4	0.0	75.647619	33.902323	22.782796	2.713333
5	8.0	78.580927	33.821106	24.189299	8.815668
6	28.0	84.183810	32.930571	25.457972	16.608571
7	171.0	86.428571	31.914706	25.465268	17.993548
8	346.0	86.494009	32.157235	25.560893	14.363134
9	334.0	85.295238	32.556765	25.294470	9.651429
10	184.0	82.778802	32.106728	23.334911	6.281106
11	36.0	78.782857	30.070476	18.194654	0.379048
12	11.0	80.924424	26.389862	14.305625	0.025806

Most Dengue Incident by Month

Figure 3 describes the monthly median DENGUE incidents. It shows August and September are the most DENGUE incidental months. We can say that dengue broke

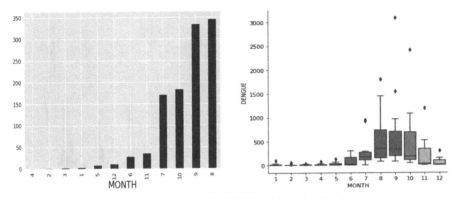

Fig. 3. Monthly DENGUGE incidents (median)

out more in August, September, October, and November of the year. First 4 months of the year, the number of dengue patients is less.

Figure 4 clearly describes that Dengue incidence increase with the increasing value of Humidity. Most of the Dengue incidents occur within the Humidity range of 80 and above.

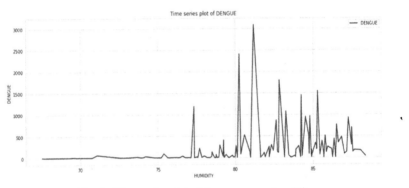

Fig. 4. Time series plot of dengue versus humidity

Figure 5 clearly describes that most of the Dengue incidents occur when the minimum temperature cross 22 °C.

Figure 6 describes that the number of Dengue incidence has increased over the year and in 2018 the highest dengue incidents occurred in Bangladesh. The second highest Dengue incidents occurred in 2016.

ANOVA Test

To test the difference of weather parameters in each month, we performed an ANOVA test. Table 4 shows the test result. As per the test result of each separate variable, we found that Null Hypothesis is Rejected for each test. DENGUE incidents, MIN temperature, MAX temperature, and HUMIDITY aren't the same in each month.

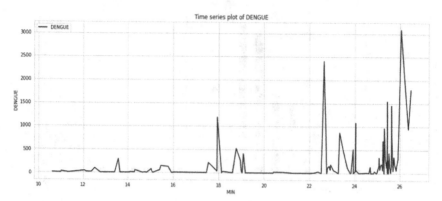

Fig. 5. Time series plot of dengue versus minimum air temperature

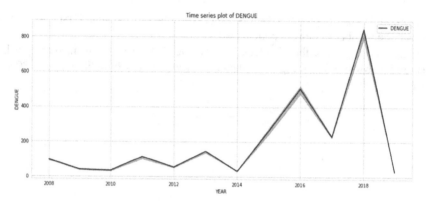

Fig. 6. Time series plot of dengue versus year

Table 4. ANOVA test result

Variable	Hypothesis	Result	Decision
Dengue	Are the Dengue incidents same in every Month?	stat = 4.601, p = 0.000	Null Hypothesis REJECTED
Min	Is the MIN temperature the same in every Month?	stat = 124.502, p = 0.000	Null Hypothesis REJECTED
Max	Is the MAX temperature the same in every Month?	stat = 567.597, p = 0.000	Null Hypothesis REJECTED
Humidity	Is the HUMIDITY same in every Month?	stat = 55.193, p = 0.000	Null Hypothesis REJECTED

3.4   Standardization

Min-Max Normalizer scales using the maximum and minimum values of this variable, so that all data moves within a certain range to the normalized state. In this method each data is subtracted from its minimum value (of that variable), the subtraction is divided by the range. This is how each data is scaled.

Range: Range is the difference between the maximum and minimum values of a variable.

$$X_{new} = \frac{X_i - min(X)}{max(X) - min(X)} \tag{1}$$

K-means Clustering Algorithm

Figure 7 shows K-Means Clustering schematic view. It divides the unmarked dataset into dissimilar clusters. In this case, K denotes the number of pre-defined clusters that must be formed during the process; for example, if K is equal to 3, there will be 3 clusters; for K is equal to 4, there will be 4 clusters, and so on [16]. It enables us to cluster the data into various groups and provides a suitable method for discovering the group categories in the unmarked dataset but without training. It is a centroid-based model, with each cluster having its centroid. This algorithm's main goal is to lessen the sum of distances between data points along with their conforming clusters.

In short, this model starts with an unlabeled dataset, splits it into k clusters, and then recaps the process until it does not discovery the best clusters. In this algorithm, the k's value should be prearranged.

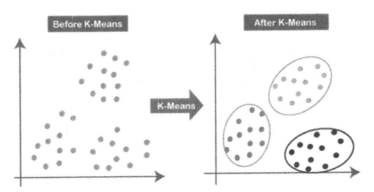

Fig. 7. K-means algorithm

The main task of the k-means clustering model is as follows.

- Iteratively determines the optimal value for K centre points or centroids.
- Appoints all data point to the nearest k-center. A cluster is formed by data points that are close to a specific k-center.

The Working Procedure of the K-Means Algorithm

- To determine the number of clusters, choose the number K.
- Choose a random set of K centroids.
- Designates all data point to the centroid that is nearest to it, which will form the predefined K clusters.
- Estimate the variance and move the cluster centroid.
- Repeat the 3 step, reassigning all data point to the cluster's current closest centroid.
- If any reassignment occurs, proceed to 4 number step; otherwise, proceed to complete.
- The model is finished.

In K-means clustering, we utilize Euclidean distance [17] to calculate the distance between any 2 data points shown in Eq. 2.

$$d(x, x') = \sqrt{(x_1 - x_1')^2 + \cdots + (x_n - x_n')^2} \tag{2}$$

4 Result and Discussion

The performance of the K-means clustering technique is predicated on the extremely efficient clusters that it produces. However, identifying the ideal number of clusters is a tough task. There are numerous methods for obtaining the best number of clusters, but we utilize the elbow method here because it is the most appropriate method for estimating the number of clusters or the value of K.

4.1 Elbow Method

The Elbow method is one of the most widely used methods for determining the optimal number of clusters. This technique makes use of the WCSS value idea. Within Cluster Sum of Squares (WCSS), we get the total variations within a cluster. The equation WCSS is shown in 3 containing 3 clusters.

$$WCSS = \sum P_{i \text{ in } Cluster1}(P_iC_1)^2 + \sum P_{i \text{ in } Cluster2}(P_iC_2)^2 + \sum P_{i \text{ in } Cluster3}(P_iC_3)^2$$
$$+ \sum P_{i \text{ in } Cluster4}(P_iC_4)^2 \tag{3}$$

In the above equation of WCSS,
$\sum P_{i \text{ in } Cluster1}(P_iC_1)^2$ is the sum of the squares of the distances between all data point and its center within a cluster1 and the same for other three term.

The elbow method employs the following steps to determine the optimal value of clusters:

- It does K-means clustering on a prearranged dataset for several K values.
- Computes the value of WCSS for each point of K.
- Draws a line connecting the designed WCSS values as well as the number of clusters K.

– If a point on the scheme look like an arm, that point is considered the most like value of K

The Fig. 8 shows that when the value of K drops from 1 to 2, the sum of squared distance decreases from 40 to 28. After that, after going down from 2 to 3, this value has come down from 28 to 18. Again after going down from 3 to 4, this value has come down from 28 to 10. So we will take the value of K as 4 optimal values.

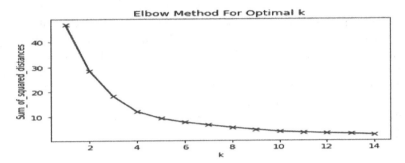

Fig. 8. Elbow method of optimal number of K

The clustering result has described in Table 5. It shows 4 clusters. They are- 0, 1, 2, and 3. In the 1st Cluster, an average 155 number of Dengue incidents occur when on average the Maximum Temperature is 28.15, Minimum Temperature is 16.50, Humidity is 79.98 and Rainfall is 1.457. In the 2nd Cluster, an average 15.71 number of Dengue incidents occur when on average the Maximum Temperature is 33.24, Minimum Temperature is 22.3, Humidity is 75.01 and Rainfall is 25.72.

In the 3rd Cluster, an average 12.08 number of Dengue incidents occur when on average the Maximum Temperature is 26.90, Minimum Temperature is 13.56, Humidity is 75.98 and Rainfall is 3.27. In the 4th Cluster, an average 431.23 number of Dengue incidents occur when on average the Maximum Temperature is 32.22, Minimum Temperature is 24.04, Humidity is 84.84 and Rainfall is 49.94.

Table 5. Clustering result

	Cluster mean					
Cluster	Month	Max	Min	Humidity	Rainfall	Dengue
0	11.500000	28.152681	16.503607	79.987957	1.457495	155.000000
1	3.968750	33.244019	22.354495	75.019204	25.724617	15.718750
2	1.500000	26.903963	13.569695	75.989150	3.274906	12.083333
3	7.946429	32.229173	25.041458	84.846397	49.942636	431.232143

5 Conclusion

Dengue incidents in Bangladesh have increased over the years. After performing Exploratory Data Analysis, it was found that dengue incidents increase every July to October and mostly it becomes extreme in August and September. Dengue Incidents have a relationship among the Minimum Air Temperature, Humidity & Rainfall. The clustering result shows four numbers of clusters with different values of the variables. The most extreme cluster shows on an average 431 dengue incidents with 7.96 on an average value of Month, 32.22 on the average value of Maximum Temperature, 25.04 on an average value of Minimum Temperature, 84.84 on an average value of Humidity, and 49.94 on an average value of Rainfall. Other clusters show 155, 15, and 12 Dengue incidents accordingly. The more environmental variable including sunshine, sosquito control program, and air quality could be helpful to identify the association of dengue incidents. We will try to include more variables and observations to expand our research findings. Time series forecasting using statistical models and artificial neural networks could be included to forecast dengue incidents based on an exogenous environmental variables.

References

1. Mutsuddy, P., Tahmina Jhora, S., Shamsuzzaman, A.K.M., Kaisar, S.M., Khan, M.N.A.: Dengue situation in Bangladesh: an epidemiological shift in terms of morbidity and mortality. Can. J. Infect. Dis. Med. Microbiol. (2019)
2. Huang, X., Clements, A.C., Williams, G., Milinovich, G., Hu, W.: A threshold analysis of dengue transmission in terms of weather variables and imported dengue cases in Australia. Emerg. Microbes Infect. 2(1), 1–7 (2013)
3. Tran, B.L., Tseng, W.C., Chen, C.C., Liao, S.Y.: Estimating the threshold effects of climate on dengue: a case study of Taiwan. Int. J. Environ. Res. Public Health 17(4), 1392 (2020)
4. Xu, J., et al.: Forecast of dengue cases in 20 Chinese cities based on the deep learning method. Int. J. Environ. Res. Public Health 17(2), 453 (2020)
5. Duarte, J.L., Diaz-Quijano, F.A., Batista, A.C., Giatti, L.L.: Climatic variables associated with dengue incidence in a city of the Western Brazilian Amazon region. Revista da SociedadeBrasileira de Medicina Tropical 52 (2019)
6. Pinto, E., Coelho, M., Oliver, L., Massad, E.: The influence of climate variables on dengue in Singapore. Int. J. Environ. Health Res. 21(6), 415–426 (2011)
7. Carvajal, T.M., Viacrusis, K.M., Hernandez, L.F.T., Ho, H.T., Amalin, D.M., Watanabe, K.: Machine learning methods reveal the temporal pattern of dengue incidence using meteorological factors in metropolitan Manila. Philippines. BMC Infectious Diseases 18(1), 1–15 (2018)
8. Iguchi, J.A., Seposo, X.T., Honda, Y.: Meteorological factors affecting dengue incidence in Davao. Philippines. BMC Public Health 18(1), 1–10 (2018)
9. CorreiaFilho, W.L.F.: Influence of meteorological variables on dengue incidence in the municipality of Arapiraca, Alagoas, Brazil. Revista da SociedadeBrasileira de Medicina Tropical 50(3), 309–314 (2017)
10. Noor, R.: Reemergence of dengue virus in Bangladesh: current fatality and the required knowledge. Tzu-Chi Med. J. 32(3), 227 (2020)

11. Sang, S., et al.: Predicting local dengue transmission in Guangzhou, China, through the influence of imported cases, mosquito density and climate variability. PLoS ONE **9**(7), e102755 (2014). https://doi.org/10.1371/journal.pone.0102755.PMID:25019967;PMCID: PMC4097061

12. Shen, J.C., et al.: The impacts of mosquito density and meteorological factors on dengue fever epidemics in Guangzhou, China, 2006–2014: a time-series analysis. Biomed. Environ. Sci. **28**(5), 321–329 (2015). https://doi.org/10.3967/bes2015.046. PMID: 26055559

13. Liu, K.K., et al.: Risk assessment of dengue fever in Zhongshan, China: a time-series regression tree analysis. Epidemiol Infect. **145**(3), 451–461 (2017). https://doi.org/10.1017/S09502 6881600265X. Epub 2016 Nov 22 PMID: 27873572

14. Liu, J., et al.: Risk factors associated with dengue virus infection in Guangdong Province: a community-based case-control study. Int. J. Environ. Res. Public Health **16**(4), 617 (2019). https://doi.org/10.3390/ijerph16040617.PMID:30791547;PMCID:PMC6406885

15. Gu, H., et al.: Meteorological factors for dengue fever control and prevention in South China. Int. J. Environ. Res. Public Health **13**, 867 (2016). https://doi.org/10.3390/ijerph13090867

16. Likas, A., Vlassis, N., Verbeek, J.J.: The global k-means clustering algorithm. Pattern Recogn. **36**(2), 451–461 (2003)

17. Islam, M.M., Uddin, J., Kashem, M.A., Rabbi, F., Hasnat, M.W.: Design and implementation of an IoT system for predicting aqua fisheries using arduino and KNN. In: Intelligent Human Computer Interaction. IHCI 2020. Lecture Notes in Computer Science, vol. 12616. Springer, Cham. https://doi.org/10.1007/978-3-030-68452-5_11

AI Reception: An Intelligent Bengali Receptionist System Integrating with Face, Speech, and Interaction Recognition

Rahad Arman Nabid[1], Shehan Irteza Pranto[1], Nabeel Mohammed[2],
Farhana Sarker[3], Mohammad Nurul Huda[4],
and Khondaker A. Mamun[1,4(✉)]

[1] Advanced Intelligent Multidisciplinary Systems Lab, United International University, Dhaka, Bangladesh
ran.nabid@gmail.com
[2] Department of CSE, North South University, Dhaka, Bangladesh
[3] Department of CSE, University of Liberal Arts Bangladesh, Dhaka, Bangladesh
[4] Department of CSE, United International University, Dhaka, Bangladesh

Abstract. Artificial Intelligence enabled automated reception to perform as a human receptionist to avoid face-to-face interaction among mass people regarding their daily service in the current pandemic. Inspired by their current problem of mass congestion, our proposed AI-based Smart Reception can authenticate users and interact in Bangla language with humans by responding to university-domain-related queries, resulting in better business service and outcomes. We used OpenFace face recognition for authentication, having an accuracy of 92.92% with 1×10^{-5} second training time for a new image by saving the image dataset as a collection of an array file. The Interaction Recognition system consists of three modules: Automatic Speech Recognition (ASR), Interactive Agent, and Text-to-Speech (TTS) Synthesis. We used the OpenSLR-Large Bengali ASR Training Data to train the Deep Speech 2 model for ASR with a Word Error Rate (WER) of 42.15%. We tested our developed database management architecture for the Interaction Recognition system with the three-step evaluation using BERT sentence transformer (paraphrase-mpnet-base-v2) that provided satisfactory responses with 92% accuracy, increasing the receptionist performance significantly. TTS module relays on WavNet gTTS model. Our research also demonstrated that a developed AI-based system could be an adaptive solution for any domain-specific reception system responsible for systematic and efficient customer service offline and online.

Keywords: Automated speech recognition · Text to speech synthesis · Sentence transformer · Face recognition · Support vector machine

© The Author(s), under exclusive license to Springer Nature Switzerland AG 2022
A. K. M. M. Islam et al. (Eds.): ICBBDB 2021, CCIS 1550, pp. 76–91, 2022.
https://doi.org/10.1007/978-3-031-17181-9_7

1   Introduction

Artificial Intelligence (AI) has revolutionized Human-Robot Interaction (HRI) as an intervention strategy to make customer services more adequate. AI helps people work smarter, resulting in better business outcomes, and requires them to develop new demand capabilities, from technological expertise to social, emotional, and creative skills. The development of Natural Language Processing (NLP), Computer Vision, Speech Recognition, Text to Speech (TTS) synthesis paves the way to build automated reception management robots that can perform as service receptionists.

In the last decade, face recognition has achieved remarkable accuracy due to continuous research that degrades analog viewing conditions [7,8]. The human face carries information about his identity, age [9], gender [10], and facial expressions that reflecting the emotions as well as mental states [10,11]. This technology is recognized as bio-metric data since it usually does not violate personal info by direct cooperation with users [12]. Moreover, passport agencies, police station offices, and numerous online applications nowadays use facial expressions to provide better and secure customer services. [7,8]. As speech is the most straightforward and convenient method of communication, researchers made an interaction through the medium of speech without resorting to the deployment of traditional interfaces like keyboards or pointing devices. This technology is made possible by developing an Automatic Speech Recognition (ASR) technique that converts speech signals into text with the help of Natural Language Processing (NLP) algorithms [13]. Besides, automatic manipulation of text and speech opens doors to reduce the human workload associated by interrogating text-free modules [14]. NLP application is now widespread among sentiment analysis, clinical analysis, [16] summary of text [15]. Combining these machine learning technology causes human talent to be replaced by technology, leading hospitality businesses to reshape their human service structures [3]. Furthermore, around 37% of customers in e-commerce use automated management services like- chatbots to get quick answers in case of an emergency because of 24/7 customer support and responsiveness [2]. Studies found from 40 articles that analyzed chatbot taxonomy and specified its challenges define the types and contexts of chatbots in the health sector [4]. It is expected that by 2024, all the patients, especially in many developed countries, will have digital access to primary care consultations that reduce the need for face-to-face outpatient visits [1]. Other systems have also been proposed with the help of automation of hospitality or reception via machine learning act as symptom checkers [5], online triage services or health promotion assistants, interactively providing live feedback [6]. Moreover, as customer service is a top priority for many universities, they also aspire to automate information for their students and guardian by integrating conversation bots for interactive media conversation [17] offline and online.

In our work, we integrate face recognition, Automated Speech Recognition (ASR), Interaction Recognition system, Text to Speech (TTS) synthesis to emulate a human receptionist that can work via Human-Robot Interaction (HRI) in the Bengali Language. Our architecture used in a receptionist robot can answer necessary queries in university visiting students and their parents instead of a physical receptionist to avoid public gatherings. According to our knowledge, the developed AI Reception is the first system interacting verbally in the Bengali language. We used OpenFace [18] for face recognition that has accuracy up to 0.9292 ± 0.0134 on Labeled Faces in the Wild (LWF)- HRBLM07 [19] dataset. With the help of OpenFace face recognition, the receptionist robot can recognize the identity of the specific customer and take some necessary info such as date, phone no, name, name of parents/children, National ID (NID) numbers. The Interaction Recognition system comprises three parts: Automatic Speech Recognition (ASR), BERT sentence transformer model for an interactive agent, and Text to Speech (TTS) synthesis. Bengali Speech is recognized by deep speech 2, where we used the OpenSLR- Large Bengali-Automatic Speech Recognition Training Data (LB-ASRTD) [33] prepared by Google researchers to train our model. Bengali text is encoded by "paraphrase-mpnet-base-v2," having average accuracy of 76.84% with a speed of 2800. Input sentence and reference sentence similarity checks are done by cosine similarity algorithms using words vector, giving 92% accuracy in the three-step evolution method. The response of Text to Speech(TTS) is made of gTTS to respond with humans instantly. These modules build up responsive Human-Robot Interaction (HRI) in the Bengali language that evolves the modern-day reception system in university reception.

2   Related Works

Researchers have been trying to find various solutions to supplant analog reception systems with AI-based interactive robots. Several studies have been conducted in the last 15 years regarding various features of AI-based customer reception. Jefri Yushendri et al. [17] developed a voice-enabled interactive bot for the improvement of customer service. They found 80.0% accuracy on speech recognition using Sphinx-4 besides 89.3% for Interaction Recognition system and 100% for text-to-speech module by using FreeTTS library written in Java. Ho Seok Ahn et al. [20] proposed a Healthbot that can perform face recognition and verbal interaction with humans by using a speech recognition system where they presented three outlines in which the robot can be used as an assistant: reception, medical server, and as a nurse. Quang-Minh Ky et al. [21] emphasized the integration of the face recognition module with a human interactive robot. Besides, they have developed their AI-based robot for two purposes: Receptionist and Security system and found improved accuracy by using the KNN classifier for face recognition. Nicola Bellotto et al. [22] presented Lux (an interactive receptionist robot) with multi-sensory detection and human recognition ability in university circumstances. Their proposed intelligent system can recognize not only faces but also track clothes and measure the heights of the persons. For the interactive robot, Claudia Cruz et al. [23] also proposed a real-time face recognition module in their paper. They developed the method in such a way that the system tracks three sections of the face, and afterward, SIFT features were extracted from each portion and processed for recognition. The bayesian method had been used for the enhancement of the recognition accuracy. W.S. Mada Sanjaya et al. [24] designed SyPEHUL: a social robot

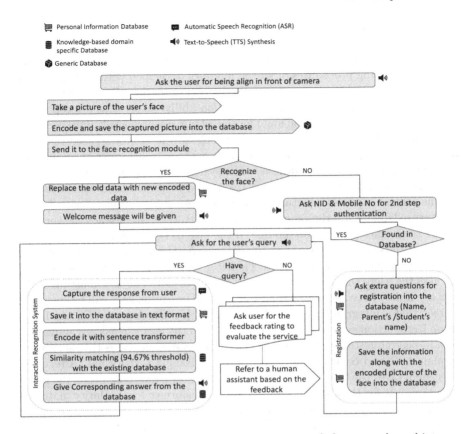

Fig. 1. System architecture of AI reception integrating with face, speech, and interaction recognition

with face tracking and recognition ability. They used Cascade Classification and OpenCV library-based LBPH (Local Binary Pattern Histogram) face recognizer for the face tracking and recognition method having 92.73% accuracy. Jiakailin Wang et al. [7] mentioned an integrated real-time face recognition system with a security service robot distinguishing strangers from known faces. They used the SVM (Support Vector Machine) classifier for face recognition which attained 86% accuracy on the LFW (Labeled Faces in the Wild) dataset. They tested their application in realistic environments and obtained better performance on real-time and multi-face recognition testing. Nataliya Shakhovska et al. [25] presented the possibilities and procedures of using Google API as a speech recognition module that can be integrated with a chatbot. They also investigated several well-known chatbots and found out their improvement methodology along with their advantages and disadvantages. Mohammad Nuruzzaman et al. [26] Proposed IntelliBot: a domain-specific chatbot. They used a deep neural network to train their chatbot using Cornell movie dialogue and a custom-built insurance dataset.

3   Material and Methods

This section demonstrates the robust architecture of AI-based Bangla Receptionist and syncing procedures of all the modules developed with multiple deep-learning and natural language processing-based approaches. Developing a Bengali AI Reception system with face recognition ability to serve as a receptionist at the university premises is the main motive of our research study. Furthermore, we automated the whole system by integrating all the modules (Face Recognition, Automatic Speech Recognition, BERT sentence transformer as an interactive agent, Text-to-Speech Synthesis). The system requires the registration process from a user for the very first time. Users need to stay in front of the camera, and the camera captures a picture of their faces. Afterward, it encodes and saves the captured image into the generic database. Next, the system sends the encoded picture to the face recognition module. If the face recognition module recognizes the image, the system updates the personal information database by replacing the old data with new encoded face data. Then it gives a predefined welcome message and asks the users whether they have any queries or not. The user must press the YES key if they have any queries and vice versa. The option keys will be shown on a screen that is integrated with the AI Reception. If the user press YES, the Interaction Recognition system will be activated. Then the user can ask any university domain-based question to the AI Reception. The system captures the user's voice through ASR and converts the speech into the Bangla text format. Afterward, the system saves the text into the personal information database inside the user's id and sends it for the encoding via sentence transformer for similarity matching with the knowledge-based domain-specific information database. Through assessing the best score by similarity matching, the system responds with the best answer from the knowledge-based database. Moreover, for irrelevant queries, the system refers to a human assistant when the score of the similarity match doesn't cross the threshold (94.67%). As our collected question database is not a reference database and the Bangla language has a different local accent, we didn't comprehensively analyze the threshold value.

On the other hand, if the face recognition module doesn't recognize the user's face, the system performs the second step authentication process by asking the user's National Identity (NID) and mobile number to find the user's history into the personal information database. Suppose the user's information is located inside the database. In that case, it means the particular user is previously registered with the system. Then the system activates the Interaction Recognition system and serves the users by performing the developed Human-Robot Interaction system. In contrast, if the user's given information isn't stored in the database, the user is required to register into the database by providing their name, parent's (in case of student's use)/student's (in case of guardian's use) name. Then the system stores the user's information along with their encoded picture of the face into the personal information database. Next, the Interaction Recognition system is activated like before. The user can ask multiple questions, but they have to select the YES key; they have more queries after getting each response from the user. Finally, if the user presses the NO key, the system takes feedback (negative or positive) from the user to rate the service and refers to a human assistant in case of negative feedback. Figure 1 illustrates the system architecture of our developed intelligent reception.

3.1 Face Recognition

OpenFace works on 2D face recognition near-human accuracy on LFW benchmark, released October 2015 [18]. OpenFace is trained with 500k images from combining the two largest labeled face recognition datasets for research, CASIA-WebFace [29], and FaceScrub [30]. Total training and testing workflow is given in Fig. 2. OpenFace uses a modified version of FaceNet's nn4 network where nn4 is based on the GoogLeNet [31] architecture, and OpenFace nn4.small2 model reduces the number of parameters that uses inception net followed by CNN architecture Table 1.

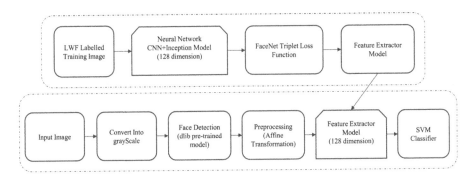

Fig. 2. Training and validation workflow of OpenFace face recognition

Table 1. The OpenFace nn4.small2 network definition

Type	Outputsize	1 × 1	3 × 3 reduced	3 × 3	5 × 5 reduced	5 × 5	Pool proj
conv1(#1 × 1 × 3,2)	48 × 48 × 64						
max pool + norm	24 × 24 × 64						m3 × 3,2
inception(2)	24 × 24 × 192		64	192			
norm + max pool	12 × 12 × 192						m3 × 3,2
inception(3a)	12 × 12 × 256	64	96	128	16	32	m, 32 p
inception(3b)	12 × 12 × 320	64	96	128	16	64	l2,64 p
inception(3c)	6 × 6 × 640		128	256,2	32	64,2	m m3 × 3,2
inception(4a)	6 × 6 × 640	256	96	192	32	64	l2 128p
inception(4e)	3 × 3 × 1024		160	256,2	64	128,2	m3 × 3,2
inception(5a)	3 × 3 × 736	256	96	384			l2, 96p
inception(5b)	3 × 3 × 736	256	96	382			m,96p
avg pool	736						
linear	128						
l2 normalization	128						

Just like other face recognition techniques, OpenFace uses frontal greyscale 2D face images in lower dimensions by detecting faces. The lower dimension images are pre-processed by normalization and detecting 68 landmarks using dib's face landmark detector [7]. The affine transformer resizes and crops the image to the edge of landmarks resulting in images of network 96 × 96.

OpenFace architecture maps unique images from a single network into triplets shown in Eq. 1. The gradient of the triplet loss is back-propagated back through the mapping to the unique images which is shown Fig. 3. In each mini-batch, we sample at most P images per person from Q people in the dataset and send all M = PXQ images through the network in a single forward pass on the GPU to get M Embedding.

$$\sum_{i}^{N} [\| f(x_i^a) - f(x_i^p) \|_2^2 - \| f(x_i^a) - f(x_i^n) \|_2^2 + \alpha] \tag{1}$$

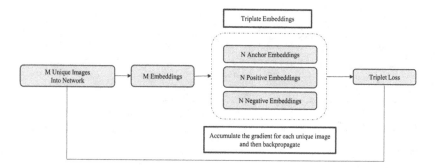

Fig. 3. Triplet loss architecture of OpenFace face recognition

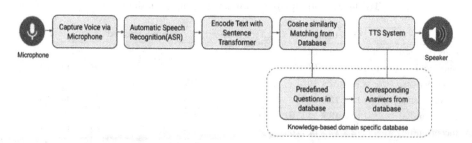

Fig. 4. Workflow of interaction recognition system integrating with automatic speech recognition (ASR), interactive agent, and text-to-speech (TTS) synthesis

OpenFace uses a linear SVM classifier with regularization weights 1, which performs well than other regularization techniques. Moreover, the SVM library uses a pretty fast CPU though GPU performs slightly better. The OpenFace uses a squared Euclidean distance on the pairs to distinguish between face to face and label pairs under a threshold as being the same person and above the threshold as different people. The best threshold on the training folds in our environment is 0.95 that gives better accuracy.

3.2   Interaction Recognition System

Our developed AI Reception is enriched with ASR (Automatic Speech Recognition), Interactive Agent, and TTS (Text-to-Speech) synthesis module shown in Fig. 4. So it can communicate with humans in the Bengali Language. Firstly, the system receives a question in a spoken form from the user; then, it converts the speech into Bengali text using the ASR. The converted text is used as an input in our domain-specific interactive agent, which provides the text response in the Bengali language. Finally, the TTS system transforms the text response of the interactive agent into speech.

Automatic Speech Recognition: We have trained a Baidu Research's Deep Speech 2 [32] model, an RNN-based end-to-end deep learning approach, for the Bengali Language, which converts the speeches in the Bengali Language into text format. Our model was trained to utilize a publicly available annotated Bangla speech corpus- OpenSLR- Large Bengali-Automatic Speech Recognition Training Data (LB-ASRTD) [33], which is currently the largest open-source speech corpus in Bangla and contains nearly 210 h of speeches. The whole dataset is split into three sets, namely train, validation, and test sets, with 171 h, 18 h, and 18 h of speeches in each set, respectively. The primary reason for using the Deep Speech 2 model is it enables us to use the ASR in noisy environments. Besides, it can handle a variety of accents and different languages. Moreover, It can serve in both online and offline environments. In this architecture, batch normalization is used in combination with RNN, and a novel optimization curriculum is used called SortaGrad showed in the following Eq. 2.

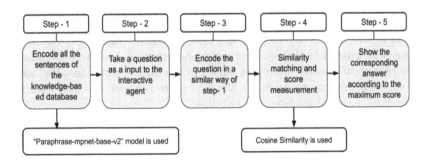

Fig. 5. Steps of interactive agent

$$L(x, y;) = -log \sum_{l \in Align(x,y)}^{\infty} \Pi Pctc(lt|x; \theta) \qquad (2)$$

Here, Align (x, y) denotes the set of all possible combinations of the characters of the transcription y to frames of input x, lt is either a character in the alphabet or the blank,

Interactive Agent in Bengali: The main task of our Interaction Recognition system is to receive a question as a text from the ASR system, then give the most relevant answer from the knowledge-based database. Our Interactive Agent is mainly designed for a specific domain to give service for only admission-related queries from the users.

Our knowledge-based database is created with admission-related queries with corresponding answers in the Bengali language. A sentence transformers model "paraphrase-mpnet-base-v2" [28] has been used to perform the sentence embedding of the sentences. We used sentence transformer, a python-based framework that offers miscellaneous tunable pre-trained models trained on the various datasets. As seen in Fig. 5, our customized Interactive Agent can be classified into six steps.

Step-1: Encode all the sentences of the database: A Python-based framework Sentence Transformer is used to encode all the sentences of the knowledge-based database. The database consists of the question section and the corresponding answer section. The "Paraphrase-mpnet-base-v2" model has been used for sentence embedding, which converts each standardized question and corresponding answers into a vector format.

Step-2: Take a question as the input to the Interactive Agent: The following procedure is taking a question from a registered user of the system. ASR receives admission-related questions from a user as voice input. Then it converts into the Bangla text via the Deep Speech 2 model and sends it to the Interactive Agent.

Step-3: Encode the question: It is required to encode the received sentence from users. The same procedures mentioned in step-1 have been taken for sentence embedding.

Step-4: Similarity Matching & Score Measurement: The approach of counting common words between the question section of our database and the user input might be a solution for developing the closed domain Interactive Agent. But problems will arise if the size of our predefined texts is too large because the number of common words increases with the size of the database. We use the cosine similarity metric to calculate the best score between the user's question and standardize questions from the database.

Step-5: Show the corresponding answer according to the maximum score: By calculating the maximum score using cosine similarity between the predefined questions and user input and maintaining a threshold (94.67%), the system shows the corresponding response of that question. The output delivered by the Interactive Agent remains as a text format which works as the input of the text-speech-synthesis [27].

Text-to-Speech Synthesis: For building a voice-enabled conversational agent for replying to various admission-related queries, the output of the response must be in the spoken form. Initially, we used a python-based "gTTS" library to convert text input into speech. This library is supported by both Python 2 and 3 versions. The main reason for using this library for our developed system is that "gTTS" serves the best quality sound among all the TTS-based python libraries available in the python programming language. Furthermore, the speech generation speed from text response is quite impressive. Figure 6 represents the basic architecture of text-to-speech synthesis.

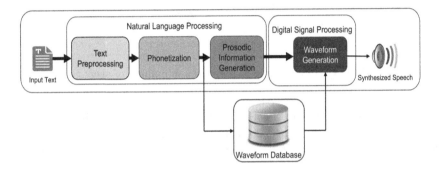

Fig. 6. Text-to-Speech (TTS) synthesis

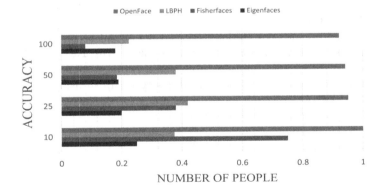

Fig. 7. Classification accuracy vs number of images in database

4   Result Analysis

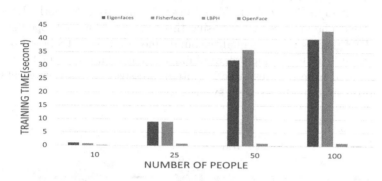

Fig. 8. Training time for new user vs number of users

We evaluated our system in a local machine operated with Linux Operating System (Ubuntu 20.04 version), 32 GB Ram, RTX 2070 GPU with 8 GB VRam, and Core i7 9th generation CPU. The database has been created using CSV format.

The first module of the receptionist robot is face recognition built with the OpenFace algorithm. Then the model is trained with an LFW dataset having 13,233 images from 5750 people. The training process provides 6000 pairs broken into ten folds where squared Euclidean distance on the pair is used, selecting threshold 0.95 in our case to get a good result. Moreover, the accuracy of nn4.small2.v1 is near the human level having an accuracy of 0.9292 ± 0.0134. This model performs well compared to Eigenfaces, FaceNet, DeepFace-ensemble within this Small dataset Table 2. When our system collects images and personal info from the database, it stores the data in a local machine or a remote database. OpenFace loses some accuracy for the increasing number of

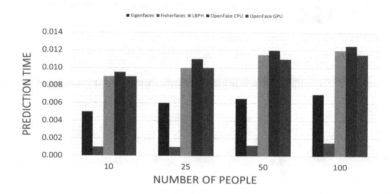

Fig. 9. Prediction time vs number of users

faces stored in the database. Moreover, OpenFace works quite well with respect to another traditional model where training time and prediction are usable for face-to-face communication and recognition. As an increasing number of faces give customers service a little bit of latency every time for training, we applied weight-saving technique in NumPy for existing users recognition. The new user's face is immediately encoded with the OpenFace model and append the encoded NumPy model with existing saved weight. This technique reduces the time to train multiple faces to less than 1×10^{-5} second show in Fig. 8. Moreover, predicting time for a single person is usable in real-time on the reception desk compared to Eigenfaces, FaceNet, DeepFace-ensemble. In our test single image recognition time is less than 1×10^{-2} shown in Fig. 9.

For our Deep Speech 2 model, we first extract the MFCC features from the utterances, and then these input features are fed into the neural network. We utilize 10 Gated Recurrent Unit (GRU) layers and 800 hidden nodes in each hidden layer. We set the learning rate to 3×10^{-4} and momentum to 0.9. Our ASR model has trained for 30 epochs, and then the training has been stopped to avoid over-fitting. We achieved 42.15% WER on the OpenSLR-LB-ASRTD dataset from our trained ASR model that is easy to deploy offline and online servers.

Paraphrase-mpnet-base-v2pre-trained weight is used from the BERT sentence transformer, having average accuracy 76.84% shown in Table 3. We use this weight as accuracy and response time is quite good for real-time use in our testing.

Table 2. Results comparison of different face recognition models

Technique	Accuracy
Human-level (cropped)	0.9753
Eigenfaces	0.6002 ± 0.0079
FaceNet	0.9964 ± 0.009
DeepFace-ensemble	0.9735 ± 0.0025
OpenFace	0.9292 ± 0.0134

Table 3. Accuracy of paraphrase-mpnet-base-v2

Dataset	Accuracy (%)
STSb	86.99
DupQ	87.80
TwitterP	76.05
SciDocs	80.57
Clustering	52.81

Table 4. Performance result of interaction recognition for test-1

Serial No	Question Asked to the Interactive Agent	Prepared Questions in Database	Avg Accuracy(%)
1	এডমিশন ফর্ম পাবো কোথায়?	এডমিশন ফর্ম কোথা থেকে সংগ্রহ করব?	80
2	ক্রেডিট ট্রান্সফারের উপায় গুলা কি কি?	ক্রেডিট ট্রান্সফার করতে চাই, কি করতে হবে?	
3	গ্র্যাজুয়েট প্রোগ্রামের জন্য কি ইভিনিং ক্লাস আছে?	ইভিনিং ক্লাস কাদের হবে	

We evaluated the performance of our Interactive Agent, where the cosine similarity metric was used for similarity matching between the predefined questions and user input. Initially, we had 100 unique admission-related questions with their corresponding answers in our database. As the receptionist system works in a real-time environment, it is quite obvious that different users might ask the same question differently. We prepared another database by considering 25 unique questions from the parent database to evaluate our system.

In test-1, we asked all the 25 selected questions but differently from the Interactive Agent. Average accuracy was calculated based on the accuracy of each response from the Interactive Agent. Sometimes, our Interactive Agent gave some irrelevant responses while testing. Because we had only one unique question for each topic in our newly created database. Table 4 illustrates the sample of a few questions asked to the Interactive Agent along with the list of corresponding predefined questions in the database. Average accuracy during the test is also mentioned in Table 4.

In test-2, we prepared our knowledge-based database so that we had two questions available in a slightly rephrased form for a single answer. So in this stage, we had 50 questions available in our new database. We asked the same queries that were asked before in test 1, observed the responses, and calculated average accuracy for this evaluation according to the responses from the system. Table 5 reflects the test evaluation process and results for this test-2. The performance of the Interactive Agent at this stage has improved than before.

In test-3, we added five rephrased questions for a single response in our database, and we repeated the same procedures taken in tests 1 and 2. This time, we measured the average result according to the performance of the Interactive Agent. Table 6 illustrates the performance result for test-3, and it is clearly observable that the Interactive Agent's performance has considerably increased since test-1 and test-2.

Table 5. Performance result of interaction recognition for test-2

Serial No	Question Asked to the Interactive Agent	Prepared Questions in Database	Avg Accuracy(%)
1	এডমিশন ফর্ম পাবো কোথায়?	এডমিশন ফর্ম কোথা থেকে সংগ্রহ করব?, এডমিশন ফর্ম কোথা থেকে নিবো?	88
2	ক্রেডিট ট্রান্সফারের উপায় গুলা কি কি?	ক্রেডিট ট্রান্সফার করতে চাই, কি করতে হবে?, স্টুডেন্টদের জন্য ক্রেডিট ট্রান্সফারের নিয়মগুলা কি কি?	

Table 6. Performance result of interaction recognition for test-3

Serial No	Question Asked to the Interactive Agent	Prepared Questions in Database	Avg Accuracy(%)
1	এডমিশন ফর্ম পাবো কোথায়?	এডমিশন ফর্ম কোথা থেকে সংগ্রহ করব?, এডমিশন ফর্ম কোথা থেকে নিবো?,?, এডমিশন ফর্ম পেতে কি করতে হবে?, এডমিশনের ফর্ম পেতে চাই। কি করতে হবে?, ভর্তি ফর্ম কোথায় পেতে পারি?	92
2	ক্রেডিট ট্রান্সফারের উপায় গুলা কি কি?	ক্রেডিট ট্রান্সফার করতে চাই, কি করতে হবে?, স্টুডেন্টদের জন্য ক্রেডিট ট্রান্সফারের নিয়মগুলা কি কি?, ক্রেডিট ট্রান্সফার কিভাবে করতে পারি?, ক্রেডিট ট্রান্সফার সম্পর্কে জানতে চাই, কিভাবে আমি ক্রেডিট ট্রান্সফার করতে পারি?	

5   Conclusion

We developed an AI-based framework for the reception system that ensures user satisfaction by providing voice-enabled domain-specific question-answering Bengali language at university premises. In addition to this, we trained the Deep Speech 2 model for ASR and OpenFace model for face recognition to achieve the best outcomes in customized environments. Although the WER of the Deep Speech 2 model is not up to the mark, in the future, we will train a neural network-based language model and perform noise augmentation to reduce the WER at a significant level. Our domain-specific database for Interaction Recognition ensures most of the university admission-related queries. In the future, the system can be made more user-friendly and robust by integrating face identification and sentence summarizing.

Acknowledgement. The authors extend their appreciation to the ICT Innovation Fund (a2i), ICT Division, Ministry of Posts, Telecommunications and Information Technology, the People's Republic of Bangladesh for funding the research work. The total technical computational resources are supported by the AIMS Lab of United International University, Bangladesh.

References

1. Nadarzynski, T., et al.: Acceptability of artificial intelligence (AI)-led chatbot services in healthcare: a mixed-methods study. Digit. Health **5**, 2055207619871808 (2019)
2. https://www.smallbizgenius.net/by-the-numbers/chatbot-statistics/#gref
3. Ivanov, S., Webster, C.: Conceptual framework of the use of robots, artificial intelligence and service automation in travel, tourism, and hospitality companies. In: Robots, Artificial Intelligence, and Service Automation in Travel, Tourism and Hospitality. Emerald Publishing Limited (2019)
4. Montenegro, J.L.Z., da Costa, C.A., da Rosa Righi, R.: Survey of conversational agents in health. Expert Syst. Appl. **129**, 56–67 (2019)
5. Ghosh, S., Bhatia, S., Bhatia, A.: Quro: facilitating user symptom check using a personalised chatbot-oriented dialogue system. Stud. Health Technol. Inform. **252**, 51–56 (2018)
6. Razzaki, S., et al.: A comparative study of artificial intelligence and human doctors for the purpose of triage and diagnosis. arXiv preprint arXiv:1806.10698 (2018)
7. Kanade, T.: Picture processing system by computer complex and recognition of human faces. Doctoral dissertation, Kyoto University, vol. 3952, pp. 83–97 (1973)
8. Phillips, P.J.: Multiple biometric grand challenge kick-off workshop. In: MBGC Workshop 2008 (2008)
9. Dantcheva, A., Brémond, F.: Gender estimation based on smile-dynamics. IEEE Trans. Inf. Forensics Secur. **12**(3), 719–729 (2016)
10. Erdem, C.E., Turan, C., Aydin, Z.: BAUM-2: a multilingual audio-visual affective face database. Multimedia Tools Appl. **74**(18), 7429–7459 (2015)
11. Zhalehpour, S., Akhtar, Z., Erdem, C.E.: Multimodal emotion recognition based on peak frame selection from video. Signal Image Video Process. **10**(5), 827–834 (2016)
12. Taskiran, M., Kahraman, N., Erdem, C.E.: Face recognition: past, present and future (a review). Digital Signal Process. **106**, 102809 (2020)
13. Haridas, A.V., Marimuthu, R., Sivakumar, V.G.: A critical review and analysis on techniques of speech recognition: the road ahead. Int. J. Knowl.-Based Intell. Eng. Syst. **22**(1), 39–57 (2018)
14. Young, I.J.B., Luz, S., Lone, N.: A systematic review of natural language processing for classification tasks in the field of incident reporting and adverse event analysis. Int. J. Med. Inform. **132**, 103971 (2019)
15. Adhikari, S.: NLP based machine learning approaches for text summarization. In: 2020 Fourth International Conference on Computing Methodologies and Communication (ICCMC). IEEE (2020)
16. Rajput, A.: Natural language processing, sentiment analysis, and clinical analytics. In: Innovation in Health Informatics, pp. 79–97. Academic Press (2020)
17. Yushendri, J., et al.: A speech intelligence conversation bot for interactive media information. In: 2017 Second International Conference on Informatics and Computing (ICIC). IEEE (2017)

18. Amos, B., Ludwiczuk, B., Satyanarayanan, M.: Openface: a general-purpose face recognition library with mobile applications. CMU Sch. Comput. Sci. **6**(2), 20 (2016)

19. Huang, G.B., et al.: Labeled faces in the wild: a database for studying face recognition in unconstrained environments. University Massachusetts, Amherst, MA, USA (2007)

20. Ahn, H.S., et al.: Hospital receptionist robot v2: design for enhancing verbal interaction with social skills. In: 2019 28th IEEE International Conference on Robot and Human Interactive Communication (RO-MAN). IEEE (2019)

21. Ky, Q.-M., Huynh, D.-N., Le, M.-H.: Receptionist and security robot using face recognition with standardized data collecting method. In: 2020 5th International Conference on Green Technology and Sustainable Development (GTSD). IEEE (2020)

22. Bellotto, N., Rowland, S., Hu, H.: Lux-an interactive receptionist robot for university open days. In: 2008 IEEE/ASME International Conference on Advanced Intelligent Mechatronics. IEEE (2008)

23. Cruz, C., Sucar, L.E., Morales, E.F.: Real-time face recognition for human-robot interaction. In: 2008 8th IEEE International Conference on Automatic Face & Gesture Recognition. IEEE (2008)

24. Cor, K., Alves, C., Gierl, M.J.: Three applications of automated test assembly within a user-friendly modeling environment. Pract. Assess. Res. Eval. **14**, 14 (2009)

25. Shakhovska, N., Basystiuk, O., Shakhovska, K.: Development of the speech-to-text chatbot interface based on google API. In: MoMLeT (2019)

26. Nuruzzaman, M.,Hussain, O.K.: IntelliBot: a dialogue-based chatbot for the insurance industry. Knowl.-Based Syst. **196**, 105810 (2020)

27. Reimers, N., Gurevych, I.: Sentence-BERT: sentence embeddings using siamese BERT-networks. arXiv preprint arXiv:1908.10084 (2019)

28. Louw, J.A.: Speect: a multilingual text-to-speech system (2008)

29. Yi, D., Lei, Z., Liao, S., Li, S.Z.: Learning face representation from scratch. arXiv preprint arXiv:1411.7923 (2014)

30. Ng, H.-W., Winkler, S.: A data-driven approach to cleaning large face datasets. In: IEEE International Conference on Image Processing (ICIP), no. 265, vol. 265, p. 530 (2014)

31. Szegedy, C., et al.: Going deeper with convolutions. In: Proceedings of the IEEE Conference on Computer Vision and Pattern Recognition, pp. 1–9 (2015)

32. Amodei, D., et al.: Deep speech 2: end-to-end speech recognition in English and mandarin. In: International Conference on Machine Learning. PMLR (2016)

33. Kjartansson, O., et al.: Crowd-sourced speech corpora for Javanese, Sundanese, Sinhala, Nepali, and Bangladeshi Bengali (2018)

A Real-Time Junk Food Recognition System Based on Machine Learning

Sirajum Munira Shifat$^{(\boxtimes)}$, Takitazwar Parthib,
Sabikunnahar Talukder Pyaasa, Nila Maitra Chaity, Niloy Kumar,
and Md. Kishor Morol

Department of Computer Science, American International University-Bangladesh,
Dhaka, Bangladesh
munirasirajum13@gmail.com, kishor@aiub.edu

Abstract. As a result of bad eating habits, humanity may be destroyed. People are constantly on the lookout for tasty foods, with junk foods being the most common source. As a consequence, our eating patterns are shifting, and we're gravitating toward junk food more than ever, which is bad for our health and increases our risk of acquiring health problems. Machine learning principles are applied in every aspect of our lives, and one of them is object recognition via image processing. However, because foods vary in nature, this procedure is crucial, and traditional methods like ANN, SVM, KNN, PLS etc., will result in a low accuracy rate. All of these issues were defeated by the Deep Neural Network. In this work, we created a fresh dataset of 10,000 data points from 20 junk food classifications to try to recognize junk foods. All of the data in the data set was gathered using the Google search engine, which is thought to be one-of-a-kind in every way. The goal was achieved using Convolution Neural Network (CNN) technology, which is well-known for image processing. We achieved a 98.05% accuracy rate throughout the research, which was satisfactory. In addition, we conducted a test based on a real-life event, and the outcome was extraordinary. Our goal is to advance this research to the next level, so that it may be applied to a future study. Our ultimate goal is to create a system that would encourage people to avoid eating junk food and to be health-conscious.

Keywords: Machine learning · Junk food · Object detection · YOLOv3 · Custom food dataset

1 Introduction

The Machine Learning approach for perceiving food is a significant recognizable factor nowadays. Numerous scientists applied this methodology in their experiments, while a portion of the investigation made noticeable progress. Recently, deep learning has been used in image recognition. The most distinguishing aspect is that better image features for recognition are extracted automatically through training. One of the approaches that meet the criteria of the deep learning approach is the convolutional neural network (CNN) [1]. Image recognition of food

A. K. M. M. Islam et al. (Eds.): ICBBDB 2021, CCIS 1550, pp. 92–105, 2022.
https://doi.org/10.1007/978-3-031-17181-9_8

products is usually frequently challenging due to the wide variety of forms of food. Deep learning, on the other hand, has recently been proved to be a highly successful image recognition tool, and CNN is a state-of-the-art deep learning solution. Using computer vision and AI approaches, researchers have been focusing on automatically detecting foods and associated dietary data from images recorded over the past two decades. The main objective of this research is to recognize junk foods. Junk food is one of the popular variants in food. Michael Jacobson, who was a director of the Center for Science the expressed his feeling by saying that junk food can be considered as a dialect for foods of inadequate or has low beneficial value for the human body which is also considered as HFSS (High fat, sugar, or salt) [2].

The lack of a rapid and accurate junk food detector in the medical field has yet to be addressed, so a new deep learning-based food image recognition system is implemented at the end of this study. The suggested method uses a Convolutional Neural Network (CNN) with a few key improvements. The effectiveness of our solution has been proved by the outcomes of using the suggested approach on two real-world datasets. In our study, we have used CNN for the detection of images of junk food where we have applied YOLO technology to train our manually created datasets. A system is created to identify specific junk food using YOLO or the "You Only Look Once," framework. The YOLO model comes from the family of Fully Convolutional Neural Networks (FCN) by which the best available result can be achieved where real-time object detection is possible with every single end-to-end model.

In the current period, Food acknowledgment has stood out enough to be noticed for holding different concerns. Junk food has certainly carved the Third World for globalization [3]. It is an integral part of the lives of developed and developing countries, and the problems associated with obesity are greatly increased. Our goal is to take this research to the next level so that it can be applied to another study in the future. Our long-term objective is to develop a system that encourages individuals to eat less junk food and to be more health-conscious. This study has been conducted by following the Formal Method and Experimental Method, which will be followed throughout the whole process. Food identification and nutritional assessment studies in recent years, they have been steadily improving to establish a good dietary assessment system. Several approaches for feature extraction and categorization as well as deep learning methods have been presented.

2   Literature Review

Junk food consumption and its effects on health are becoming a major concern around the world. Everyone should receive health education so that they can recognize which foods are more helpful. Healthy eating is one of the most important tasks that will always result in a healthy lifestyle [4]. To prevent illness diet is one of the key factors [5]. Since 1966 consumption of fast food is growing at a rapid speed [4]. Any food that is simple to make and consume in a short amount of time is considered fast food. Fast food, on the other hand, lacks the necessary nourishment for human health, which is why it is less expensive. In the long run, fast food has many damaging effects on the human body due to its content of fat have excessive cholesterol levels and sugar [7]. People are now more aware of and concerned about their health. Because individuals are the main emphasis for a better future, health should be a major concern for everyone. Food identification is gaining popularity these days, like computers and mobile phones can readily detect food and its dietary fiber content using a machine learning approach [8]. In the real-time junk food image detecting process, optical sensors are used. Using optical sensors after capturing the food images every image can be labeled [9]. The work in this research is to detect junk food using the YOLOv3 algorithm detector with custom data set. The full form of YOLOv3 is 'You Only Look Once' and it is one of the fastest and commonly used deep learning-based object detection methods. It uses the k-means cluster technique to evaluate the initial width and height of the foretold bounding boxes [10, 11]. Numerous algorithms were proposed to make food recognition fast and precise. A lot of people are still working on Food Detection to make wide-ranging use of deep learning. In 2005, N. Dalal introduced Histogram of oriented gradients (HOG). Essentially, this approach is a feature descriptor that is utilized in image processing and other computer vision methods to differentiate objects. An experiment by [20] on multiple food image detection using HOG obtained 55.8% classification rate, which enhanced the standard result in case of using only DPM by 14.3 points. CNN, which means Convolutional Neural Networks is one of the most advanced methods for image recognition [12]. This technique contains a multi-layer of a neural network similar to the function of the brain [32]. The neurons take minor areas of the previous layer as input. CNN includes two layers. As a result, CNN achieved much improvement than other traditional approaches using handcrafted structures. Finished reflection of trained convolution kernels, established that color features are vital to food image recognition. Overall the output was prosperous that specifies that it would have been difficult for humans to recognize such images [13, 14].

Mask R-CNN was used for Chinese food image detection by Y. Li, X. Xu, and C. Yuan in their paper named Enhanced Mask R-CNN for Chinese Food Image Detection. To reach their aim they first built Chinese food images. A deep separable convolution as an alternative of traditional convolution for decreasing model consumption which can significantly decrease the resource consumption and increase the detection productivity of the Chinese food images with great accuracy [17].

The Single Shot Detector (SSD) method uses a single deep neural network to recognize objects in photos. SSD eliminates the proposal generation and subsequent pixel or feature resampling stages, allowing all calculations to be consolidated into a single network. It is a direct and simple method to assimilate into systems that have need of a detection module. In both training and meddling SDD is has a great speed [28]. Spatial Pyramid Pooling (SPP-net) is a network assembly that can produce a fixed-length demonstration irrespective of pictures size and scale. It is a strong method that recovers altogether CNN-based image detection approaches. It can receive both input image of different size and fixed-length piece demonstration [16].

The most efficient and precise algorithm of all is YOLO (You Only Look Once) proposed by Joseph Redmon. It can detect multiple object from one image. YOLOv3 is very robust and has nearly on par with RetinaNet and far above the SSD alternatives. The recommended method decreases the layer number in the current YOLOv3 network model to shorten the failures and feature mining time [29]. A deep convolutional neural network is combined with YOLO, a contemporary object identification approach, to identify two objects at the same time. The accuracy rate was around 80% [15].

Centered on Faster R-CNN with Zeiler and Fergus model (ZF-net) and Caffe framework. p-Faster R-CNN algorithm for healthy diet detection was projected. By comparing it with Fast R-CNN and Faster R-CNN the performance of p-Faster R-CNN was weighed. Faster R-CNN rises the AP value of each kind of food by more than 2% paralleled with Faster R-CNN, and p-Faster R-CNN, Faster R-CNN is superior to Fast R-CNN correctness and speed [16,17].

To test the proposed algorithm's accuracy and speed against current YOLOv3 and YOLOv3-tiny network models using WIDER FACE and datasets, it was compared to existing YOLOv3 and YOLOv3-tiny network models. As a consequence, the accuracy performance comparison results for YOLOv3 were 88.99%, 67.93% for YOLOv3-tiny, and 87.48% for YOLOv3-tiny. When compared to the present YOLOv3-tiny, this result reveals a 19.55% improvement accuracy. In comparison to YOLOv3, the outcome was 1.51% lower. In addition, the speed was 54.7 FPS lower than YOLOv3-tiny. On the other hand, 70.2 frames per second are quicker than YOLOv3 [18,19].

When a person looks at an image they can immediately determine the object, notice their position and even know how to react to that. A human can detect an object precisely even if the image is blurred or in complex structure [20]. However, the difficulty is that the globe is vast, and not everyone is aware of the variety of junk food available. Junk food is different in different countries. With the use of a prediction model, the system will alert the user to the food's effect. The majority of people have food allergies. One of the most prevalent scenarios is an adverse reaction. People can be more conscious of their meal choices by detecting these types of food [21]. Contemporary object detection approaches, such as the CNN family and YOLO, are briefly discussed in this work. In actuality, YOLO has a wider use than CNNs. A unified object detection model is the YOLO object detection model. It's simple to put together and can be quickly trained on whole photographs. Unlike classifier-based approaches, YOLO is trained on a loss function that is directly related to detection. Furthermore, because YOLO provides a more generalizing representation of objects than other models, it is well suited to applications requiring speedy and accurate object detection [22].

3   Method

The research method is selected based on a machine learning approach with 20 different classes of various junk food. The process is followed in machine learning problem solving technique. YOLO (You Only Look Once) object detector is chosen since the detector is rapid and reliable at the same time. The detector configuration was tuned to get the most efficient outcome of 98.05% accuracy. The following workflow are followed for the experiment (Fig. 1):

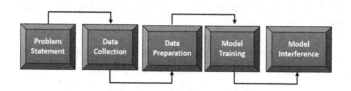

Fig. 1. Research workflow

3.1   About Model (YOLOV3)

The YOLO model comes from the family of Fully Convolutional Neural Networks (FCN) by which best available result can be achieved where real time object detection is possible with every single end-to-end model. In YOLO object detection model, the train image is divided into several grid (13×13). On these grids 5 bounding boxes are created [30]. One bounding box may intersect several grids as well. Confidence level is assigned for each bounding box. With a certain threshold the bounding boxes are selected for classification. The model can already recognize 15 objects. 20 more items were manually added with the given model. 100 Pictures were selected for each class. Then with the help of data augmentation method the dataset was increased to around 500 Pictures for individual class. Later, the images were labeled with YOLO format using "labelImg".

It has 75 convolutional layers. Due to the Residual layer, it can contain skip connections. It has upsampling layers as well. There is no use of pooling in YOLO v3. To avoid loss of low-level features stride 2 is being used in each convolutional layer. YOLO can handle different shape of input images but if the shapes are similar it makes it less complicated to debug. After the convolution a feature map is generated which contains ($B \times (5+C)$) entries (where B is number of bounding boxes and C is the class confidence for specific bounding box) [30]. Each bounding box has $5+C$ attributes- (x, y) co-ordinates, w (width), h (height), objective-ness score and C class confidences. The specialty of YOLO v3 is, it can predict 3 bounding boxes (Anchors) for individual cell. Anchors are preset bounding boxes that have been pre-defined. The backbone of YOLOv3 is Darknet-53. Other models like SSD and RetinaNet, on the other hand, use the common ResNet family of backbones [31]. Also, YOLOv3 is an incremental upgrade from previous models. It preserves fine-grained features by sampling and concatenating feature layers with earlier feature layers. Another enhancement is the use of three detection scales. As a consequence, the model can recognize objects of varying sizes in images. The link of the process of the whole algorithm is given: https://github.com/MasterS007/YOLOV3-Process-for-detecting-Junk-Food.git.

3.2 Dataset Collection

Dataset was collected manually for 20 different classes of junk food such as biryani, burger, chicken nuggets, hotdog, chips, Kabab, Mac and Cheese, Meatloaf, Muffin, Nachos, Cookies, French Fry, Ice-cream, Pizza, Processed Cheese, cheesecake, crispy chicken, sandwich, noodles and waffles (Fig. 2). The pictures were captured by smartphones and Digital Cameras. Foods from restaurants, food courts, and Cart parked on street were taken into consideration to add variety to the dataset. The pictures were searched from internet. The most popular pictures were taken from Google Images. Along with that some social media (Facebook) was used as well to get latest pictures of the classified foods. 100 images were selected per class resulting in $100 \times 20 = 2000$ images in total. Link of the dataset is: https://www.kaggle.com/sirajummunirashifat/junk-food-recognition-system-based-on-ml.

3.3 Data Augmentation

Since the number of classes was comparatively high, a simple test was conducted by training with initial 2000 images. The training results with such a low amount of dataset only provided 61.6% accuracy. Data augmentation was used to further increase the dataset since a low dataset might cause low accuracy. Rotation of random degrees, horizontal and vertical flip, zoom in rescaling was taken into consideration for augmentation. This was used so that the variety of the data can be trained with the same image. After the augmentation, there were 500 images for each class. Which resulted in $500 \times 20 = 10000$ images.

3.4 Data Preparation

The pictures were all in various formats so they had to be resized to a 416×416 and renamed in a certain order to reduce complexity. All the pictures were converted to jpg for YOLO bounding box creation. All the 10000 images were labeled manually. The open-source software labelImg [23] also supported multiple bounding boxes in a single picture which increased the number of total bounding box helping the accuracy of the training. Coordinates (Tx, Ty, Th, Tw) and the class number of the object were extracted from each image by labeling to accommodate it for training.

Fig. 2. Sample images of classes

3.5   Model Tuning

The working mechanism of the object detection model is based on custom configuration YOLO v3. Darknet-53 was used as a base to start the tuning. The detection is completed with 3 phases of detection in the RGB channel. Inputs were taken as 416×416 to save training time. The model uses 9 anchor boxes generated with K-Means clustering. 75 Convolution Layers are executed with filters size varied from 32, 64, 128, 256 and max up to 512. The filter size was increased to get more accurate results while sacrificing very little detection time. Stride and Padding 1, 2 is used for all convolution layers with Leaky Relu (Eq. 2) as an activation function. Binary cross-entropy loss is used as an error function to avoid overlapping classes. Simple Logistic regression is applied to measure objectness score. Tensor number $75 \times 75 \times [3*(4+1+80)]$ were calculated from (Eq. 1) for 80 classes.

$$T = S.S.B(4+1+C) \tag{1}$$

Here 75×75 kernel size was inserted in the 3 detection layers. The higher layers are responsible for the smaller case of the object whereas the lower layer (82nd) is accurate with larger object enabling detection across all scaling. SGD optimizer is applied with a learning rate of 0.001 for adaptive learning. Many models were trained to tune in for the best outcome. Models kernel size for each convolution was increased to notice the performance increase. Batch normalization was applied with testing on subdivisions 16 and 32.

$$f(x) = 1(x < 0)(0.1x) + 1(x >= 0)(x) \tag{2}$$

3.6   Internal Architecture

Approaches for each epoch that have been applied to train the model using Darknet-53 are shown in Fig. 3. The batch size was taken 64 and subdivision was taken 16. Max batch was 10000, used SGD optimizer.

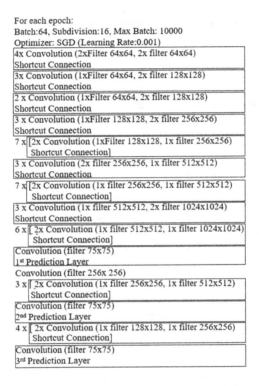

Fig. 3. Internal architecture of the model

3.7   Model Training

The model was conducted with an Nvidia RTX 2060 GPU and Google Colab using the python Tensorflow library. The training data was split into training, validating, and testing sections. 100 Epochs were selected for each iteration. A total of 80% of the data was chosen for training, while the remaining 20% was retained for testing and validation. A total of 40000 epochs were iterated with the required time of 3 days. Each iteration kept decreasing the neat loss. The weights were generated after 100 epochs which could be used on any platform for testing.

4   Model Evaluation

4.1   Training and Testing

The experimental findings of our system employing the dataset of junk food of 20 classes are shown in this chapter where each item consists of 500 images, which we created ourselves. To recognize junk food, the Yolov3 algorithm was proposed and the results were more accurate. We needed to move this properly structured dataset into VM (Virtual Machine) cloud because Google Colab was used to train this model. After moving the dataset into the VM cloud the yolov3-custom.cfg file was configured. To configure the file, the batch size was changed to 64, and the subdivision was changed to 16. We set our max-batches to 40000, steps to 32000, and 36000, the class value was altered to 20 in all three YOLO layers, and filters were set to 75 in all three convolutional layers before the YOLO layers.

4.2   Model Performance

After successfully training the model, we made a quick test with some junk food images captured by our cellphone. The model was testing with unseen image dataset. (Figure 4) shows some testing results of images.

Our trained model has a very low loss, as shown in the graph (Fig. 5). For our model to be 'accurate' we would aim for a loss below 2. In this graph, we can see that the model's loss is less than 2, indicating that we achieved our projected aim. For the training dataset, our suggested model has an accuracy of 98.05%. The exam on random photos went reasonably well when the training was completed. We succeeded to achieve a pretty consistent pace.

In Fig. 6 it is shown that the test image dataset was used in the model which trained to test the accuracy in Google Colab with 16 number of subdivision and also used in the model which trained in local GPU machine with 32 number of subdivision.

With the help of image augmentation, a dataset of 10000 images with 3 days of training was able to produce results with upwards of 98.05% confidence. Given the complexity of the food images, the model did exceptionally well. We also trained the model on a local GPU system, changing the batch size and subdivisions to 64 and 32, respectively. The major motivation for this was to make subdivision 32 so that training the model would take less time. If the subdivision number is higher, the amount of time spent training will be reduced. As a result, the model's subdivision number was increased. Even though training time was reduced and training accuracy was excellent, test accuracy was dismal. We can see from the above comparison that when the subdivision was 16, the model was more accurate 98.05% confidence, and when the subdivision was 32, the model was less accurate 87% confidence.

Fig. 4. Result of food recognition

4.3   Result Comparison with Previous Research

A sliding window was used in conventional computer vision systems to scan for things at different locations and sizes. The aspect ratio of the item was typically thought to be fixed because this was such a costly task. Selective Search was employed by early Deep Learning-based object detection algorithms like the R-CNN and Fast R-CNN to reduce the number of bounding boxes that the algorithm had to examine. Another method, termed Overfeat, included scanning the picture at various scales using convolutional sliding windows-like techniques. Faster R-CNN was then used to identify bounding boxes that were to be tested using a Region Proposal Network (RPN). The traits retrieved for object recognition were also employed by the RPN for proposing probable bounding boxes, which saved a lot of work.

YOLO, on the other hand, takes an entirely new approach to the object detection problem. It merely sends the entire image via the network once. SSD is another object detection approach that passes the picture through a deep learning network once, although YOLOv3 is significantly quicker and achieves similar accuracy. On an M40, TitanX, or 1080 Ti GPU, YOLOv3 produces results that are quicker than real-time with more accuracy.

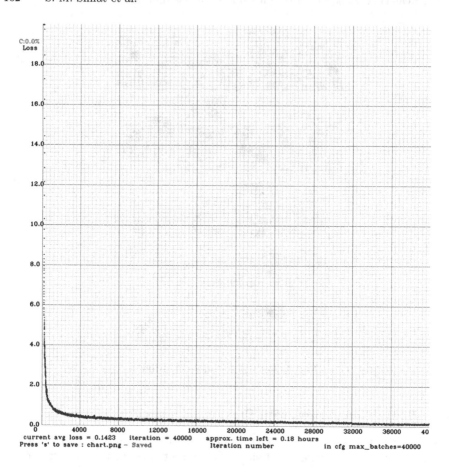

Fig. 5. Graphical view of loss of training

	Predicted duration		Percentage of Error		Percentage of Accuracy	
	Colab GPU with subdivision 16	Local GPU with subdivision 32	Colab GPU with subdivision 16	Local GPU with subdivision 32	Colab GPU with subdivision 16	Local GPU with subdivision 32
Total Average	40.34ms	40.33ms	1.95%	12.8%	98.05%	87%

Fig. 6. Accuracy of food recognition from testing images

Yolo Implementation model is like a normal CNN model. There are many CNN based algorithm like RCNN, Yolo model and many more. But R-CNN algorithm requires thousands of network evolution to predict one image which are very time consuming. R-CNN algorithm focuses on specific area of the image and trains separately each component. To solve this problem YOLO model has been proposed. The main purpose of use this algorithm is, it is computationally very fast and also used on real time environment.

It is difficult to find research that identifies this type of junk food. However, there are a few papers that are comparable to this one. The table below (Fig. 7) shows some of the connections between our research and previous studies on food classification.

Work	Technology Used	Accuracy
Food image recognition using deep convolutional network with pre-training and fine-tuning [25].	DCNN	70.4%
Im2calories: towards an automated mobile vision food diary [26].	Google net/food101	79.0%
A food recognition system for diabetic patients based on an optimized bag-of-features model [27].	ANNnh	75.0%
Yelp Food Identification via Image Feature Extraction and Classification [28].	CNN & SVM	68.49%
Food recognition: a new dataset, experiments and results [29].	CNN	79.0%
A Real-time Junk Food Recognition System based on Machine Learning.	**CNN with YOLOV3**	**98.05%**

Fig. 7. Result comparison with previous research

5   Conclusion

In this study, A CNN-based algorithm was implemented by modifying Darknet-53 architecture. The model was heavily tuned to achieve an outcome of 98.05% accuracy. Our model was trained in The dataset contains 20 classes and 500 images were taken for each class. It's evident that our object detection model outperforms other categorization methods. The model provided almost 30 FPS on a real-time windows desktop app on an Intel Core I5-7400 desktop. The generated weights can be used on Android, IOS devices to create a portable application. With a single snap, people will be able to capture and detect the desired food. In the future, our team intends to develop such an app. Though the testing was conducted on a small test set of 1000 images, further testing is expected to keep an average accuracy of more than 90%. In this research, we also introduced a dataset of 10000 images of junk food which was captured and gathered by us. The limitation we have faced while training our model is a lack of resources such as a strong enough GPU to reduce the training time.

Because junk food is linked to a variety of severe diseases, we will be able to utilize our model to determine the link between those diseases and junk food in the future. With the use of this technology, new research in the medical and technological fields can be undertaken so that people can avoid eating foods that are detrimental to them.

References

1. LeCun, Y., Bottou, L., Bengio, Y., Haffner, P.: Gradient-based learning applied to document recognition. Semanticscholar.org (2021). https://www.semanticscholar.org/paper/Gradient-based-learning-applied-to-document-LeCun-Bottou/162d958ff885f1462aeda91cd72582323fd6a1f4
2. Bhaskar, R.: Junk food: impact on health. J. Drug Deliv. Ther. **2**(3) (2012). https://doi.org/10.22270/jddt.v2i3.132
3. Europe PMC: Europe PMC. Europepmc.org (2021). http://europepmc.org/abstract/MED/6905150
4. Chowdhury, M., Haque Subho, M., Rahman, M., Islam, S., Chaki, D.: Impact of fast food consumption on health: a study on university students of Bangladesh. In: 2018 21st International Conference of Computer and Information Technology (ICCIT) (2018). https://doi.org/10.1109/iccitechn.2018.8631962
5. Skerrett, P., Willett, W.: Essentials of healthy eating: a guide. J. Midwifery Women's Health **55**(6), 492–501 (2010). https://doi.org/10.1016/j.jmwh.2010.06.019
6. Islam, M.: The impact of fast food on our life: a study on food habits of Bangladeshi people. Global J. **20**(8) (2020)
7. Diet: World Health Organization (2021). http://www.who.int/dietphysicalactivity/diet/en/
8. Khan, T., Islam, M., Ullah, S., Rabby, A.: A machine learning approach to recognize junk food. In: 2019 10th International Conference on Computing, Communication and Networking Technologies (ICCCNT) (2019). https://doi.org/10.1109/icccnt45670.2019.8944873
9. Lee, G., Huang, C., Chen, J.: AIFood: A Large Scale Food Images Dataset for Ingredient Recognition (2019)
10. Zhao, L., Li, S.: Object detection algorithm based on improved YOLOv3. Electronics **9**(3), 537 (2020). https://doi.org/10.3390/electronics9030537
11. Zhu, L., Spachos, P.: Support vector machine and YOLO for a mobile food grading system. Internet Things **13**, 100359 (2021). https://doi.org/10.1016/j.iot.2021.100359
12. Ciocca, G., Napoletano, P., Schettini, R.: Food recognition: a new dataset, experiments, and results. IEEE J. Biomed. Health Inform. **21**(3), 588–598 (2017). https://doi.org/10.1109/jbhi.2016.2636441
13. Kagaya, H., Aizawa, K., Ogawa, M.: Food detection and recognition using convolutional neural network. In: Proceedings of the 22nd ACM International Conference on Multimedia (2014). https://doi.org/10.1145/2647868.2654970
14. Subhi, M.A., Ali, S.M.: A deep convolutional neural network for food detection and recognition. In: IEEE-EMBS Conference on Biomedical Engineering and Sciences (IECBES) 2018, pp. 284–287 (2018). https://doi.org/10.1109/IECBES.2018.8626720
15. Sun, J., Radecka, K., Zilic, Z.: FoodTracker: A Real-time Food Detection Mobile Application by Deep Convolutional Neural Networks. Montreal, Quebec, Canada (2019)
16. Wan, Y., Liu, Yu., Li, Y., Zhang, P.: p-faster R-CNN algorithm for food detection. In: Romdhani, I., Shu, L., Takahiro, H., Zhou, Z., Gordon, T., Zeng, D. (eds.) CollaborateCom 2017. LNICST, vol. 252, pp. 132–142. Springer, Cham (2018). https://doi.org/10.1007/978-3-030-00916-8_13

17. Li, Y., Xu, X., Yuan, C.: Enhanced mask R-CNN for Chinese food image detection. Math. Probl. Eng. **2020**, 1–8 (2020). https://doi.org/10.1155/2020/6253827
18. Won, J., Lee, D., Lee, K., Lin, C.: An improved YOLOv3-based neural network for de-identification technology. In: 2019 34th International Technical Conference on Circuits/Systems, Computers and Communications (ITC-CSCC) (2019). https://doi.org/10.1109/itc-cscc.2019.8793382
19. Srivastava, S., Divekar, A., Anilkumar, C., Naik, I., Kulkarni, V., Pattabiraman, V.: Comparative analysis of deep learning image detection algorithms. J. Big Data **8**(1), 1–27 (2021). https://doi.org/10.1186/s40537-021-00434-w
20. Matsuda, Y., Yanai, K.: Multiple-food recognition considering co-occurrence employing manifold ranking. In: 2012 21st International Conference on Pattern Recognition (ICPR), pp. 2017–2020 (2012)
21. Sampson, H.A., Ho, D.G.: Relationship between food-specific IgE concentrations and the risk of positive food challenges in children and adolescents. J. Allergy Clin. Immunol. **100**(4), 444–451 (1997). https://doi.org/10.1016/s0091-6749(97)70133-7
22. Du, J.: Understanding of object detection based on CNN family and YOLO. J. Phys. Conf. Ser. **1004**, 012029 (2018). https://doi.org/10.1088/1742-6596/1004/1/012029
23. LabelImg is a graphical image annotation tool and label object bounding boxes in images, GitHub (2021). https://github.com/tzutalin/labelImg
24. Yanai, K., Kawano, Y.: Food image recognition using deep convolutional network with pre-training and fine-tuning. In: 2015 IEEE International Conference on Multimedia & Expo Workshops (ICMEW) (2015). https://doi.org/10.1109/icmew.2015.7169816
25. Myers, A., et al.: Im2Calories: towards an automated mobile vision food diary. In: 2015 IEEE International Conference on Computer Vision (ICCV) (2015). https://doi.org/10.1109/iccv.2015.146
26. Anthimopoulos, M., Gianola, L., Scarnato, L., Diem, P., Mougiakakou, S.: A food recognition system for diabetic patients based on an optimized bag-of-features model. IEEE J. Biomed. Health Inform. **18**(4), 1261–1271 (2014). https://doi.org/10.1109/jbhi.2014.2308928
27. Sun, F., Gu, Z., Feng, B.: Yelp Food Identification via Image Feature Extraction and Classification, Bloomington, IN (2019)
28. Choudhury, A.: Top 8 Algorithms For Object Detection One Must Know, Analytics India Magazine (2021). https://analyticsindiamag.com/top-8-algorithms-for-objectdetection/
29. Won, J., Lee, D., Lee, K., Lin, C.: An improved YOLOv3-based neural network for deidentification technology. In: 2019 34th International Technical Conference on Circuits/Systems, Computers and Communications (ITC-CSCC) (2019). https://doi.org/10.1109/itc-cscc.2019.8793382
30. What's new in YOLO v3? Medium. https://towardsdatascience.com/yolo-v3-object-detection-53fb7d3bfe6b
31. YOLOv3 Object Detector — ArcGIS for Developers. Developers.arcgis.com (2021). https://developers.arcgis.com/python/guide/yolov3-object-detector/
32. Faruk, A.M., Faraby, H.A., Azad, M.M., Fedous, M.R., Morol, M.K.: Image to Bengali caption generation using deep CNN and bidirectional gated recurrent unit. In: 2020 23rd International Conference on Computer and Information Technology (ICCIT), pp. 1–6 (2020). https://doi.org/10.1109/ICCIT51783.2020.9392697

Inference of Gene Regulatory Network (GRN) from Gene Expression Data Using K-Means Clustering and Entropy Based Selection of Interactions

Asadullah Al Galib[1]([✉])(ID), Mohammad Mohaimanur Rahman[1],
Md. Haider Ali[2](ID), and Eusra Mohammad[3]

[1] BRAC University, 66, Dhaka 1212, Bangladesh
asadullah.al.galib@g.bracu.ac.bd
[2] University of Dhaka, Nilkhet Rd, Dhaka 1000, Bangladesh
haider@du.ac.bd
[3] Max Planck Institute for Biophysical Chemistry, Am Faßberg 11,
37077 Göttingen, Germany
eusra.mohammad@mpibpc.mpg.de

Abstract. Inferring regulatory networks from gene expression data alone is considered a challenging task in systems biology. The introduction of various high-throughput DNA microarray technologies has significantly increased the amount of data to be analysed and various inference algorithms have inherent limitations in dealing with different types of datasets due to their specialized nature. In this paper, we propose a novel method to infer gene regulatory network from expression data which utilises K-means clustering along with some properties of entropy from information theory. The proposed method, first groups the genes of a dataset into a given number of clusters and then finds statistically significant interactions among genes of each individual cluster and selected nearby clusters. To achieve this, an information theoretic approach based on Entropy Reduction is used to generate a regulatory interaction matrix consisting of all genes. The purpose of grouping genes in clusters based on the similarity of expression level is to minimise the search space of regulatory interactions among genes. The performance of the algorithm is measured using precision-recall and compared with the result of ARACNE, a popular information theoretic approach to reverse engineer gene regulatory networks from expression dataset.

Keywords: Unsupervised machine learning · K-means clustering · Information theory · Entropy · Gene regulatory networks · Gene expression dataset

1 Introduction

In our approach to infer gene regulatory network, we focus on merging a powerful gene expression analysis technique, clustering with the Entropy Reduction Technique (ERT) from information theory in an attempt to achieve better

A. K. M. M. Islam et al. (Eds.): ICBBDB 2021, CCIS 1550, pp. 106–120, 2022.
https://doi.org/10.1007/978-3-031-17181-9_9

performance than existing information theoretic approaches such as ARACNE (Algorithm for the Reconstruction of Accurate Cellular Networks). The goal is to merge these two techniques in order to handle large datasets without being provided any information regarding the type of experimental conditions in which the expression levels of genes were measured. With the knowledge of the regulatory network and the role that each gene plays in a network, fields such as drug discovery and personalized medicine will be revolutionized.

1.1   Gene Regulatory Network

Genes of a biological system do not act independently of each other. They work in a complex regulatory network with other genes and gene products such as RNA and protein to control the expression level of certain genes in the network, either through activation or inhibition regarding the expression level. Two genes can be considered connected by a regulatory interaction link if the expression level of one influences the expression level of the other.

1.2   Clustering of Gene Expression Data

As a useful data mining technique, clustering has been used in the context of gene expression data to identify grouping that exists in the data and also to find hidden patterns among data points. In our algorithm, we use k-means clustering because of its simplicity and ability to cluster large datasets containing 4000 to 5000 genes along with hundreds of samples in an efficient manner to be later used with the Entropy Reduction Technique (ERT). We also use the Elbow Method (see Fig. 2) to find the optimal value for the number of clusters.

1.3   Entropy Reduction (ER)

We use the entropy reduction approach in our algorithm for the purpose of determining statistically significant regulatory interactions among genes. In Information Theory, proposed by Shannon, Entropy is a fundamental concept. It can be defined as the measurement of uncertainty of a random variable [2].

$$H(x) = -\sum_{x \in X} p(x) \log p(x) \tag{1}$$

where H is the entropy, x is a discrete random vector with alphabet X, and p(x) is the probability mass function.

Entropy is very closely related to Mutual Information (MI), which is the measurement of the amount of information about one random variable that is contained in another variable. So it reduces the uncertainty of one variable given that the information about another variable is provided [2]. In the biological context, if two genes have a regulatory interaction among them, then the mutual information between those two genes will be high. On the other hand, if two genes act independently in the biological process, they will have a mutual information measure close to zero. The main component of entropy reduction technique is, if a variable A shares a regulatory link with another variable B, then

$$H(A|B) < H(A) \tag{2}$$

where, $H(A|B)$ is the Conditional Entropy of A given B and H (A) is the Entropy of A [2].

Entropy Reduction Technique (ERT) is a relatively new approach to be applied to the task of inferring biological networks. Previously it has been used to generate regulatory networks for small biological networks [2]. In order to apply ERT in the context of large datasets where we would like to avoid calculating large three dimensional matrices, we use a clustering algorithm to minimize the search space so that ERT then can be applied on smaller groups of genes in an efficient way.

1.4   Contribution

We are proposing a novel approach to infer gene regulatory network that combines clustering of genes with Entropy Reduction Technique to make this effective idea applicable on large datasets. We evaluate the performance of our algorithm using Precision and Recall on the dataset from DREAM5-Network Inference Challenge [5] as well as in-silico dataset generated by GeneNetWeaver [10]. The resultant network is compared with the regulatory network generated by ARACNE. We also compare the results from No-Clustering, Unmerged-Clustering and Selected-Merged-Clustering versions of our algorithm to assess the effectiveness of clustering in the regulatory networks. Even though the No-Clustering version is the most effective one in determining regulatory interactions among genes, Selected-Merged-Clustering version also performs well across all datasets. Different threshold values are used after the ERT step to eliminate less significant interactions and outputs of multiple versions of the algorithm are compared to highlight the range of effective threshold values.

2   Related Work

Several types of information theoretic approaches have been used to reverse engineer gene regulatory networks from expression data. Here, we will discuss ARACNE and the Entropy Reduction Technique (ERT) that we have used in our algorithm:

2.1   ARACNE

ARACNE (Algorithm for the Reconstruction of Accurate Cellular Networks) is an information theoretic algorithm that uses microarray gene expression data to generate transcriptional regulatory network [3]. It identifies links between genes as true regulatory interactions if the statistical dependency is irreducible between those genes. ARACNE defines potential regulatory interactions between two genes based on their Mutual Information (MI). After generating pair-wise mutual information, it uses a threshold value to eliminate links between gene pairs as not significant if they are below the threshold value. But the problem with this MI-based approach is that it also labels indirect interactions between genes which are highly co-regulated due to their relationship with a third gene, as true regulatory interactions, which results in large amount of false positives. ARACNE solves this problem by using a technique called the **Data Processing Inequality (DPI)** [3].

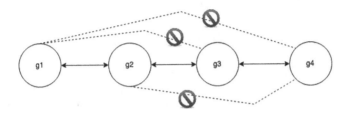

Fig. 1. DPI technique.

The idea of DPI is, if Gene g1 and Gene g3 (see Fig. 1) have indirect interactions through a third Gene g2 then the link between g1 and g3 will be removed by DPI.

$$I(g1, g3) <= min[I(g1, g2), I(g2, g3)] \tag{3}$$

where I is the MI between gene pairs.

2.2 Entropy Reduction Technique

The reason for using concepts from information theory such as Entropy, Mutual Information is to generate biological networks without any background theoretical knowledge.

Entropy is closely related to Mutual Information which is the measurement of how much information one variable contains about another. Mutual Information, I can be described in terms of both Joint Entropy $H(X, Y)$ and Conditional Entropy, $H(Y|X)$ in the following way [2]

$$H(X, Y) = -\sum_x \sum_y p(x, y) \log p(x, y) \tag{4}$$

$$H(Y|X) = -\sum_x \sum_y p(x, y) \log p(y|x) \tag{5}$$

$$I(X, Y) = H(X) - H(X|Y) = H(X) + H(Y) - H(X, Y) \tag{6}$$

The basic idea of Entropy Reduction technique is, if a variable A does not depend on variable B, then the Entropy of A given B is equal to the Entropy of A. But if variable A has dependency on variable B, then the Entropy of A given B is less than the Entropy of variable A [2].

$$H(B) = H(A), \textbf{A and B are independent of each other} \qquad (7)$$

$$H(A|B) < H(A), \textbf{A and B have dependency relationship} \qquad (8)$$

This works well when the regulatory network is very small [2]. But for large networks containing thousands of genes, this is extremely time consuming and unfeasible to be applicable in real applications.

3   Clustering of Gene Expression Data

The main goal of clustering is to group data points which are similar into the same cluster from a set of clusters and dissimilar data points into a different cluster. In the context of genetics, the similarity measure can be the similar expression or co-expression level of genes [7]. If Gene A and Gene B are grouped in the same cluster based on expression level, then it can be deduced that they are part of the same biological process. Moreover, strong co-expression level among genes also suggests co-regulation [7]. Various supervised, semi-supervised and unsupervised algorithms have been used in systems biology [9,11], but considering the globular shape of regulatory networks, we focus primarily on K-means clustering.

3.1   K-Means Clustering

K-means clustering falls into the subgroup of clustering called Partitioning Clustering, which is a clustering technique where each data point belongs to only one of the non-overlapping groups or clusters. It is a very simple and fast unsupervised clustering technique.

To measure the quality of the clustering, Sum of Squared Error (SSE) is computed for a clustering of data points.

$$SSE = \sum_{i=1}^{k} \sum_{X \in C_i} dist(C_i, X)^2 \qquad (9)$$

Here dist is the Euclidean distance between two points in Euclidean space and C_i is the centroid of i-th cluster which is defined by,

$$C_i = \frac{1}{m} \sum_{X \in C_i} X \qquad (10)$$

For our algorithm, we use Lloyd's version of K-means [8] with twenty runs for each value of K to find the minimum SSE. To find the optimal value of K for a given dataset, we run the K-means algorithm on that dataset for K = 2 to K = 100, and plot a within-cluster SSE against the number of clusters to identify the maximum reduction of SSE at any given point. This is also known as the Elbow Method (see Fig. 2).

Gene expression data can be clustered in two ways – i) by row (genes), to cluster genes in different groups and treating samples as features and ii) by column (samples), to cluster samples and treating genes as features. Both of them have their practical purposes. For our method we use row-based or gene-based clustering to group genes by their similar co-expression levels.

Assessing Optimal Number of Clusters with the Elbow Method

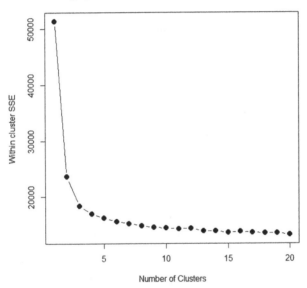

Fig. 2. Elbow method to find the optimal value of K.

We use three different versions of clustering together with the ERT step, to be compared for their effects on the efficiency of the ERT process. The versions are described below:

No Cluster Version: In this version, we avoid clustering the dataset; instead we run the ERT step on the entire dataset to find the true regulatory interactions among genes. Given the complexity of the ERT step, it takes a significant amount of time to complete generating the connection matrix.

Unmerged Version: For this version, we cluster the dataset into a given number of clusters and run ERT on genes of each cluster separately. Then we merge the connection matrices returned from each cluster and generate a n-by-n connection matrix where n is the number of genes. In this version, the genes which have true regulatory interactions with genes in a different cluster are not identified.

Selected Merged Version: With this version, after running the unmerged version of the algorithm, an additional merging among "close" clusters is carried out. We calculate which clusters are close to a given cluster by first finding the Euclidean distance of the nearest cluster and then multiplying the distance by two. And then we identify which clusters' centroids fall within this doubled distance and consider them to be "close" clusters. Finally we merge all the connection matrices from individual and close clusters after applying the Entropy Reduction step into a n-by-n connection matrix where n is the number of genes.

4   Method

In this section, we will describe different components of our algorithm in detail. The algorithm can be divided in two main parts, the Clustering part and the Entropy Reduction (ERT) part.

4.1   The Clustering Part

Input: Data matrix A of dimension n × m, where n is the number of genes and m is the number of samples or experiments, the value of number of clusters K, algorithm for K-means clustering and maximum number of iterations for K-means.

Algorithm:

1. Cluster the dataset into K different clusters using the given algorithm.
2. Generate a list of K elements L, where each element contains all the data points assigned to a cluster. This list is used in the Cluster Merging and ERT steps.
3. Calculate a distance matrix D of dimension $K \times K$ where distance between each pair of cluster centers is stored.

Output: L, list of K elements and distance matrix D

4.2   Entropy Reduction Part for One Cluster [2]

Input: Cluster ID

Algorithm:

1. Collect data points n of the given cluster ID from the list L, generated in Clustering Part.
2. Generate data matrix TD of the genes from the main data matrix A, where columns contain genes and rows contain samples.
3. Discretize TD.

4. Calculate Mutual Information (MI) matrix M of dimension n × n and normalize the mutual information in an n × n dimensional matrix NMI using Linfoot definition of normalization to have the mutual information values in the range of 0 to 1 [2].

$$\mathbf{M\ [i,\ j]\ =\ MutualInformation(TD[,\ i],\ TD[,\ j])}$$

5. Calculate the single entropy matrix E of dimension n.

$$\mathbf{E[i]\ =\ Entropy(TD[,i])}$$

6. Calculate an n × n dimensional Conditional Entropy matrix, CE between all pairs of variables.

$$\mathbf{CE\ [i,\ j]\ =\ ConditionalEntropy(TD[,\ i],\ TD[,\ j])}$$

7. Calculate an n × n dimensional Reduced Entropy matrix, RE between each pair of variables i, j using mutual information matrix M and single entropy matrix E using the equation,

$$\mathbf{RE\ [i,\ j]\ =\ (M[i,\ j])/E[i]}$$

8. Generate an n × n dimensional ERT matrix ERTM using the following condition,

$$\mathbf{If\ CE\ [i,\ j]\ =\ E[i],\ then\ ERTM\ [i,\ j]\ =\ 1\ Else\ ERTM\ [i,\ j]\ =\ 0}$$

9. Generate a connection matrix C of n × n dimension using the following condition,

$$\mathbf{If\ ERTM\ [i,\ j]\ ==\ 1,\ then\ C\ [i,\ j]\ =\ RE\ [i,\ j]\ Else\ C\ [i,\ j]\ =\ 0}$$

After this step, each cell of the connection matrix contains the reduced entropy between two genes.

Output: Connection matrix C.

To apply the ERT algorithm on two clusters for the Selected-Merged version of the algorithm, first identify the closest clusters of a given cluster by the process described in Sect. 3.1 under Selected-Merged-Clustering Version and then run the ERT algorithm described above. The output connection matrix C is of dimension n × m, where n is the number of genes in the first cluster and m is the number of genes in the second cluster.

After running ERT on all individual clusters and all pairs of closest clusters, all the returned matrices are combined together in a connection matrix of dimension n × n. Different threshold values are applied on the connection matrix to evaluate the performance of the algorithm.

The overall algorithm can be described as follows:

1. Cluster the dataset into given number of clusters.
2. Apply ERT algorithm on each cluster.
3. Merge a cluster with its closest clusters.
4. Apply ERT algorithm on all the merged clusters and combine all the results of connection matrices from ERT to generate an n × n final connection matrix where n is the number of genes.

We also experimented with the Data Processing Inequality (DPI) technique [3] from ARACNE algorithm after the final connection matrix of genes is generated in an attempt to verify whether combining the DPI technique with our algorithm improves the accuracy of the generated regulatory network even further. In the result section, we only present the "Before DPI" results, meaning the results obtained without applying the DPI technique.

5   Results

To evaluate our algorithm, we use the DREAM5 - Network Inference Challenge from DREAM Challenges [5]. We use precision and recall as performance measures for our algorithm. Precision is defined by,

$$Precision = \frac{TP}{TP + FP} \tag{11}$$

where TP is the True Positive prediction of a regulatory interaction between a pair of genes and FP is the False Positive prediction.

Recall is defined by,

$$Recall = \frac{TP}{TP + FN} \tag{12}$$

where FN is a False Negative Prediction of regulatory interaction.

5.1   Results for DREAM5-Network Inference Challenge Dataset [5]

First, we look at the effect of different threshold values (see Fig. 3, top) which are used as cutoff points to identify the true positives or regulatory interactions among genes. If the reduced entropy value between a pair of gene is above a certain threshold value, we deduce from that the genes share a regulatory interaction. At the same time, we also measure the effectiveness of clustering (see Fig. 3, bottom) in identifying interactions. Our goal is to find out whether clustering the datasets prior to applying ERT yields similar results as no-clustering approach (denoted as NC in the Fig. 3, bottom).

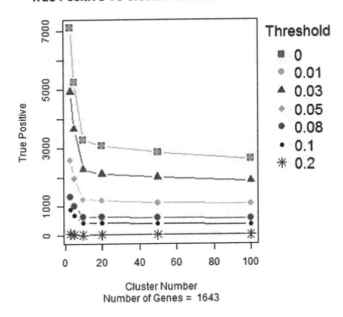

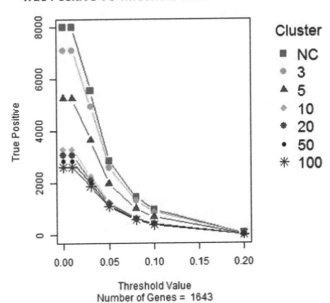

Fig. 3. True positive vs clusters for different threshold values (top), true positive vs threshold for different cluster numbers (bottom)

Next, we compare the results from ARACNE (denoted as ARC in Fig. 4) and three different versions of our algorithm in identifying correct regulatory interactions under different threshold values (see Fig. 4).

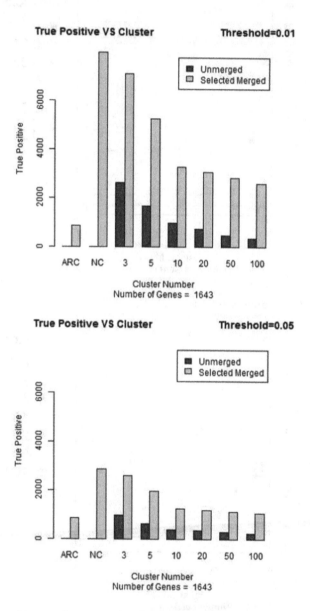

Fig. 4. True positive vs cluster number for ARACNE, no-clustering, selected-merged, unmerged clustering

We then compare the false positive results from ARACNE and different clustering versions (see Fig. 5) for similar threshold values.

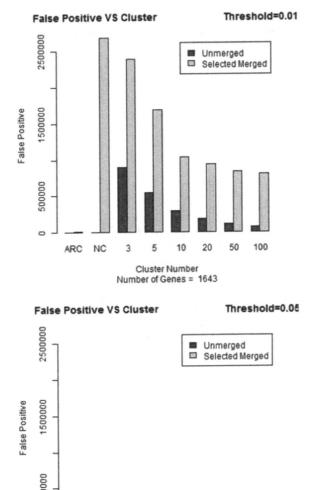

Fig. 5. False positive vs cluster for ARACNE, no-clustering, selected-merged, unmerged clustering

Precision and Recall Graphs for Different Threshold Values

Finally, we compare the precision and recall rate derived from ARACNE, no-clustering and selected-merged clustering versions of our algorithm (Fig. 6).

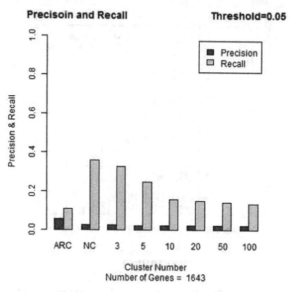

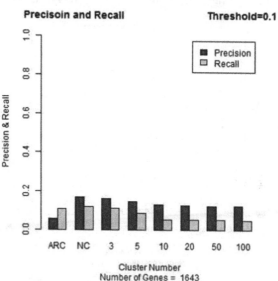

Fig. 6. Precision and recall for ARACNE, no-clustering and selected-merged clustering

6   Discussion

The performance of our algorithm in inferring true regulatory interactions without using DPI technique shows great improvements for lower threshold values over the ARACNE approach. We also find that the No-Clustering version of our algorithm is ranked highest among ARACNE, Unmerged-Clustering and Selected-Merged-Clustering versions of our algorithm in identifying true interactions before using DPI technique. But lower values for the number of clusters in the Selected-Merged version also produce similar results to the No-Clustering version in finding true interactions. For higher values of cluster numbers, both the true positives and false positives are reduced compared to lower values of cluster numbers. Using threshold values lower than the mean of all non-zero values of the final connection matrix generated by the algorithm which contained the reduced entropy for each pair of genes, result in a high number of true and false positives. For values greater than the mean, the reduction of false positives is much greater than the reduction of true positives. As it is evident from the graph of precision and recall for different cluster numbers, our algorithm produces high recall rate before using DPI technique. Another important observation from the precision and recall graph is that the algorithm produces a high recall rate for smaller threshold values. On the other hand, using higher threshold values produce a high precision rate. So for our algorithm to be useful in real-world applications, reasonable threshold values depending on the goal of the task have to be chosen for it to perform well.

7   Conclusion and Future Work

In this work, we have proposed a novel algorithm that enables entropy reduction technique to be used in real-world applications by reducing the search space of regulatory interactions for large networks. The algorithm showed significant improvements in generating accurate regulatory networks when used with appropriate threshold values. For the clustering part of our algorithm we have only used K-means clustering for its simplicity. But in future we want to use different types of clustering algorithms such as spectral clustering and affinity propagation clustering with the Entropy Reduction Technique to compare the performance with our current approach. For the Selected-Merged-Clustering version of the algorithm we hope to use better measurement techniques to identify close clusters. For the current implementation, we consider each gene pair to have true interactions if the conditional entropy is less than the single entropy. In future, it would be better to gain insights regarding the threshold values from the datasets in order to consider interactions to be true only if they are above those threshold values.

References

1. Marbach, D., et al.: Wisdom of crowds for robust gene network inference. Nat. Methods **9**(8), 796–804 (2012)
2. Villaverde, A.F., Ross, J., Morán, F., Banga, J.R.: MIDER: network inference with mutual information distance and entropy reduction. PLoS One **9**(5) (2014). https://doi.org/10.1371/journal.pone.0096732
3. Margolin, A.A., et al.: ARACNE: an algorithm for the reconstruction of gene regulatory networks in a mammalian cellular context. BMC Bioinform. **7**(Suppl 1) (2006). https://doi.org/10.1186/1471-2105-7-s1-s7
4. Dimitrakopoulos, G.N., Maraziotis, I.A., Sgarbas, K., Bezerianos, A.: A clustering based method accelerating gene regulatory network reconstruction. Procedia Comput. Sci. **29**, 1993–2002 (2014). https://doi.org/10.1016/j.procs.2014.05.183
5. Sage Synapse: Contribute to the Cure (n.d.). https://www.synapse.org/#!Synapse:syn2787209/wiki/70349. Accessed 08 Apr 2017
6. Lee, W., Tzou, W.: Computational methods for discovering gene networks from expression data. Brief. Bioinform. **10**(4), 408–423 (2009). https://doi.org/10.1093/bib/bbp028
7. Jiang, D., Tang, C., Zhang, A.: Cluster analysis for gene expression data: a survey. IEEE Trans. Knowl. Data Eng. **16**(11), 1370–1386 (2004). https://doi.org/10.1109/tkde.2004.68
8. Tan, P., Steinbach, M., Kumar, V.: Introduction to Data Mining. Dorling Kindersley: Pearson (2015)
9. Maetschke, S.R., Madhamshettiwar, P.B., Davis, M.J., Ragan, M.A.: Supervised, semi-supervised and unsupervised inference of gene regulatory networks. Brief. Bioinform. **15**(2), 195–211 (2013). https://doi.org/10.1093/bib/bbt034
10. Schaffter, T., Marbach, D., Floreano, D.: GeneNetWeaver: in silico benchmark generation and performance profiling of network inference methods. Bioinformatics **27**(16), 2263–2270 (2011). https://doi.org/10.1093/bioinformatics/btr373
11. Mordelet, F., Vert, J.: SIRENE: supervised inference of regulatory networks. Bioinformatics **24**(16), I76–I82 (2008). https://doi.org/10.1093/bioinformatics/btn273
12. Cerulo, L., Elkan, C., Ceccarelli, M.: Learning gene regulatory networks from only positive and unlabeled data. BMC Bioinform. **11**(1), 228 (2010). https://doi.org/10.1186/1471-2105-11-228

From Competition to Collaboration: Ensembling Similarity-Based Heuristics for Supervised Link Prediction in Biological Graphs

Md Kamrul Islam$^{(\boxtimes)}$ 🆔, Sabeur Aridhi🆔, and Malika Smail-Tabbone🆔

Universite de Lorraine, CNRS, INRIA, LORIA, 54000 Nancy, France
{kamrul.islam,sabeur.aridhi,malika.smail}@loria.fr

Abstract. Link prediction is a fundamental problem in the field of graph mining. The aim of link prediction is to infer/discover unobserved links in graphs. Link prediction in biological graphs is highly challenging. There exist many similarity-based methods in the literature for link prediction. These methods compete for victory in graphs from various domains. Unfortunately, they are efficient only in some specific graphs, and no one wins in all graphs. In this paper, we study some well-known similarity-based methods and consider them as independent features to define a feature set. The feature set is then used to train traditional supervised learning methods for link prediction in biological graphs. We evaluate the methods on ten biological graphs from different organisms. Experimental results show that the similarity-based methods collaboratively improve prediction performance, and are even comparable to high-performing embedding-based methods in some biological graphs. We compute the importance score of similarity-based features in order to explain the leading features in a graph.

Keywords: Biological graphs · Link prediction · Similarity-based heuristics · Supervised learning

1 Introduction

Many complex biological systems can be well-represented with graphs where a node represents a biological entity (e.g. protein, gene, etc.) and a link represents the interaction between two entities. Most real-world biological graphs are incomplete in nature. For example, 99.7% of the molecular interactions in human cells are still not known [1]. The links in biological graphs must be validated by field and/or laboratory experiments, which are expensive and time consuming. Researchers have developed link prediction methods to compute the plausibility of a link between two unconnected nodes in a graph to avoid the blind checking of all possible interactions. Formally, link prediction is the task of predicting the likelihood of a link between two nodes based on available topological/attribute

A. K. M. M. Islam et al. (Eds.): ICBBDB 2021, CCIS 1550, pp. 121–135, 2022.
https://doi.org/10.1007/978-3-031-17181-9_10

information of a graph [2]. Link prediction methods help us toward a deep understanding of the structure, evolution, and functions of biological graphs [3].

Similarity-based methods are the simplest and unsupervised methods of link prediction in biological graphs, which define the proximity of a link by the similarity between its end nodes. The great advantage of these methods is their interpretibility which is essential for any biological system [4]. However, each of the similarity-based methods performs well only in some particular graphs and no one wins in all graphs. These methods necessitate manually formulating various heuristics based on prior beliefs or extensive knowledge of various biological graphs. The lack of universal applicability of similarity-based methods motivates researchers to study machine learning methods to automatically learn the heuristics from a graph. To learn the appropriate heuristics automatically from a graph, researchers have developed embedding-based methods which represent nodes, edges, graphs in low dimensional vector space [5]. The embedding-based method has become a popular link prediction tool in graphs over the last decade. These methods show impressive link prediction performance in most of the graphs. The downside of embedding-based methods is that they seriously suffer from the well-known 'black-box' problem. As the link decisions in biological graphs are critical, a link prediction method should be sufficiently interpretable to achieve trust among stakeholders [6]. The requirement for link prediction methods to be interpretable may limit the use of embedding-based methods in real-world biological systems. Researchers are still working on opening the 'black-box' of embedding-based methods [9, 10].

Another group of link prediction methods is developed based on traditional supervised learning-based methods. These methods extract features from a graph and train a traditional classifier for the link prediction task [11–17]. These methods are nearly as performant as embedding-based methods and as interpretable as similarity-based methods in many biological graphs. These methods describe the link prediction problem as a link classification problem with two classes: existence and absence of a link. In this paper, we intend to investigate whether the existing similarity-based heuristics collaboratively improve the link prediction performance in biological graphs. We study similarity-based heuristics for feature extraction and utilize the features in supervised learning-based classifiers for link prediction in biological graphs. We find that this is not the first attempt to study supervised learning methods to link prediction problem in graphs. But there are important differences between past works [12, 18, 19] and this study. The existing methods mostly focus on node attributes for extracting features which are application dependent. However, node attributes are not available in many real-world biological graphs. In contrast, our supervised learning-based method is developed based on only the topological features (similarity-based heuristics). Kumari et al. [17] studied a few local (four) and global (three) similarity heuristics for supervised link predictions, which is the closest work in the literature to our study. However, for large graphs, global methods are not the best option as they are computationally expensive [20]. In this study, we enrich the feature set by including fourteen local similarity-based heuristics. In addition, we extract few other topological features of nodes and derive link-based features based on end node features. We study these features in supervised machine learning methods for link prediction in biological graphs. We see that supervised learning methods show comparable prediction results in many of the biological graphs. We also demonstrate the feature importance in different datasets for different supervised learning-based methods.

1.1   Similarity-Based Link Prediction

Link prediction is the task of discovering or inferring a set of non-existing links in a graph based on the current snapshot of the graph. Similarity-based is the simplest category of link prediction methods, which is formulated based on the assumption that two nodes interact if they are similar in a graph [20]. Generally, these methods compute similarity scores of non-existent links, sort the links in decreasing order of their scores and top-L links are predicted as potential existent links. Defining the similarity is a crucial and non-trivial task which differs from graphs to graphs [20]. Consequently, numerous similarity-based methods exist in the literature. These methods are broadly categorized into three categories: local, global and quasi-local methods. Local methods are developed based on local topological or neighbourhood information, whereas global methods use the global topological information of graphs to define similarity functions [20]. Quasi-local methods consider the neighbourhood up-to a predefined hop for defining the similarity function. The high computational time of global methods motivates us to study only local and quasi-local methods. We study fourteen well-known local similarity-based methods for link prediction in graphs, thirteen of which are summarized in Table 1 local and one quasi-local. We summarize the similarity-based methods and the rest one (Preferential Attachment (PA)) in Table 2 with basic principles and the definition of similarity functions.

2   Methodology

In a broader sense, we consider the similarity-based heuristics as individual features to generate the feature set for a supervised learning-based classifier.
    We describe each of the steps in Sects. 2.1–2.3.

2.1   Feature Extraction

The most crucial task of a supervised learning-based classifier is to define an appropriate feature set [12]. Given a graph and a train set of links, we extract structural features for the train links. When extracting the features of a link, the link is temporarily removed from the graph and re-connected after feature extraction to ensure that the extracted features are not biased by the existence of the train link. We are motivated to use only topological features for defining our feature set as they exist in all kinds of graphs. Our feature set contains twenty topological features which are broadly categorized into two categories: similarity-based and derived link features (Fig. 1).

Table 1. Summary of similarity-based methods. Each method is considered as an individual link feature. $S(x, y)$ is the similarity function between two end nodes x and y. Γx and Γx denote the neighbour sets of nodes x and y respectively. A is the adjacency matrix and λ is a free parameter.

Methods	Principles	Similarity-functions
Common Neighbours (CN) [21]	Two nodes are more likely to be linked if they have more neighbours in common	$CN(x,y) = \|\Gamma x \cap \Gamma y\|$
Adamic-Adar (AA) [22]	A variant of CN in which each common neighbour is penalized logarithmically by its degree	$AA(x,y) = \sum_{z \in \Gamma x \cap \Gamma y} \frac{1}{\log\|\Gamma z\|}$
Resource Allocation (RA) [23]	Based on the resource allocation mechanism, the high degree common neighbours will be penalized even more	$RA(x,y) = \sum_{z \in \Gamma x \cap \Gamma y} \frac{1}{\|\Gamma z\|}$
Jaccard Index (JA) [24]	The score is punished for each non-common neighbour in the normalization of CN	$JA(x,y) = \frac{\|\Gamma x \cap \Gamma y\|}{\|\Gamma x \cup \Gamma y\|}$
Salton Index (SA) [25]	The cosine similarity between adjacency vectors for a pair of nodes is used to compute the link probability	$SA(x,y) = \frac{\|\Gamma x \cap \Gamma y\|}{\sqrt{\|\Gamma x\| \times \|\Gamma y\|}}$
Sørensen Index (SO) [26]	The overall fraction of common neighbours from a local perspective is what the link prediction is described as	$SO(x,y) = \frac{2 \times \|\Gamma x \cap \Gamma y\|}{\|\Gamma x\| + \|\Gamma y\|}$
Hub Promoted Index (HPI) [27]	Link establishment between high-degree nodes and hubs is encouraged.	$HPI(x,y) = \frac{\|\Gamma x \cap \Gamma y\|}{max(\|\Gamma x\|, \|\Gamma y\|)}$
Hub Depressed Index (HDI) [27]	Link establishment between low-degree nodes and hubs is encouraged	$HDI(x,y) = \frac{\|\Gamma x \cap \Gamma y\|}{min(\|\Gamma x\|, \|\Gamma y\|)}$
Local Leicht-Holme-Newman (LLHN) [28]	The real and expected number of shared neighbours are used to define the similarity between two nodes	$LLHN(x,y) = \frac{\|\Gamma x \cap \Gamma y\|}{\|\Gamma x\| \times \|\Gamma y\|}$
Cannistrai-Alanis-Ravai (CAR) [29]	In measuring the similarity score between two end nodes, level-2 linkages are combined with shared neighbourhood information	$CAR(x,y) = \sum_{z \in \Gamma x \cap \Gamma y} 1 + \frac{\|\Gamma x \cap \Gamma y \cap \Gamma z\|}{2}$
Clustering Coefficient-based Link Prediction (CCLP) [30]	The influence of each shared neighbour is quantified by using the node's local clustering coefficient	$CCLP(x,y) = \sum_{z \in \Gamma x \cap \Gamma y} CC_z$
Node and Link Clustering (NLC) [31]	The contribution of each common neighbor is quantified by using the node's node and link clustering coefficients	$NLC(x,y) = \sum_{z \in \Gamma x \cap \Gamma y} \left(\frac{CN(x,z)}{\|\Gamma z\| - 1} \times CC_z + \frac{CN(x,z)}{\|\Gamma z\| - 1} \times CC_z \right)$
Local Path Index (LPI) [32]	Similarity is calculated using the second and third order paths between the end nodes	$LPI(x,y) = [A^2 + \lambda A^3]_{x,y}$

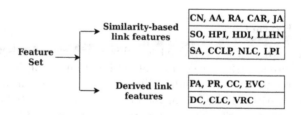

Fig. 1. Feature set for supervised learning

Table 2. Summary of derived link features: the derived link feature function $S(x, y)$ is defined based on end nodes features.

Features	Principles	Link feature functions
Preferential Attachment (PA) [33]	Based on the rich-get-richer principle, in which the link likelihood between two high-degree nodes is greater than that between two low-degree nodes	$PA(x, y) = |\Gamma x| \times |\Gamma y|$
Pager Rank (PR) [34]	PageRank computes a ranking of the nodes based on the structure of the links	$PR(x, y) = PR(x) + PR(y)$
Clustering Coefficient (CC) [35]	The clustering coefficient of a node is the fraction of possible triangles through that node that exist	$CC(x, y) = CC(x) + CC(y)$
Degree Centrality (DC) [36]	The degree centrality for a node is the fraction of nodes it is connected to	$DC(x, y) = DC(x) + DC(y)$
Eigen vector centrality (EVC) [37]	Eigenvector centrality computes the centrality for a node based on the centrality of its neighbors	$EVC(x, y) = EVC(x) + EVC(y)$
Closeness Centrality (CLC) [38]	Closeness centrality of a node is the reciprocal of the average shortest path length to other reachable nodes	$CLC(x, y) = CLC(x) + CLC(y)$
Vote Rank Centrality (VRC) [39]	Ranking of the nodes based on a voting scheme where a node casts votes to its neighbours. A node with the highest votes has the best (lowest) ranking	$VRC(x, y) = \frac{1}{VRC(x)} + \frac{1}{VRC(y)}$

Similarity-Based Link Features: We define the link-based features as the features which are related to the common topological information of end-nodes of a link. We use thirteen existing similarity-based heuristics as link-based features, which are summarized in Table 1. For instance, the number of common neighbours of end nodes of a link is used as the common neighbour (CN) feature.

Derived Link Features: Few link-based features are derived from the individual features of the link's end nodes. We summarized six derived features in Table 2. These features are related to the topological information of individual nodes only. For example, the degree of end nodes is multiplied in Preferential Attachment (PA) to define the similarity score. Note that the link features in Table 2 except PA are not directly defined in the literature. We derive the link features based on the end node feature. To compute the link feature, features of end nodes are simply added except PA. As the voterank centrality computes low ranks for high-influencing nodes in a graph, the reciprocals of the voterank scores of end nodes are summed to define the voterank centrality feature.

2.2 Feature Scaling

In general, the magnitude scale for different features in different graphs varies [7,8]. Supervised learning-based methods are easily affected by the non-uniform scaling as there is a high chance that features with higher magnitude play a more decisive role during the training of a classifier. But, it is not desirable for the classifier to be biased towards one particular feature. Hence, we normalize each feature in the range of 0–1.

2.3 Classifier Training and Link Prediction

For the link prediction task, we train a traditional supervised machine learning classifier to classify a link into either existent or non-existent classes. There exist many classifiers in the literature which perform better than others in some particular datasets. In this paper, we study three traditional classifiers: Support Vector Machine (SVM) with RBF kernel, Decision Tree, and Logistic Regression. We extract the features of the test links and classify them into existent or non-existent classes using a trained classifier to evaluate the link prediction performance.

3   Experiments

3.1   The Baselines

To evaluate the prediction performance of supervised learning methods, we consider two categories of link prediction methods: similarity-based and embedding-based methods.

For the similarity-based category, we consider all the heuristics in Table 1 in Table 2. For the embedding-based methods, we choose two popular methods: Node2Vec [40] and SEAL [41]. We shortly describe Node2Vec and SEAL methods. For more details, we refer to the original papers. **Node2Vec** [40] is a classical skip-gram model-based graph embedding method which learns node embeddings by optimizing a neighbourhood preserving objective function. It makes an interpolation between BFS (Breadth First Search) and DFS (Depth First Search) to define a 2nd order random walk. A fixed size neighbourhood is sampled using the 2nd order random walk and fed into the well-known skip-gram model [42] to learn the node embedding. The link embedding is then computed as the Hadamard product of the end node embeddings. A logistic regression-based classifier is then trained for the link prediction task. SEAL, the second embedding-based approach, is based on neural networks (NN). **Learning from Sub-graphs, Embeddings and Attributes (SEAL)** utilizes the latent and explicit features of end nodes and structural information of the graph to learn the link embedding. SEAL starts with extracting a h-hop neighbouring sub-graph and node labeling by a double radius node labeling (DRNL) algorithm. In the second step, the labelled sub-graph is then used to generate the structural encoding. The link embedding is the concatenation of structural encoding, pre-computed latent encoding and explicit feature encoding. In the final step, a neural network (NN) is trained for link prediction task.

3.2   Experimental Datasets

In this study, we focus on only biological graphs. For evaluating performance, we collect six biological graphs from the Network Repository[1]. Table 3 summarizes the topological statistics and descriptions of the graph datasets.

Table 3. The graph datasets: number of nodes ($|\mathbf{V}|$), links ($|\mathbf{E}|$), average node degree (NDeg), average clustering coefficient (CC), and description.

Graphs	Organism	$|\mathbf{V}|$	$|\mathbf{E}|$	NDeg	CC	Description
CE-GT [43]	Worm	924	3239	7.01	0.605	Nodes: Genes in C. elegans Links: Gene functional associations in C.elegans
CE-HT [43]	Worm	2617	2985	2.28	0.008	Nodes: Proteins in C. elegans Links: High-throughput protein-protein interactions
Celegans [43]	Worm	453	2040	9.01	0.647	Nodes: Substrates in Caenorhabditis elegans Links: Metabolic reactions between substrates in C.elegans
CE-LC [44]	Worm	1387	1648	2.37	0.076	Nodes: Proteins in C.elegans worm Links: Small/medium-scale protein-protein interactions (compiled from protein-protein interaction data bases)
Diseasome [45]	Human	516	1188	4.61	0.636	Nodes: Known genetic disorders in H.sapiens Links: Connections between pair of disorders when they share minimum one gene
DM-HT [45]	Fly	2989	4660	3.12	0.009	Nodes: Proteins in D.melan-ogaster fly Links: High-throughput protein-protein interactions
DM-LC [44]	Fly	658	1129	3.43	0.105	Nodes: Proteins in D.melanogaster fly Links: Small/medium-scale protein-protein interactions (compiled from protein-protein interaction data bases)
HS-HT [44]	Human	2570	13691	10.65	0.169	Nodes: Proteins in human Links: Protein-protein interactions in human protein network
SC-LC [44]	Yeast	2004	20452	20.41	0.168	Nodes: Proteins in S.cerevisiae yeast Links: Small/medium-scale protein-protein interactions in yeast network
Yeast [44]	Yeast	2114	2277	2.15	0.059	Nodes: Proteins in S.cerevisiae yeast Links: Protein-protein interactions in yeast network

The link prediction performance is evaluated using a random sampling validation protocol [7,8,41]. For a graph dataset, train and test sets are prepared by splitting the existent links. The train set consists of 90% existent and an equal number of non-existent links. The test set contains the remaining 10% existent and equal number of non-existent links. To prepare five train and five test sets for each graph, we repeat the link splitting operation five times independently. The datasets are available in a GitLab repository[2].

---

[1] https://networkrepository.com/bio.php.
[2] https://gitlab.inria.fr/kislam/supervised-lp.

3.3   Evaluation Metrics

The link prediction problem is considered as a binary classification problem [46]. A traditional classifier, in general, learns a threshold to classify links as existent or non-existent. However, for similarity-based link classification methods, we find no standard approach for computing the threshold. The threshold is calculated in an optimistic manner. We first normalize the link scores to a range of 0–1 and then use the normalized scores to compute a ROC curve. The curve gives the true positiverate (TPR) and false positive rate (FPR) for different score threshold settings. The threshold point with the highest [TPR + (1 − FPR)] is computed as the *threshold* as we want to maximize TPR as well as minimize FPR. We classify links based on this threshold. A link with a *score >= threshold* is classified as existent and non-existent otherwise. Based on the true and predicted classes of links, we define four metrics: true positive (TP), true negative (TN), false positive (FP), and false negative (FN). TP is the number of existent links predicted to be existent, TN is the number of non-existent links predicted to be non-existent, FP is the number of non-existent links predicted to be existent, and FN is the number of existent links predicted to be non-existent links. We compute the following three well-known metrics using these four metrics.

$$Recall = \frac{TP}{TP + FN} \tag{1}$$

$$Precision = \frac{TP}{TP + FP} \tag{2}$$

$$F1 = 2 \times \frac{Precision \times Recall}{Precision + Recall} \tag{3}$$

3.4   Results and Discussion

In this section, we describe the prediction performance of supervised learning-based methods on six biological graphs. We also illustrate the importance of the features in graphs.

Prediction Performance: The prediction performance is computed for all methods over all the five sets for each graph, and the average scores are recorded. We do not include the standard deviation results as the values are very low in all the experiments. The precision, recall and F1 scores are tabulated Table 4, where the best two similarity-based methods are denoted with Sim^1 and Sim^2. We compute the precision scores of similarity-based methods in a optimistic way. The precision scores of similarity-based methods (best and second best) are very high and highest among all the methods in all the graphs, as shown in the table. This demonstrates the ability of similarity-based methods to predict high-quality links. However, the recall scores are low, implying that these methods identify the majority of existing test links as non-existent. As a result, the F1 score for similarity-based methods is very low. We also see that, as expected, the two

Table 4. Performance metrics: the dataset-wise best and second best precision, recall and F1 scores are indicated in bold and underline. The best and second best similarity-based methods are denoted with Sim^1 and Sim^2 respectively. For Sim^1 and Sim^2 methods, the methods are specified and the performance scores are given in ().

Datasets	Metric	Sim^1	Sim^2	N2V	SEAL	SVM	DT	LR
CE-GT	Precision	NLC (**0.960**)	JA (0.896)	0.707	0.842	0.842	0.828	<u>0.901</u>
	Recall	NLC (0.039)	JA (0.042)	0.707	**0.931**	0.827	0.776	<u>0.900</u>
	F1	NLC (0.075)	JA (0.078)	0.707	<u>0.885</u>	0.834	0.801	**0.901**
CE-HT	Precision	RA (**0.996**)	AA (0.996)	0.596	0.705	0.753	0.745	<u>0.752</u>
	Recall	RA (0.001)	AA (0.001)	0.593	**0.791**	<u>0.529</u>	0.519	0.510
	F1	RA (0.002)	AA (0.002)	0.594	**0.745**	<u>0.622</u>	0.612	0.608
Celegans	Precision	RA (**0.938**)	CCLP (0.932)	0.778	0.806	0.899	0.850	<u>0.907</u>
	Recall	RA (0.042)	CCLP (0.041)	0.777	0.888	<u>0.899</u>	0.830	**0.906**
	F1	RA (0.08)	CCLP (0.079)	0.778	0.845	<u>0.899</u>	0.840	**0.906**
CE-LC	Precision	AA (**0.969**)	RA (0.969)	0.658	0.763	0.715	0.763	<u>0.789</u>
	Recall	AA (0.009)	RA (0.009)	0.647	**0.794**	0.620	0.584	<u>0.673</u>
	F1	AA (0.028)	RA (0.028)	0.652	**0.778**	0.664	0.662	<u>0.726</u>
Diseasome	Precision	NLC (**0.991**)	AA (0.988)	0.757	0.914	0.926	0.800	<u>0.927</u>
	Recall	NLC (0.035)	AA (0.040)	0.756	0.896	<u>0.919</u>	0.692	**0.920**
	F1	NLC (0.067)	AA (0.078)	0.756	0.905	<u>0.922</u>	0.742	**0.924**
DM-HT	Precision	CCLP (**0.999**)	NLC (0.998)	0.712	0.720	0.780	<u>0.796</u>	0.770
	Recall	CCLP (0.001)	NLC (0.001)	**0.704**	<u>0.703</u>	0.657	0.661	0.644
	F1	CCLP (0.002)	NLC (0.002)	0.708	0.712	<u>0.714</u>	**0.722**	0.701
DM-LC	Precision	PA (**0.979**)	CCLP(0.944)	0.696	0.790	0.829	0.828	0.812
	Recall	PA (0.02)	CCLP (0.007)	0.688	**0.835**	0.771	0.770	<u>0.777</u>
	F1	PA (0.039)	CCLP (0.014)	0.692	0.812	**0.799**	<u>0.798</u>	0.794
HS-HT	Precision	NLC (**0.954**)	CCLP (0.949)	0.797	0.854	<u>0.861</u>	0.847	0.861
	Recall	NLC (0.031)	CCLP (0.031)	0.794	0.815	<u>0.840</u>	0.791	**0.848**
	F1	NLC (0.060)	CCLP (0.061)	0.796	0.834	0.850	0.818	**0.854**
SC-LC	Precision	NLC (**0.893**)	AA (0.873)	0.772	0.784	<u>0.868</u>	0.850	0.853
	Recall	NLC (0.035)	AA (0.036)	0.770	0.815	**0.849**	0.810	<u>0.844</u>
	F1	NLC (0.067)	AA (0.068)	0.771	0.799	**0.859**	0.829	<u>0.849</u>
Yeast	Precision	CCLP (**0.971**)	RA (0.967)	0.699	0.705	0.753	0.746	<u>0.755</u>
	Recall	CCLP (0.006)	RA (0.008)	<u>0.699</u>	**0.726**	0.567	0.551	0.598
	F1	CCLP (0.012)	RA (0.015)	<u>0.699</u>	**0.716**	0.647	0.634	0.668

best-performing similarity-based methods differ for different datasets. Among the supervised learning methods (SVM, DT, LR), DT shows the worst prediction results, but it is still much better than similarity-based methods. The other two classifiers have similar performance scores. The performance of the other two classifiers in terms of prediction scores is impressive. Yet in many graphs, supervised learning-based classifiers show superior prediction performance than embedding-based methods. Relating the performance to graph properties, we see that traditional classifiers outperform embedding-based methods in dense graphs. This is intuitive as the majority of the studied similarity-based heuristics are based on common neighbours (see Table 1). The performance scores of traditional classifiers are worse in the sparse graphs (CE-HT, CE-LC, Yeast), where embedding-based methods show better performance scores.

Feature Importance: In this section, we investigate the influence of each feature in a classifier for the link prediction task. To compute the feature importance coefficient, we use the Permutation importance module from the sklearn

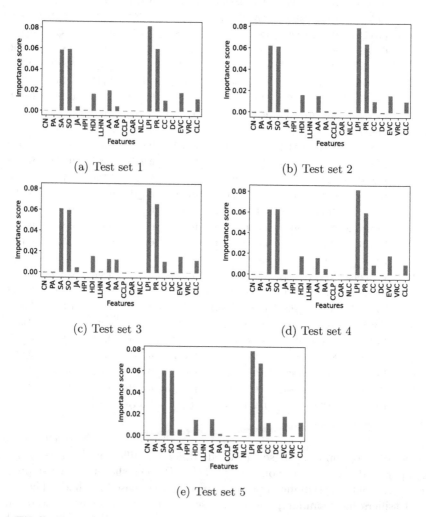

(a) Test set 1

(b) Test set 2

(c) Test set 3

(d) Test set 4

(e) Test set 5

Fig. 2. Feature importance in HS-HT graph by logistic regression classifier

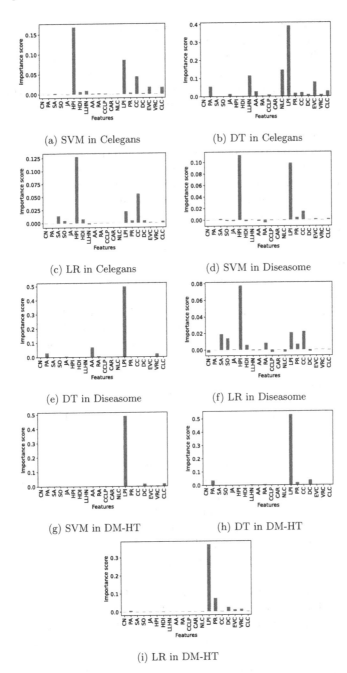

Fig. 3. Feature importance in different datasets by different supervised methods: (a)–(c) in Celegans, (d)–(f) in Diseasome, (g)–(i) in DM-HT

python-based machine learning tool[3]. When a feature is unavailable, the coefficient is calculated by looking at how much the score (accuracy) drops [47]. The higher the coefficient, the higher the importance of the feature. In Fig. 2, we demonstrate the feature importance in the HS-HT biological graph in the logistic regression (LR) classifier to investigate how the importance of features differs in different sets of the same biological graph. In the LR classifier for the HS-HT biological graph, four features dominate. The dominance of multiple heuristics or features in a graph shows that heuristics that work collaboratively perform better than heuristics that work alone. We can also find that the feature importance coefficients in all five sets in the HS-HT graph are substantially identical.

We further investigate the importance score of features in three classifiers (SVM, DT, LR) for three different datasets. We evaluate the importance score of features for only one set for each graph. We see that different classifiers give different importance coefficients to different features in different datasets. In DM-HT dataset, all the classifiers compute high coefficient for LPI feature and they have close prediction performance (in Table 4). In the Celegans dataset, the HPI feature dominates in SVM and LR classifiers whereas LPI dominates in the DT classifier. In the Celegans dataset, SVM and LR outperform DT in terms of prediction (in Table 4), demonstrating that LR and SVM compute feature importance scores more correctly. Surprisingly, we see that DT has a tendency to give more importance to the LPI feature in these three datasets (Fig. 3).

4   Conclusion

Do similarity-based heuristics compete or collaborate for link prediction task in graphs? In this article, we study this question. We study fourteen similarity-based heuristics in six biological graph from three different organisms. As expected, we observe they perform well only in some particular biological graphs and no one wins in all graphs. Rather than using them as standalone link prediction methods, we consider them as features for supervised learning methods. In addition, we derive six link features based on the node's topological information. Based on the twenty features, we train three traditional supervised learning methods: SVM, DT and LR-based classifiers. We see that the similarity-based heuristics collaboratively improve link prediction performance remarkably, even outperforming embedding-based methods in some graphs.

We propose three future dimensions of this study. Firstly, studying collaboration of similarity-based heuristics in large scale biological as well as social graphs could be a potential future work as the graphs in the current study are small/medium in size. Secondly, exploring some other heuristics might improve prediction performance in sparse graphs. The final future research could be studying other classifiers like Random Forest, AdaBoost, K-Neighbors for the link prediction task in graphs.

---

[3] https://scikit-learn.org/stable/modules/generated/sklearn.inspection.permutation_importance.html.

References

1. Stumpf, M.P., et al.: Estimating the size of the human interactome. Proc. Natl. Acad. Sci. **105**(19), 6959–6964 (2008)
2. Xu, Z., Pu, C., Yang, J.: Link prediction based on path entropy. Phys. A **456**, 294–301 (2016)
3. Shen, Z., Wang, W.X., Fan, Y., Di, Z., Lai, Y.C.: Reconstructing propagation networks with natural diversity and identifying hidden sources. Nat. Commun. **5**(1), 1–10 (2014)
4. Zhou, T., Lee, Y.L., Wang, G.: Experimental analyses on 2-hop-based and 3-hop-based link prediction algorithms. Phys. A Stat. Mech. Appl. **564**, 125532 (2021)
5. Cui, P., Wang, X., Pei, J., Zhu, W.: A survey on network embedding. IEEE Trans. Knowl. Data Eng. **31**(5), 833–852 (2018)
6. Gerke, S., Minssen, T., Cohen, G.: Ethical and legal challenges of artificial intelligence-driven healthcare. In: Artificial Intelligence in Healthcare, pp. 295–336. Academic Press (2020)
7. Islam, M.K., Aridhi, S., Smail-Tabbone, M.: Appraisal study of similarity-based and embedding-based link prediction methods on graphs. In: Proceedings of the 10th International Conference on Data Mining & Knowledge Management Process, pp. 81–92 (2021)
8. Islam, M.K., Aridhi, S., Smaïl-Tabbone, M.: An experimental evaluation of similarity-based and embedding-based link prediction methods on graphs. Int. J. Data Min. Knowl. Manag. Process **11**, 1–18 (2021)
9. Faber, L., Moghaddam, A.K., Wattenhofer, R.: Contrastive graph neural network explanation. In: Proceedings of the 37th Graph Representation Learning and Beyond Workshop at ICML 2020, p. 28. International Conference on Machine Learning (2020)
10. Yuan, H., Yu, H., Wang, J., Li, K., Ji, S.: On explainability of graph neural networks via subgraph explorations. In: Proceedings of the 38th International Conference on Machine Learning (2021)
11. Cukierski, W., Hamner, B., Yang, B.: Graph-based features for supervised link prediction. In: The 2011 International Joint Conference on Neural Networks, pp. 1237–1244. IEEE, July 2011
12. Al Hasan, M., Chaoji, V., Salem, S., Zaki, M.: Link prediction using supervised learning. In: SDM 2006: Workshop on Link Analysis, Counter-Terrorism and Security, vol. 30, pp. 798–805, April 2006
13. Berton, L., Valverde-Rebaza, J., de Andrade Lopes, A.: Link prediction in graph construction for supervised and semi-supervised learning. In: 2015 International Joint Conference on Neural Networks (IJCNN), pp. 1–8. IEEE, July 2015
14. Benchettara, N., Kanawati, R., Rouveirol, C.: A supervised machine learning link prediction approach for academic collaboration recommendation. In: Proceedings of the Fourth ACM Conference on Recommender Systems, pp. 253–256, September 2010
15. Ahmed, C., ElKorany, A., Bahgat, R.: A supervised learning approach to link prediction in Twitter. Soc. Netw. Anal. Min. **6**(1), 1–11 (2016). https://doi.org/10.1007/s13278-016-0333-1
16. Shibata, N., Kajikawa, Y., Sakata, I.: Link prediction in citation networks. J. Am. Soc. Inform. Sci. Technol. **63**(1), 78–85 (2012)
17. Kumari, A., Behera, R.K., Sahoo, K.S., Nayyar, A., Kumar Luhach, A., Prakash Sahoo, S.: Supervised link prediction using structured-based feature extraction in social network. Concurr. Comput. Pract. Exp. **34**(13), e5839 (2020)

18. Liben-Nowell, D., Kleinberg, J.: The link-prediction problem for social networks. J. Am. Soc. Inform. Sci. Technol. **58**(7), 1019–1031 (2007)
19. De Sá, H.R., Prudêncio, R.B.: Supervised link prediction in weighted networks. In: The 2011 International Joint Conference on Neural Networks, pp. 2281–2288. IEEE, July 2011
20. Martínez, V., Berzal, F., Cubero, J.C.: A survey of link prediction in complex networks. ACM Comput. Surv. (CSUR) **49**(4), 1–33 (2016)
21. Lorrain, F., White, H.C.: Structural equivalence of individuals in social networks. J. Math. Sociol. **1**(1), 49–80 (1971)
22. Adamic, L.A., Adar, E.: Friends and neighbors on the web. Soc. Netw. **25**(3), 211–230 (2003)
23. Zhou, T., Lü, L., Zhang, Y.C.: Predicting missing links via local information. Eur. Phys. J. B **71**(4), 623–630 (2009). https://doi.org/10.1140/epjb/e2009-00335-8
24. Jaccard, P.: Étude comparative de la distribution florale dans une portion des Alpes et des Jura. Bull Soc. Vaudoise. Sci. Nat. **37**, 547–579 (1901)
25. Salton, G., McGill, M.J.: Introduction to Modern Information Retrieval. McGraw-Hill (1983)
26. Sorensen, T.A.: A method of establishing groups of equal amplitude in plant sociology based on similarity of species content and its application to analyses of the vegetation on Danish commons. Biol. Skar. **5**, 1–34 (1948)
27. Ravasz, E., Somera, A.L., Mongru, D.A., Oltvai, Z.N., Barabási, A.L.: Hierarchical organization of modularity in metabolic networks. Science **297**(5586), 1551–1555 (2002)
28. Leicht, E.A., Holme, P., Newman, M.E.: Vertex similarity in networks. Phys. Rev. E **73**(2), 026120 (2006)
29. Cannistraci, C.V., Alanis-Lobato, G., Ravasi, T.: From link-prediction in brain connectomes and protein interactomes to the local-community-paradigm in complex networks. Sci. Rep. **3**(1), 1–14 (2013)
30. Wu, Z., Lin, Y., Wang, J., Gregory, S.: Link prediction with node clustering coefficient. Phys. A **452**, 1–8 (2016)
31. Wu, Z., Lin, Y., Wan, H., Jamil, W.: Predicting top-L missing links with node and link clustering information in large-scale networks. J. Stat. Mech: Theory Exp. **2016**(8), 083202 (2016)
32. Lü, L., Jin, C.H., Zhou, T.: Similarity index based on local paths for link prediction of complex networks. Phys. Rev. E **80**(4), 046122 (2009)
33. Barabási, A.L., Albert, R.: Emergence of scaling in random networks. Science **286**(5439), 509–512 (1999)
34. Langville, A.N., Meyer, C.D.: A survey of eigenvector methods for web information retrieval. SIAM Rev. **47**(1), 135–161 (2005)
35. Onnela, J.P., Saramäki, J., Kertész, J., Kaski, K.: Intensity and coherence of motifs in weighted complex networks. Phys. Rev. E **71**(6), 065103 (2005)
36. Dubitzky, W., Wolkenhauer, O., Cho, K.H., Yokota, H. (eds.): Encyclopedia of Systems Biology, vol. 402. Springer, New York (2013). https://doi.org/10.1007/978-1-4419-9863-7
37. Bonacich, P.: Power and centrality: a family of measures. Am. J. Sociol. **92**(5), 1170–1182 (1987)
38. Freeman, L.: Centrality in networks: I. Conceptual clarifications. Soc. Netw. **1**(3), 215–239 (1979)
39. Zhang, J.X., Chen, D.B., Dong, Q., Zhao, Z.D.: Identifying a set of influential spreaders in complex networks. Sci. Rep. **6**, 27823 (2016)

40. Grover, A., Leskovec, J.: node2vec: scalable feature learning for networks. In: Proceedings of the 22nd ACM SIGKDD International Conference on Knowledge Discovery and Data Mining, pp. 855–864, August 2016
41. Zhang, M., Chen, Y.: Link prediction based on graph neural networks. Adv. Neural. Inf. Process. Syst. **31**, 5165–5175 (2018)
42. Mikolov, T., Chen, K., Corrado, G., Dean, J.: Efficient estimation of word representations in vector space. In: International Conference on Learning Representations (2013)
43. Duch, J., Arenas, A.C.: Community identification using extremal optimization. Phys. Rev. E **72**, 027104 (2005)
44. Cho, A., et al.: WormNet v3: a network-assisted hypothesis-generating server for Caenorhabditis elegans. Nucleic Acids Res. **42**(W1), W76–W82 (2014)
45. Goh, K.I., Cusick, M.E., Valle, D., Childs, B., Vidal, M., Barabási, A.L.: The human disease network. Proc. Natl. Acad. Sci. **104**(21), 8685–8690 (2007)
46. Kumar, A., Singh, S.S., Singh, K., Biswas, B.: Link prediction techniques, applications, and performance: a survey. Phys. A **553**, 124289 (2020)
47. Breiman, L.: Random forests. Mach. Learn. **45**(1), 5–32 (2001). https://doi.org/10.1023/A:1010933404324

Mental Disability Detection of Children Using Handwriting Analysis

Shammi Akhtar[1] ⓘ, Regina Kasem[1], Afrin Linza[1], Mithun Chandra Das[1],
Md. Rashedul Islam[1(✉)], and Raihan Kobir[2]

[1] Department of Computer Science and Engineering, University of Asia Pacific, Dhaka,
Bangladesh
shammi@uap-bd.edu.com, rashed.cse@gmail.com
[2] School of Computer Science and Engineering, University of Aizu, Fukushima, Japan

Abstract. Handwriting analysis also known as graphology is a way of knowing particular traits and behavior respective of a person. So far studies related to graphology are mostly concerned with the prediction of behaviors and so this paper focuses on the use of handwriting for other mental conditions classification. With the increase in mental disorder found in children, having an automated system could be diagnosis friendly. And so, the proposed methodology is concerned with the development of a device for predicting the mental condition of children through automated handwriting analysis. In this paper, a pen tablet is used for the collection of handwriting data samples measuring features. A parameter selection process is used for top dominant parameters and features are extracted from selected parameters, which are act as the input to the model. For the classification of the model that is the mental condition of the child, we used six different algorithms as classifiers, and among these SVM and Decision tree holding the highest accuracy of 72.7%.

Keywords: Graphology · Child mental disability · Parameter selection · KNN · SVM · Random forest · Regression · AUC

1 Introduction

Graphology also is known as brainwriting, used to get an insight into a person's mental state and individual traits, which is a study of analyzing human handwriting. It is a scientific method that considers characteristics like pen pressure, angle, slant, size, spacing, and many other writing features to disclose specific personality traits. Handwriting uses the central nervous system and has been shown to link directly to emotions and feelings held deep within the mind. Since writing is done by our brain which is why it is called brainwriting, it prints out exactly how a person feels or thinks that very instant. It is a great tool that has many applications in medical, recruitment, and even forensic analysis.

In this study, the focus is on the handwriting of children aged 7 to 16 years. Rules applied for children are mostly similar to adult handwriting except for their roundness and unsteady strokes due to untrained motor skills in younger ones. Even from their scribbles, their behavior can be analyzed. Rough swirls and marks indicate their activeness and vigorous temperament while little and fine marks indicate their subtle and accepting mindset. For the early detection of learning difficulties and emotional exertions, the National Handwriting Academy acknowledges the importance of graphology. Studies have shown that poor handwriting and motor skills are usually linked with children having autism compared to their peers. Attention deficit hyperactivity disorder (ADHD) is a mental health disorder that can cause above-normal levels of hyperactive and impulsive behaviors which also shows a link to poor handwriting found in many studies according to an article published in Learning Disabilities Research and Practice. University of Haifa studied and conducted, two groups of children one having autism and the other that doesn't, significant changes in the way they write were observed. They were given two different tasks. One was to copy some text that was given and the other was to write whatever they wanted to. It was seen that waiting time on paper and in the air was longer and had produced broader and tall letters with a smaller degree of slant by children with high functioning autism. It also took them longer to copy text than to write their own [1]. And this concluded that unique handwriting pattern is usually found in children with high functioning autism spectrum disorder.

Children with mental disorder show serious changes in the way they learn, behave, or handle their emotions affecting their daily lifestyle. Estimating children having difficulty in mental health can be done in many ways. CDC (Centers for disease control and prevention) uses surveys like the National Survey of Children's Health to make such deduction. So, in this study, the main objective is to apply graphology to detect whether a child has autism or not with accuracy to monitor the mental health of a developing child. In most cases, the state-of-the-art method monitors the children's mental health by examining the handwriting on paper, where human interacting and expertness is needed. Thus, the main idea is to make the children's mental disability by writing on a digital pen tablet and analyze the handwriting for automatic prediction using machine learning techniques. In this proposed system, a digital pen-tablet is used to collect data of handwriting. The handwriting data are analyzed and optimal parameters are selected. A set of discriminant features are extracted from selected parameters. The features of selected parameters are used to train the machine learning algorithm and detect the mental disability of children.

The rest of the paper is organized as follows. Related works are described in Sect. 2. Section 3 describes the proposed model. The results are presented in Sect. 4 and Sect. 5 concludes the paper.

2 Related Works

There have been many studies conducted in graphology to detect the personality traits of individuals by applying several machine learning algorithms which has several applications in real life such as for recruitment. This section covers some of the recent and relevant studies discussed shortly.

In recent statistics in the United States, it has been seen that depression and anxiety have increased over time [2]. Ghandour RM et al. studied that 7.4% of children aged 3–17 years (approximately 4.5 million) have a diagnosed behavior problem, 7.1% of children aged 3–17 years (approximately 4.4 million) have diagnosed anxiety, 3.2% of children aged 3–17 years (approximately 1.9 million) have diagnosed depression [3]. David S. Mandell et al. studied that children with mental disorder show serious changes in the way they learn, behave, or handle their emotions affecting their daily lifestyle. Also, in certain cases, autism is diagnosed late only when faced with new social challenges and school demands. In these cases, children are first diagnosed by either ADHD or other sensory processing issues which are also quite common in autistic children which delays the diagnosis and as a result miss out the therapy required for autism [4].

Champa and Kumar proposed a system to predict the personality of a person from handwriting analysis using an artificial neural network [5]. The baseline, the pen pressure, and the letter "t" are the inputs parameter to ANN which reveal the personality traits and the outputs are the personality trait of the writer. The polygonization method and grey level threshold value has been used to evaluate baseline and pen pressure. The height of 't' bar has been evaluated by template matching. The backpropagation method has been used in this paper.

Hemlata et al. review and analysis on handwriting which provides an outline of handwriting analysis and features on handwriting that is related to personality traits and an overview of the Handwriting Analysis System (HAS). The attribute of a person can be dug up by the Handwriting Analysis System (HAS). A scanned image of a handwriting sample is given as input and a set of personality traits are produced as output by following some steps using various handwriting features, i.e. baseline, size, slant, spacing, margin, pressure, etc. For more accurate analysis features such as zone, the speed of handwriting can also be considered. The entire module is broken into several sections such as scanning, preprocessing, segmentation, feature extraction, and classification [6].

Prachi Joshi et al. discussed a method for identifying personality traits from handwriting analysis using a machine learning approach like KNN classifier which improves the efficiency of the handwriting analysis. This system has been aimed at individuals who face many interviews, especially in the age group of 20–35 years, and obtain their characteristic traits. The baseline, margin, slant of the words, and height of the 't' bar are explored in this paper which reveals the personality traits. The polygonization method has been used to evaluate the baseline. The margin and the height of the 't' bar have been evaluated using vertical scanning and template matching. The baseline, margin, and the height of 't' bar were extracted from handwriting samples using image processing tools and converted into feature vector which is then compared with the trained data set and mapped to the class of personality trait [7].

Parmeet and Deepak discussed a method for behavior prediction using handwriting analysis explored features such as baseline, letter slant, pen pressure, letter 'i', and letter 'f' are explored. These features are the inputs to the artificial neural network and output the personality traits of the writer. The baseline and letter slant were also evaluated by the polygonization method. The pen pressure was evaluated by grey-level threshold value and the letter 'i' and letter 'f' was evaluated by template matching. MATLAB tool was used for implementation in this paper. Multiple samples were examined for obtaining the performance result [8].

So, we can see that identifying personality traits were always the main focus of handwriting analysis. And so, this study was aimed particularly for children with special care to see the difference in their writing with that of normal children and if this could be used to classify their mental condition. Handwriting features pressure and average time in particular were major contributions in the classification.

3 Proposed Model

We used 6 different classifiers for the classification of our dataset. The following flow graph represents the workflow that we have maintained during this study starting with the collection of data and then data preprocessing and partitioning using k fold cross-validation method. Figure 1 shows the proposed methodology Flow diagram.

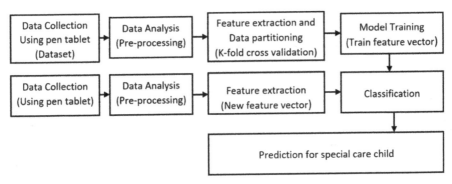

Fig. 1. Methodology flow diagram.

3.1 Device and Data Collection

In this study, for the collection of handwriting as input, pen tablet as shown in Fig. 2. is used, which is an input device that converts the information of the motions of hand from a pen-like instrument called Stylus. We have collected data from different special education institutes namely Beautiful Mind, Proyas, and some normal schools, and made our dataset.

Children were given a set of totals of five different texts and shapes to be written and drawn on a pen tablet. Each set was taken twice from each child to improve the accuracy. Table 1 shows the writing task set.

For each input text of the sample set, the output is continuous data and so the average of each of the six parameters time, pressure, x-axis, y-axis, horizontal angle, and pen altitude is then calculated. After that, the average for all the five text samples was calculated which serves as the final output for an individual child.

3.2 Data Analysis

Figure 3 (a–f) shows the variation in values for each child for parameters average time, pressure, x-axis, y-axis, horizontal angle, and pen altitude.

Fig. 2. A pen tablet was used for collecting handwriting data.

Table 1. Writing task set

No.	Sample
1.	Hello World
2.	Thank You
3.	UAP CSE
4.	
5.	

3.3 Dominant Parameter Selection

An important process for assessing which feature contributes mostly to predicting the target class. Accuracy of models can be greatly affected by irrelevant features so tracking them is very crucial for better performance of the models. It also reduces overfitting and training time. For the feature selection, we have used the Select K-Best method which selects k number of top-scoring features and score is calculated using the function chi2 that tests the dependency of two events. The value of k used in this study is 5.

$$X^2 = \sum (observed - expected)^2 \big/ expected \tag{1}$$

According to the score of parameters presented in Table 2 time and pressure are the most significant features in our study with y-axis being the least significant having a poor score of 0.028990. Based on the calculated score the top 3 parameters (i.e., pen pressure, Horizontal angle, and x-axis) are selected for feature extraction.

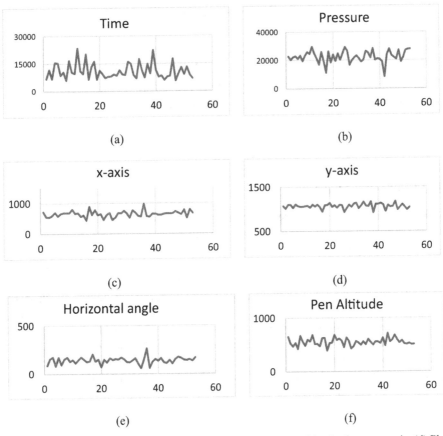

Fig. 3. (a) Plot for feature time, (b) Plot for feature pressure, (c) Plot for feature x-axis, (d) Plot for feature y-axis, (e) Plot for feature horizontal angle, (f) Plot for feature pen altitude.

Table 2. Show the feature selection score for each attribute

SN	Parameters	Score
1	Pen pressure	1095.263
2	Horizontal angle	57.926
3	x-axis	51.571
4	Pen altitude	19.635
5	y-axis	0.029

3.4   Feature Extraction from Selected Paraments

In this step, the features are extracted from the selected parameters. The extracted features are listed in Table 3. The extracted features are used for child mental growth classification.

Table 3. List of features

Features	
Start pressure	End pressure
Peak pressure	Mean pressure
Pressure acceleration	Pressure jerk
Horizontal angle mean	Horizontal angle STD
Mean of x-velocity	STD of x-velocity

3.5 Classification Models

For the classification of our model the following six classifiers are used along with all the pen features.

1. Logistic regression- Logistic regression is a popular supervised machine learning model when it comes to classification problems [9]. This estimates how the result is affected by independent variables as a probability. There are three main methods of logistic regression which are Binary logistic regression, Ordinal logistic regression, and nominal logistic regression. In our study, we used Binary logistic regression which includes binary results and makes analysis through dependent variables. That is, the binary result variable and one or more expressive variable's correlation is suggested by binary logistic regression. A logistic function known as a sigmoid function along with a linear model is defined in logistic regression.

$$P(yi = 1|X = 1) = \frac{1}{1 + e^{-(\beta 0 + \beta 1 * x)}} \qquad (2)$$

2. Random forest- Used in both regression and classification problems, in this model Breiman demonstrated that using ensembles of tree that is grown to choose the most popular class. Often random vectors are used for the growing task and this significantly improves the accuracy in classification results. Randomness in feature and input in classification yields good results. This plays a great role in targeting the most significant features. Gain ratio, Information gain, and Gini index is used for the splitting operation [10].

3. Decision tree- Another supervised machine learning algorithm is widely used in classification problems. It has a tree structure that includes a root, branches and leaf nodes where each node, branch and leaf denote attribute, test outcome and class label respectively with the topmost node being the root [11] t. In our study, we have used Gini impurity which attempts to find a decision rule which creates splits to increase impurity repeatedly until all leaf nodes are pure.

$$G(t) = 1 - \sum_{i=1}^{c} Pi^2 \qquad (3)$$

where G(t) is the Gini impurity at node t, and pi is the proportions of observations of class c at node t.

4. Naïve Bayes- A supervised machine learning algorithm [12] based on Bayes theorem where the learning is simplified with the assumption that features are independent of a given class. This model is easy to interpret, faster to predict and can be easily trained with a small dataset. The probability of class y given object x is expressed as:

$$p(x|y) = \frac{p(y|x)p(x)}{p(y)} \tag{4}$$

5. K-nearest neighbor- This technique [13] also known as Memory-Based Classification is a non-parametric algorithm and the most straightforward classifier in machine learning language that analyzes the neighboring nearest elements and using them identifies the class of an unknown query. Distance functions such as Euclidean distance, Manhattan distance and Minkowski distance are used to compute the distances among the points and the unknown point is classified based on the k number of nearest points. In our study, we have used Minkowski distance for measuring the distances.

$$\text{dminkowski} = \left(\sum_{i=1}^{n} |Xi - Yi|^p\right)^{\frac{1}{p}} \tag{5}$$

Applications of this method range from healthcare, handwriting detection to image recognition and more.

6. Support Vector Machine (SVM) – Widely used supervised machine learning algorithm [14] which produces high accuracy in terms of classification performance and were developed from statistical learning. It also has many applications such as handwritten digit recognition, tone recognition, and image classification. It classifies a point by detecting a hyperplane that maximizes the margin among classes in training data. The support vector classifier is expressed as:

$$f(x) = \beta 0 + \sum_{i \in S} \alpha i K\left(xi, \, xi'\right) \tag{6}$$

where $\beta 0$ is the bias, S is the set of all observations, αi learning parameter of the model, and K is the kernel function.

In our study we have used a linear kernel represented as

$$K(xi, xi') = \sum_{j=1}^{p} xijxi'j \tag{7}$$

where p is the number of features.

4 Experiments and Results

4.1 Dataset

The dataset is composed of 53 observations with 7 features such as time, pressure, x-axis, y-axis, horizontal angle and pen altitude and class attribute collected from children of age group 7 to 16. The class attribute column contains a binary class that indicates whether the observation is a special care child or not. Figure 4 (a–e). Shows the handwriting samples collected from a special care child and Fig. 5 (a–e). Shows handwriting samples collected from a normal child for the above sample set.

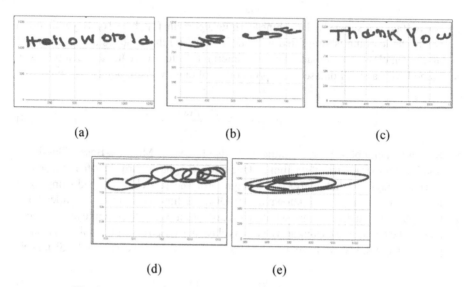

Fig. 4. (a–e) Handwriting sample obtained from a special care child.

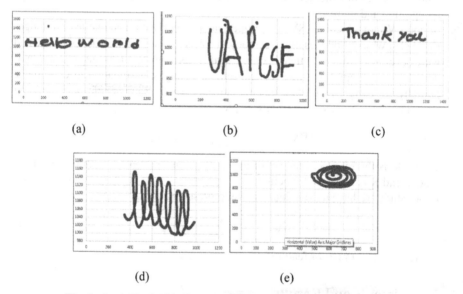

Fig. 5. (a–e) Handwriting samples were obtained from a normal child.

4.2   Experimental Results

In this study, we used six algorithms which are logistic regression, random forest, decision tree, naïve Bayes, K-nearest neighbor, and Support vector machine (SVM) for the prediction of our dataset.

According to Table 4 the result of the mean accuracy score for each classifier with Naïve Bayes, Decision tree, and Random forest having the best performance. To improve performance, we standardized our dataset by scaling the data. Table 5 shows the accuracy score after scaling. It can be seen that accuracy of all the classifiers increased and the accuracy of the Support vector machine increased by 5.7% having the highest score of accuracy among all the six classifiers.

Table 4. Performance of each classifier.

Classifier	Accuracy
Logistic regression	0.565
k-nearest neighbor	0.510
Decision tree	0.615
Naïve bayes	0.635
Support vector machine	0.440
Random forest	0.615

Table 5. Performance of classifier after scaling.

Classifier	Accuracy
Logistic regression	0.590
k-nearest neighbor	0.640
Decision tree	0.640
Naïve bayes	0.635
Support vector machine	0.670
Random forest	0.636

Since the Support Vector machine shows the best performance it was further tuned, and the parameters used in the model were linear kernel and C = 1.5 (cost parameter).

The following Table 6 shows the performance concerning different evaluation metrics of the six classifiers for the model (Fig. 6).

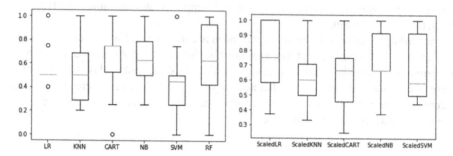

Fig. 6. (a) Comparison of the classifiers and (b) Comparison of classifiers after scaling.

Table 6. Performance of each classifier for different metrics

Classifier	Accuracy	Precision	Recall	F1 score	AUC
Logistic legression	0.636	0.67	0.64	0.63	0.650
K-nearest neighbor	0.545	0.55	0.55	0.55	0.550
Naïve bayes	0.454	0.45	0.45	0.45	0.449
Decision tree	0.727	0.74	0.73	0.73	0.733
Random forest	0.636	0.64	0.64	0.62	0.616
Support vector machine	0.727	0.74	0.73	0.73	0.733

So, tuning the parameters further increased the performance of the support vector machine by 8.5% with the final accuracy of 72.7%.

5   Conclusion

The main focus of this study is to develop a system where handwriting can be used as a means of predicting the mental condition automatically of a child similar to how it can be used to predict behaviors and traits. The collected parameters from the pen-tablet are sorted based on score and different statistical features are extracted from the selected parameters. Six different classifiers, i.e., Logistic Regression, K-nearest neighbor, Decision Tree, Naïve Bayes, Random forest, and Support Vector Machine are used for predicting the outcome of our dataset. Both drawings and writings of children were considered in this study. Scaling the data and tuning the parameters of KNN and SVM improved the accuracy of the models. SVM and Decision tree had the best results of 72.7% accuracy.

Acknowledgement. We would like to thank the Institute of Energy, Environment, Research, and Development (IEERD, UAP) and the University of Asia Pacific for financial support.

References

1. University of Haifa. Children with high-functioning autism spectrum disorder show unique handwriting patterns: Integrative education system should consider this factor, say experts. ScienceDaily, http://www.sciencedaily.com/releases/2016/06/160601084649.html. Accessed 21 Dec 2020
2. Bitsko, R.H., Holbrook, J.R., Ghandour, R.M., Blumberg, S.J., Visser, S.N., Perou, R., Walkup, J.: Epidemiology and impact of healthcare provider diagnosed anxiety and depression among US children. J. Dev. Behav. Pediatr. **39**, 395 (2018)
3. Ghandour, R.M., Sherman, L.J., Vladutiu, C.J., Ali, M.M., Lynch, S.E., Bitsko, R.H., Blumberg, S.J.: Prevalence and treatment of depression, anxiety, and conduct problems in US children. J. Pediatr. **206**, 256–267 (2018)
4. Mandell, D.S., Ittenbach, R.F., Levy, S.E., Pinto-Martin, J.A.: Disparities in diagnoses received prior to a diagnosis of autism spectrum disorder. J. Autism Dev. Disord. **37**(9), 1795–1802 (2007). https://doi.org/10.1007/s10803-006-0314-8
5. Champa, H.N., AnandaKumar, K.R.: Artificial neural network for human behavior prediction through handwriting analysis. Int. J. Comput. Appl. **2**(2), 36–41 (2010). https://doi.org/10.5120/629-878
6. Hemlata, M.S., Singh, S.K.: Personality detection using handwriting analysis: review. In: ACEC (2018)
7. Joshi, P., Agarwal, A., Dhavale, A., Suryavanshi, R., Kodolikar, S.: Handwriting analysis for detection of personality traits using machine learning approach. Int. J. Comput. Appl. (0975–8887) 130(15) (2015)
8. Grewal, P.K., Parashar, D.: Behavior prediction through handwriting analysis. IJCST **3**(2), 520–523 (2012)
9. Peng, C.Y.J., Lee, K.L., Ingersoll, G.M.: an introduction to logistic regression analysis and reporting. J. Educ. Res. **96**, 3–14 (2002)
10. Breiman, L.: Random Forests. Mach. Learn. **45**, 5–32 (2001)
11. Patel, B.N., Prajapati, S.G., Lakhtaria, K.I.: Efficient classification of data using decision tree bonfring. Int. J. Data Min. **2**(1), 6–12 (2012)
12. Kaviani, P., Dhotre, S.: Short survey on naive bayes algorithm. Int. J. Adv. Eng. Res. Dev. **4**(11) (2017)
13. Cunningham, P., Delany, S.J.: k-nearest neighbor classifiers technical report. In: UCD-CSI-2007–4 (2007)
14. Shrivastava, D.K., Bhambu, L.: Data classification using support vector machine. J. Theor. Appl. Inf. Technol. © 2005 - 2009 JATIT

Electrocardiogram Signal Analysis Based on Statistical Approaches Using K-Nearest Neighbor

Mahmudul Alam[1] , Md. Monirul Islam[2] , Md. Rokunojjaman[3] ,
Sharmin Akter[4] , Md. Belal Hossain[5] , and Jia Uddin[6(✉)]

[1] Department of Computer Science and Engineering, Bangamata Sheikh Fojilatunnesa Mujib
Science and Technology University, Melandaha, Jamalpur 2012, Bangladesh
[2] Department of Computer Science and Engineering,
University of Information Technology and Sciences, Dhaka 1212, Bangladesh
monirul.islam@uits.edu.bd
[3] Department of Computer Science and Engineering, Chongqing University of Technology,
Banan, Chongqing 400054, China
[4] Department of Mathematics, University of Dhaka, Dhaka 1230, Bangladesh
[5] Department of Computer Science and Engineering, Pabna University of Science and
Technology, Pabna 6600, Bangladesh
[6] AI and Big Data Department, Endicott College, Woosong University, Daejeon, South Korea
jia.uddin@wsu.ac.kr

Abstract. The performance of computer aided ECG analysis is very important for
doctors and patients. Analyzing the ECG signal has been shown to be very useful
in distinguishing patients from various disease. In this research, ECG signals
is investigated using statistical approaches including Standard Deviation (SD),
Coefficient of Variation (CoV), and Central Tendency Measure (CTM), and the
machine learning model named, K-nearest neighbors (K-NN) model is used to
identify them. With QRS complex extraction, the bit-to-bit interval (BBI) and
instantaneous heart rate (IHR) were computed. CTM is measured IHR for ECG
record of database. CTM highest value for IHR is detected for ten patients with
normal rhythm with average value of 0.799 and low SD average of 5.633. On the
other hand, the CTM for IHR of ten abnormal rhythm patients achived low value
with average of 0.1645 and high SD average of 21.555. To validate the model,
we utilized the standard MIT-BIH arrhythmia database. We used "twenty normal
and abnormal rhythms" from the record of MIT-BIH database where each record
is of one-hour duration. Experimental results proved that the proposed classifier
named, K-nearest neighbor (K-NN) method gives the best accuracy 98.8%, best
sensitivity 98.8%, and best specificity 89% for SD, best accuracy 98.2%, best
sensitivity 98.23%, and best specificity 90% for CoV, and best accuracy 98.2%,
best sensitivity 98.23%, and best specificity 90.2% for CTM respectively. Further,
we distinguish between proposed model and state-of-art models including support
vector machine and ensemble.

Keywords: Statistical methods · ECG signal · K-NN · CTM · Instantaneous
heart rate (IHR)

A. K. M. M. Islam et al. (Eds.): ICBBDB 2021, CCIS 1550, pp. 148–160, 2022.
https://doi.org/10.1007/978-3-031-17181-9_12

1 Introduction

ECG is a noting but a record of electrical action of heart where each heart beat is shown by 5 peaks and valleys as the series of electrical waves. They are labelled by the letters P, Q, R, S, and T. Sometimes, we also use another peak as U. Each component of the signal deflects different heart activity such as atrial depolarization, atrial repolarization, ventricular depolarization, ventricular repolarization, and so on. The accurate and dependable identification of the QRS complex, as well as T- and P-waves, is critical to the success of the ECG analyzing system. The P-wave represents the activation of the heart's upper chambers, the atria, whilst the QRS complex and T-wave represent the activation of the heart's lower chambers, the ventricles. The QRS complex is the most important task in automatic ECG signal analysis [1]. The range of normal value of heart beat is of (60–100) per minute. In normal rhythm, the interval and amplitude of all peak as well as valleys is shown in Table 1.

Table 1. The interval and amplitude of all peak for normal rhythm

Names of wave	Amplitude	Name of intervals	Duration (s)
P-wave	0.25 mV	P-R	0.12–0.20
R-wave	1.60 mV	Q-T	0.35–0.44
Q-wave	25% R-wave	S-T	0.05–0.15
T-wave	0.1–0.5 mV	QRS	0.11

ECG analysis is a very useful method for detecting cardiovascular diseases. Heart diseases can be diagnosed using ECG wave shapes, intervals of peaks and valleys, and a few other mathematical parameters. However, the full ECG signal is too large and complex to identify only a few cardiac cycles. As a result, to reduce the burden of interpreting the ECG, an automatic interpreting system must be built. Human observation was previously used to control traditional methods of monitoring and diagnosing an arrhythmia. Because of the huge amount of patients in such conditions and the lack of continuous monitoring, numerous systems for automated arrhythmia identification have been developed in an attempt to solve the problem in the last two decades. The methods worked by transforming the most subjective qualitative diagnostic criteria into a massive quantitative signal feature classification problem. As a result, an efficient method for analyzing the ECG signal and diagnosing heart diseases is required. Traditional techniques, such as frequency domain analysis, time-domain analysis, and wavelet transform analysis of electrocardiogram (ECG) for arrhythmia detection, have been used to address the problem, with the QRS complex in the ECG being used to compare between normal and abnormal rhythms [2–4].

The central tendency measure (CTM) has been proven to be a useful tool for detecting irregular heartbeats. CTM can be a useful sign of the absence of congestive heart failure when combined with clinical characteristics [5]. Intrinsic patterns of two time series, such as ECGs, and time series except a pattern, like: hemodynamic investigations, have been found to benefit from the CTM method for assessing variability in non-linear techniques [6]. To examine the underlying issue in the ECG, CTM can be utilized in concert with other techniques such as correlation dimension (CD) and Approximate entropy (ApEn) [7].

For distinguishing the normal and abnormal rhythms, many modern classifier methods are used in current days. Support Vector Machine (SVM), Analysis of Variance (ANOVA), K-nearest neighbors (KNN) are most popular among them. KNN method is very useful to identify normal and abnormal ECG signals as well as healthy patients and ailing patients [8]. In this paper, we used CTM, SD, and CoV techniques and KNN model.

The rest of the paper outline is as follows. Section 2 demonstrates the literature review as well as proposed methodology has stated in the Sect. 3. The result analysis is depicted in Sect. 4, and finally, we finish the paper at the end Sect. 5.

2 Literature Review

The identification of normal and abnormal electrocardiograms using chaotic models is a widely used research technique. Beth Israel Hospital and MIT have been collaborating on arrhythmia analysis and connected subjects since 1975. The MIT-BIH Arrhythmia Database, completed and distributed in 1980 [9], was one of the project's first major products. Following that, it quickly became the most popular data source for ECG research. This database has been used by hundreds of researchers to publish their findings. The authors [10] used Combined Models to analyze Chaotic ECG. They use a Neural Network to classify their results. They improve on their previous method two years later. This time, they investigated new chaotic methods using various signal studies such as the second-order difference plot and the CTM. The authors of [5] use chaotic models to classify ECG signals. On that project, they analyzed various non-linear techniques and classified them using variance analysis (ANOVA).

The most commonly used technique for analyzing this study is statistical techniques. The authors of [11] used nonlinear techniques of heart rate variability to analyze Cardiac Heart Failure patients. For the results, they calculated Detrended Fluctuation Analysis, Higuchi Exponent, Approximate, and Sample Entropy. The authors [12] used Statistical Tools and Non-Linear Analysis to detect Premature Ventricular Contraction of the ECG. They discovered a difference in the nonlinear results of normal and ailing patients. The authors of [13] did the same type of research on heart rate variability. To identify variability, they used phase space portrait, embedding dimension, correlation dimension, Lyapunov Exponents, and surrogate data analysis on the project [14] employs the Approximate Entropy method to assess the regularity of heart rate. The authors of [6] use chaos theory to extract features for ECG time-series mining. They used some nonlinear techniques in conjunction with an ECG chaos extractor program. The authors [15] described fourier-transform real-time discriminating of Ventricular tachyarrhythmia and classification using neural networks [16] investigated heart rate in specific subjects of various ages. They measured nonlinear parameters such as the Poincare plot, DFA, Lyapunov exponent, and approximate entropy for people of various ages and compared the differences. Classifier techniques are most commonly a criterion for distinguishing between normal and pathological data. There are numerous classifier techniques used to detect heart disease from ECG data. One of the most common classifier techniques is K-Nearest Neighbor. It is created with MATLAB, a machine learning feature, and Python programming. The authors of [17] used the KNN method to analyze ECG signals. Initially, they estimate some parameters such as R-R interval, P-R interval, QRS complex period, and S-T interval using MATLAB. The result is then compared to theoretic normal or abnormal data. Finally, they used MATLAB to convert all of the resulting data to K-nearest neighbor and calculate the form and percentage of classification accuracy. The authors [18] investigated PVC classification using K-NN. The MIT-BIH arrhythmia database [19] was used to estimate the results for the project. Finally, they compare the specificity and sensitivity of their proposed data to that of some referred author's data. Authors [19] recently researched autoregressive modeling with different ECG signal interpretations. They measured the order of the models for a specific disease and classified the results in KNN with a higher accuracy rate.

3   Proposed Methodology

We use statistical methods to depict the heart rate variability (HRV) study in the paper. First, the QRS complex of the ECG signal must be extracted and evaluated. The bit-to-bit interval (BBI) or R-R interval can be easily calculated using the QRS complex. We acquire the immediate heart rate via the BBI (IHR). Some statistical characteristics containing standard deviation (SD), coefficient of variation (CoV), and central tendency measure (CTM), can be computed using this BBI and IHR dataset. The ECG signals of a good health person and an unwell person are compared using the results produced from the petition of these non-linear approaches. Then, we measure the accuracy of non-linear techniques using machine learning models.

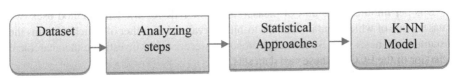

Fig. 1. Detailed block diagram of proposed methodology

The complete life cycle of proposed methodology is shown in Fig. 1. This mainly consists of 4 steps. They are- Dataset, Analyzing parts, Statistical approaches and Classifier model namely K-NN.

3.1   Dataset

The ECG data which are used in the paper using statistical methods to identify heart's electrical activity are carried out from the MIT-BIH Arrhythmia Database, where 360 Hz is the sampling rate and sample resolution is 11 bits/sample. We take the 10 normal and 10 abnormal rhythm data from MIT-BIH Arrhythmia. The number of data record is shown in Table 2.

Table 2. The number of used data record of MIT-BIH Arrhythmia

No. of 10 normal data	No. of 10 abnormal data
100	106
107	119
111	200
112	208
117	213
118	221
121	222
122	223
124	228
234	233

3.2 Analyzing Steps

The MIT-BIH database's ECG signal is first divided into periods or beats. Because the lengths of the peak-to-peak (beats) on the ECG signal are not equal because it is quasi-periodic, a beat is act as the signal between R-R intervals. The Bit-to-Bit Interval (BBI), which is the average space between two consecutive R waves, is calculated as a result of this. The BBI is timed in seconds. Using Eq. 1, we can determine Instantaneous Heart Rate (IHR) from BBI and it is vice-versa.

$$IHR = \frac{60}{BBI} \tag{1}$$

Bits per minute is the unit of measurement for IHR (bpm). This method uses two datasets, one of which contains the bit-to-bit interval and the other of which contains the instantaneous heart rate. Statistical approaches were used to investigate the anarchical behavior of the ECG on these two data sets.

3.3 Statistical Approaches

In statistical techniques, we utilized three methods named Standard Deviation, Coefficient of Variance, and Central Tendency Measure.

3.3.1 Standard Deviation

In probability and statistics, the standard deviation of a probability distribution, random variable, population, or multiset of values is a measure of the dispersion of its values. It is commonly represented by the letter (sigma). It's known as the square root of the variance.The average of the squared variances between data points and the mean is varience when computing the standard deviation. As indicated in Eq. 2, the SD is the root mean square (RMS) deviation of data from its arithmetic mean. The SD is the most commonly used statistical dispersion metric, reflecting how far values in a data collection are spread. The standard deviation is low when the data point is close to the mean. Furthermore, the standard deviation will be considered if a large number of data points vary from the mean. The standard deviation is 0 for the all equal data value.

$$\sigma = \sqrt{\left(\frac{1}{N}\Sigma_{i=1}^{N}(x_i - \bar{x})^2\right)} \tag{2}$$

3.3.2 Coefficient of Variation

The coefficient of variation is a statistical measure of the dispersion of data points in a data series around the mean. Equation 3 is used to calculate it.

$$CoV = \frac{SD}{mean} \tag{3}$$

Generally, after measuring the actual value of (CoV), it is expressed with respect to subject 100. So it is shown as a percentage in Eq. 4.

$$CoV = \frac{SD}{mean} \times 100\% \tag{4}$$

3.3.3 Central Tendency Measure (CTM)

The use of second-order difference plots to examine central tendency provides a valuable summary. It's determined by drawing a circular zone surrounding the origin with radius r, calculating the number of points that fall within the radius, and then dividing by the sum of points. Let t stand for the sum of points, and r is considering for the central area. Then,

$$n = \frac{\left[\sum_{i=1}^{t-2}\delta(d_i)\right]}{t - 2} \tag{5}$$

where,

$\delta(di) = 1$; if $\left\{(a_{i+2} - a_{i+1})^2 + (a_{i+1} - a_i)^2\right\}^{0.5} < r = 0$; otherwise

We applied the data set produced from the bit-to-bit interval and the prompt heart rate to apply the CTM. It has been shown that for a regular rhythm, the data set is restricted to a small area, resulting in a high CTM. The data set for aberrant rhythms tend to be distributed over a larger area, resulting in a poor CTM.

The central tendency measures (CTM) are calculated using the standard deviation variation, which ranges from 10% to 100% for normal and abnormal patients.

3.4 KNN-Model

The k-nearest neighbors (KNN) technique is one of the most straightforward and straight-forward Machine Learning algorithms for classifying and identifying data. The KNN algorithm thinks that new data and past data are similar and places the new data in the category that is most like the previous data's types. It saves all available data and assigns a new classification to a new data point based on similarity. This means when new data comes to the chart, it classified shortly into a type by using the KNN classifier [20].

To quantify the separations, various separation capabilities are used; a famous decision is a Euclidean separation provied by Eq. 6.

$$d\left(x, x'\right) = \sqrt{\left(x_1 - x_1'\right)^2 + \ldots + \left(x_n - x_n'\right)^2} \tag{6}$$

More specifically, took a positive full number K, a revolutionary perception x, and a comparability metric d, the KNN computation uses Eq. 7 to carry out the accompanying improvements.

It iterates through the whole dataset, calculating d between x and each preparation insight. Set A will be the K emphases in the preparation data that is closest to x. It's worth noting that K isn't usually used to break a tie.

It then evaluates the restrictive possibility for each class or the percentage of focuses in A with that particular class mark. (Note that I(x) is a marker task that evaluates to 1 when the argument x is legitimate and 0 otherwise.)

$$P(y = j | X = x) = \frac{1}{K} \sum_{i \in A} I\left(y^{(i)} = j\right) \tag{7}$$

4 Experimental Result and Analysis

For 10 normal rhythm records and ten aberrant rhythm records, we calculated the instantaneous heart rate (IHR). The Standard Deviation (SD) and Coefficient of Variation (CoV) are calculated from these data sets, and the results are given in Figs. 2 and 3.

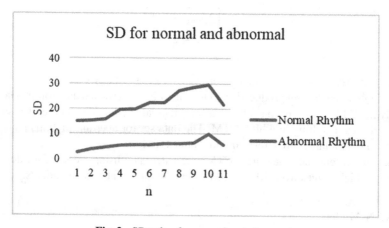

Fig. 2. SD value for normal and abnormal.

The last point of normal rhythm and abnormal rhythm line is the average value of SD. Their value is 5.633 for normal rhythm and abnormal rhythm is 21.555 respectively. Theoretically for normal patients, the standard deviation is less than 6. If any rhythm's SD value is more than 6 is considered as an abnormal patient.

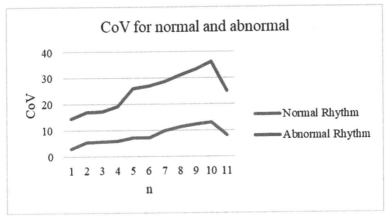

Fig. 3. CoV for normal and abnormal.

From Fig. 3, we get the average value for normal rhythm is 8.114% and for abnormal rhythm is 25.06%. The efficiency of abnormal rhythm is always greater than normal rhythm.

We determined the instantaneous heart rate (IHR) for 10 normal rhythm histories for ten abnormal rhythms records. From data sets mean, the standard deviation (SD), Variance, coefficient of variation (CoV) are achived and the results are revealed in Tables 3 and 4.

Table 3. Ten normal rhythm's ECG with the statistical analysis

Data No	SD	CoV
100	5.324	7.068%
107	5.63	7.114%
111	3.939	5.564%
112	2.586	3.062%
117	6.295	12.244%
118	9.928	13.003%
121	6.217	9.97%
122	4.686	5.68%
124	6.189	11.394%
234	5.536	6.041%

Table 3 displays the records of ten normal rhythm's electrocardiogram with the statistical analysis. The beginning column illustrates the record names. The next column provides the SD, and last column shows CoV respectively determined from IHR of those records. Table 4 demostrates the records of ten abnormal rhythm's electrocardiogram with the statistical analysis.

Table 4. Ten abnormal rhythm's ECG with the statistical analysis

Data No	SD	CoV
100	27.25	36.22%
107	22.521	31.239%
111	14.989	17.002%
112	19.544	19.146%
117	15.796	14.612%
118	22.52	26.093%
121	28.485	33.398%
122	15.254	17.163%
124	19.766	27.057%
234	29.43	28.625%

In the CTM, ten normal rhythms are recorded. The variation of r varies from 10% to 100% for normal and abnormal rhythm. Here we have shown CTM value r 10%, r 100% and average CTM.

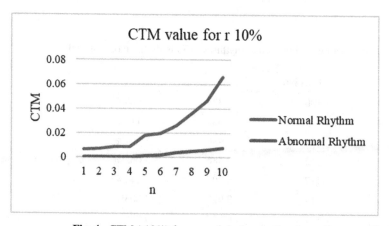

Fig. 4. CTM (r10%) for normal & abnormal patient.

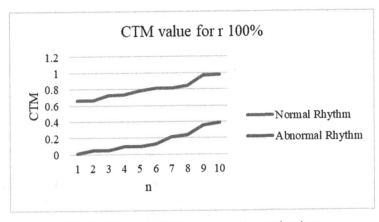

Fig. 5. CTM (r 100%) for normal & abnormal patient.

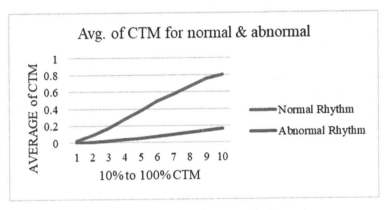

Fig. 6. Average of CTM for normal & abnormal.

From Figs. 4 to 6, it can be observed that the central tendency steadily increases with the standard deviation, although the normal rhythm does not. Similarly, for aberrant rhythms, the central tendency does not substantially increase for standard deviation, and the CTM values are always less than 0.5. With an increase in r from 10% to 100%, the CTM value of the normal rhythm increases in a similar way. However, for aberrant rhythms, CTM values are steadily increased as r increases from 10% to 100%. The CTM values of normal rhythms are substantially higher than aberrant rhythms. So, it can be perfectly said that the normal rhythm patients are much healthier than abnormal rhythm patients.

4.1 Classification

In this section, we measured accuracy, sensitivity and specificity. We can measure these from confusion matrix easily. A confusion matrix has some terminology including actual yes (tp, fn), actual no (fp, tn), predicted yes (tp, fp), and predicted no (fn, tn) where tp =

true positive, false negative = fn, fp = false positive, and tn = true negative. Accuracy, sensitivity and specificity are shown in Eq. 8, 9, 10 respectively.

$$Accuracy = \frac{tp + tn}{tp + tn + fp + fn} \tag{8}$$

$$Sensitivity = \frac{tp}{tp + fp} \tag{9}$$

$$Specificity = \frac{tn}{tn + fp} \tag{10}$$

Table 5 shows the accuracy among different machine learning models. K-NN gives the highest accuracy, 98.8% for SD, 98.2% for CoV, and 98.2% for CTM respectively. SVM [21] gives 95% for SD, 90% for CoV, and 95% for CTM respectively. Ensemble classifier [22] holds the lowest position by achieving an accuracy of 65% for SD, 75% for CoV, and 80% for CTM respectively. Table 5 also shows the sentivity among different machine learning models. K-NN gives the highest sensitivity, 98.8% for SD, 98.23% for CoV, and 98.23% for CTM respectively. SVM gives 95% for SD, 90.01% for CoV, and 95% for CTM respectively. Ensemble classifier holds the lowest position by achieving an sensitivity of 65% for SD, 74.99% for CoV, and 80.01% for CTM respectively and we get the specificity for each algorithms like K-NN gives the highest specificity, 89% for SD, 90% for CoV, and 90.2% for CTM respectively, SVM gives 85% for SD, 83% for CoV, and 82% for CTM respectively, and Ensemble classifier holds the lowest position by achieving an specificity of 56% for SD, 64% for CoV, and 65% for CTM respectively.

Table 5. Accuracy rate of different classifier methods

Name of parameters	Accuracy KNN (%)	Accuracy SVM (%)	Accuracy Ensemble (%)	Sensitivity K-NN, SVM, Ensemble	Specificity K-NN, SVM, Ensemble
SD	98.8	95	65	98.8, 95, 65	89, 85, 56
CoV	98.2	90	75	98.23, 90.01, 74.99	90, 83, 64
CTM	98.2	95	80	98.23, 95, 80.01	90.2, 82, 65

K-NN gives the highest values of each performance metrics. We know, K-NN is used as a voting system to identify which class an unclassified object belongs to, taking into account the class of the nearest neighbors in the input space.

5   Conclusion

In this paper, we applied three techniques to identify arrhythmia on the ECG data set. We take ten normal and ten abnormal rhythms from the MIT-BIH arrhythmia database for calculation of IHR and BBI along with we also show the number of data. Each data is approximately 1 h in duration, and a total of twenty data sets are analyzed. We figured out this classification using statistical techniques including Standard Deviation (SD), Coefficient of Variance (CoV), and Central Tendency Measure respectively (CTM). In this paper, we get that CTM gives much is a much higher role in identifying normal and abnormal rhythms in the ECG signals. In comparison to the aberrant rhythm data set, CTM for both IHR and BBI of the normal rhythm data set has a largest value. For showing all the performance metrics including accuracy, sensitivity and specificity of the statistical techniques, we utilized some machine learning algorithms. Among these, K-nearest neighbor (K-NN) method gives the best accuracy 98.8%, best sensitivity 98.8%, and best specificity 89% for SD, best accuracy 98.2%, best sensitivity 98.23%, and best specificity 90% for CoV, and best accuracy 98.2%, best sensitivity 98.23%, and best specificity 90.2% for CTM respectively.

References

1. Saritha, C., Sukanya, V., Narasimha Murthy, Y.: ECG signal analysis using wavelet transforms. Bulg. J. Phys. **35**(1), 68–77 (2008)
2. Thakor, N.V., Pan, K.: Tachycardia and fibrillation detection by automatic implantable cardioverter-defibrillators: sequential testing in time domain. IEEE Eng. Med. Biol. Mag. **9**(1), 21–24 (1990)
3. Martínez, J.P., Almeida, R., Olmos, S., Rocha, A.P., Laguna, P.: A wavelet-based ECG delineator: evaluation on standard databases. IEEE Trans. Biomed. Eng. **51**(4), 570–581 (2004)
4. Shufni, S.A., Mashor, M.Y.: ECG signals classification based on discrete wavelet transform, time domain and frequency domain features. In 2015 2nd International Conference on Biomedical Engineering (ICoBE), pp. 1–6. IEEE (2015)
5. de Jonge, G., Sprij, A.: 30. In: 36 zieke kinderen, pp. 117–120. Bohn Stafleu van Loghum, Houten (2012). https://doi.org/10.1007/978-90-313-8424-2_30
6. Jovic, A., Bogunovic, N.: Feature extraction for ECG time-series mining based on chaos theory. In: 2007 29th International Conference on Information Technology Interfaces, pp. 63–68. IEEE (2007)
7. Naghsh, S., Ataei, M., Yazdchi, M., Hashemi, M.: Chaos-based analysis of heart rate variability time series in obstructive sleep apnea subjects. J. Med. Sig. Sens. **10**(1), 53 (2020)
8. Gupta, V., Mittal, M., Mittal, V.: R-peak detection based chaos analysis of ECG signal. Analog Integr. Circ. Sig. Process **102**(3), 479–490 (2019). https://doi.org/10.1007/s10470-019-015 56-1
9. MIT-BIH Arrhythmia Database CD-ROM, 3rd ed., Cambridge, MA:, Harvard–MIT Div. Health Sci. Technol. (1997)
10. Cohen, M.E., Hudson, D.L.: New chaotic methods for biomedical signal analysis. In: Proceedings 2000 IEEE EMBS International Conference on Information Technology Applications in Biomedicine. ITAB-ITIS 2000. Joint Meeting Third IEEE EMBS International Conference on Information Technol, pp. 123–128. IEEE (2000)
11. Signorini, M.G., Ferrario, M., Marchetti, M., Marseglia, A.: Nonlinear analysis of heart rate variability signal for the characterization of cardiac heart failure patients. In: 2006 International Conference of the IEEE Engineering in Medicine and Biology Society, pp. 3431–3434. IEEE (2006)

12. Mou, F.A., Jerin, E., Al Mahmud, M.A., Zadidul Karim, A.H.M.: Identification of premature ventricular contraction (PVC) of electrocardiogram using statistical tools and non-linear analysis. Glob. J. Res. Eng. (2016)

13. Uzun, S., Asyali, M.H., Celebi, G., Pehlivan, M.: Nonlinear analysis of heart rate variability. In: Proceedings of the 23rd Annual EMBS International Conference, pp. 1581–1584 (2001)

14. Signorini, M.G., Sassi, R., Lombardi, F., Cerutti, S.: Regularity patterns in heart rate variability signal: the approximate entropy approach. In: Proceedings of the 20th Annual International Conference of the IEEE Engineering in Medicine and Biology Society. Biomedical Engineering Towards the Year 2000 and Beyond (Cat. No. 98CH36286), vol. 20, pp. 306–309. IEEE (1998)

15. Minami, K., Nakajima, H., Toyoshima, T.: Real-time discrimination of ventricular tachyarrhythmia with Fourier-transform neural network. IEEE Trans. Biomed. Eng. **46**(2), 179–185 (1999)

16. Acharya, R., Kannathal, N., Sing, O.W., Ping, L.Y., Chua. T.L.: Heart rate analysis in normal subjects of various age groups. Biomed. Eng. Online **3**(1), 1–8 (2004)

17. Jayalalith, S., Susan, D., Kumari, S., Archana, B.: K-nearest neighbour method of analysing the ECG signal (To find out the different disorders related to heart). J. Appl. Sci. **14**(14), 1628–1632 (2014)

18. Christov, I., Jekova, I., Bortolan, G.: Premature ventricular contraction classification by the Kth nearest-neighbours rule. Physiol. Meas. **26**(1), 123 (2005)

19. Moody, G.B., Mark, R.G.: The impact of the MIT-BIH arrhythmia database. IEEE Eng. Med. Biol. Mag. **20**(3), 45–50 (2001)

20. Islam, M.M., Uddin, J., Kashem, M.A., Rabbi, F., Hasnat, M.W.: Design and implementation of an IoT system for predicting aqua fisheries using arduino and KNN. In: Singh, M., Kang, D.-K., Lee, J.-H., Tiwary, U.S., Singh, D., Chung, W.-Y. (eds.) IHCI 2020. LNCS, vol. 12616, pp. 108–118. Springer, Cham (2021). https://doi.org/10.1007/978-3-030-68452-5_11

21. Soumaya, Z., Taoufiq, B.D., Benayad, N., Yunus, K., Abdelkrim, A.: The detection of Parkinson disease using the ge-netic algorithm and SVM classifier. Appl. Acoust. **171**, 107528 (2021)

22. Velusamy, D., Ramasamy, K.: Ensemble of heterogeneous classifiers for diagnosis and prediction of coronary artery disease with reduced feature subset. Comput. Meth. Prog. Biomed. **198**, 105770 (2021)

Telekit: An IoT Based Wearable Health Assistant with Machine Learning Approach

Md. Shahnauze Ahsan[1] and Md. Imran Uddin[2(✉)]

[1] Ahsan's Lab, Chittagong, Bangladesh
[2] Chittagong University of Engineering and Technology, Chittagong, Bangladesh
imranuddin.puc.eee@gmail.com

Abstract. Maintaining a healthier lifestyle is quite implausible for the mass people of developing countries like Bangladesh. Instead of regular health checkups, here folks only seek the treatment at the stage of enervate. To ameliorate this situation, in this study, we have proposed a low-cost wearable fitness device named "TeleKit". We envisioned targeting middle-aged people who are most of the time reluctant to take health precautions. Our developed system is capable of detecting Oxygen saturation, pulse rate, and the temperature of the human body. To monitor these physical parameters we have also developed an Android app with a pop-up notification feature. We also classified and aggregated the collected data through an IoT network. Applying a machine learning algorithm we demonstrate the correlation between the health parameters that will help us to predict and take necessary steps before any serious disease. This device will play a crucial role as an emergency, app notification will help the end-users to take necessary precautions. The outcome of this research would help the health service provider, and the decision-makers to provide low-cost health kit facilities, especially in rural areas.

Keywords: IoT · Wearable · Health assistant · Machine learning · Spo2 · Wemos

1 Introduction

The health sector is one of the most sensitive phenomena for densely populated countries. A mass number of people don't maintain a regular health checkup and suffer in a long run. To motivate those people a low-cost health kit would be a fruitful solution. Various types of health kits are available in the market and people simply avoid those expensive Health kits. A cost-effective and user-friendly device would change this scenario. Again with the immense development of information technology, the Internet of Things, cloud technology, and artificial intelligence is playing a significant impact on the progress of this health sector. Consequently, researchers are also developing varieties of e-Health and m-Health devices.

The survey showed in [1], approaches that different types of wearable sensors have the profound potential for governing and diagnosing the early symptoms of the disease concerning contagious diseases. In the field of customized healthcare, IoT technology holds enormous potential and benefits. The wireless body area network is considered the primary enabler, which consists of communication modules and wearable sensor devices. The smartphone is used as a data processing, illustration, and transmission gateway in the greater percentage of existing wearable health monitoring systems. However, such types of a system need the program to run all day long, which has a significant impact on typical mobile phone usage. Wifi-based cloud technology can utilize for such kinds of wearable sensor data acquisition [2].

Patients' health conditions could be monitored remotely on a real-time basis, emergencies can be correctly defined, and related people like doctors and family members can be notified as needed. Multiple types of wearable IoT wearable health device has been introduced in [3–5].

A rational IoT-based wearable health assistance system was also introduced in [6]. Intelligent systems like fuzzy logic, machine learning, deep learning, convolutional neural networks process are also used nowadays. Prediction systems through the ML and types of AI-based chatbots help us to take necessary precautions before any kind of serious health disease.

In our study, we tried to smooth collecting, analyzing, and evaluate the basic health parameters of the data through an IoT network. We designed a web and android application interface based on the various types of profiles. To keep the communication system running smoothly, the mobile app and web interface are linked together. Our targeted mid-aged people, who are at high risk of health issues will be able to use this device easily. Pop-up notifications from the app will notify the users to take the necessary steps. Finally, after the required data collection steps, we have applied logical regression to those data and tried to predict the illness. So, we can say that our study focuses to promote a low-cost and end user-friendly health assistant which is centered on the following objectives:

- To collect the user's health data using wearable sensors.
- To process the data, and send it to the IoT server.
- To make an authentication platform that will be capable of the store and make further notifications.
- To approach the machine learning algorithm and forecast the illness of the user.

The whole study is allocated into five parts. Where Sect. 2 is focused on the literature survey. Section 3 discusses the proposed system architecture and Sect. 4 is the machine learning approach. The result is analyzed in Sect. 5, before fulfillment of our study with the epilogue and future works in Sect. 6.

2   Literature Survey

Numerous researchers worked on IoT-based healthcare systems. In this section, we tried to feature the gist of those.

2.1   Wearable Sensors in Healthcare

Wearable devices are becoming more technologically advanced day by day. As a result, contributions in this subject will never be obsolete because it improves the daily lifestyle of health-conscious people. A person's breathing rate is a relatively new statistic that isn't often used in wearable devices. This metric by itself can reveal data about a person's health. Wearable sensors are also capable of predicting a heart attack, fall monitoring, and Cardiorespiratory inspection which could be utilized as a personal safety kit with real-time data monitoring [7, 8].

Heart rate and SpO2 detectors are primarily used for patients suffering from cardiovascular disease or respiratory arrest. Doctors suggest individuals must go through check-up his pulse rate and oxygen saturation level at least once a month. Folks can easily acknowledge their SpO2 level, heart rate, and body temperature using this health kit. Authors in [9] disclose that these sensors also can be used for patients who are unable to go to the healthcare center due to an emergency. Patient data will be encrypted, and the detector is affordable, so it saves patients time while also reducing their expenditure.

We chose three wearable sensors which are capable of monitoring heart rate, Oxigen Saturation, and body temperature.

2.2 IoT Network Platform

In the last decade, the IoT has made each thing internally connected, and it has been considered the next technical revolution. Boards and sensors are constantly monitored through various types of IoT dashboards. These IoT dashboards are modern tools and we use to display and arrange the data coming from sensing elements toward our machines. IoT platforms are loaded with graphs, charts, and various widgets.

It's tough to keep track of patients in different locations where there aren't enough skilled med techs. A researcher in [10] proposed a system use of Wi-Fi to enable access to any location having an internet service or a 3G/4G network by establishing an appropriate access point. A wireless IoT gadget that gathers ECG, respiratory airflow, and blood oxygenation of patients and communicates this information to the central database to track more patients effectively and can save working time.

The Authors in [11] implemented an IoT device that connects the fitness gears. Through IoT Network, the trainer provides a user workout prescription. According to the findings, people with an uneven exercise routine had significantly improved flexibility, power, muscular endurance, and cardiovascular fitness. We used an IoT platform "Thinkspeak" to demonstrate and store health data.

2.3 Prospect of Android Apps in Healthcare

An android mobile app helps the user to monitor fitness data easily. Various types of fitness apps are available nowadays. The Authors in [12] designed a custom app using the MIT App Inventor platform. They designed the hardware with body temperature and a pulse oximeter sensor which is connected to the App with Bluetooth.

In [13], scholars developed a Chatbot using the Convolutional Neural Network algorithm. They improvised the Facebook messenger apps API which is capable of replying to the solution of the disease.

Another m-Health approach has been developed by [14], where an android based app has been introduced for healthcare service. Their app also offers an intelligent symptom classifier, which takes user-provided symptoms and converts them into medical conditions. It then develops a collection of questionnaires and asks the user through interaction to forecast the most likely medical condition based on the user's input, which the system understands. We also developed a custom app using the Android Studio platform to monitor and notify the user of health conditions.

2.4 Machine Learning as a Tool for Disease Prediction

Nowadays ML has plenty of uses in the healthcare industry, which are currently being discovered and researched. Early recognition of disease has a significant influence on the current process and it decreases the risk of survival. There has been numerous recent progress in ML technology, which is assisting the medical industry to treat patients effectively. To forecast health parameter conditions, researchers used various types of ML algorithms for instance, CNN, ANN, K-NN, random forest, Naïve Bayes classifier [15–17].

The Authors in [18] proposed a system that can predict and monitor the children's health status applying the Ensemble technique. In another approach, Hidden Markov Model has been applied to monitor a patient's heart status remotely [19].

Multiple binary classification techniques are available that can be used to diagnose health diseases. The best classification technique for classifying the risk of health disease is logistic regression. Researchers in [20, 21] worked with logistic regression to predict health status. On the other hand authors in [22] found better accuracy in ordinal forest classification than logistic regression to predict health fitness.

Analyzing all prediction algorithms we applied Random Forest classification to predict the user's illness accessing the data from the IoT server.

3 Proposed System Architecture

Our proposed systems block diagram has been shown in Fig. 1. When the finger of a person is placed in the MAX30100 sensor the operation of the device begins, where the in-built photodiode of the sensor accomplishes the detection process of transmitted Red and IR light-based on getting power connection. By measuring the absorption ratio between Red and IR light the percentage of oxygen saturation (SpO2) is discovered. In the meantime, the variation of blood density throughout the finger facilitates the detection of pulse rate. Afterward, an Analog to Digital converter (ADC) converts the data with a renowned consecutive process of Sampling, Quantization, and Coding. The binary coded data of ADC is sent to 60 Hz Low Pass Filter where it filters out the power line and ambient noise.

On the other hand, the Temperature sensor measures the body temperature based on upgrading its output voltage by 10 mv with the increase of 1 °C of body temperature and address the data to WemosD1 mini ESP8266 Wi-Fi-based micro-controller.

The data exchange pathway among sensors and micro-controller board is facilitated with I2C serial communication where WemosD1 mini does the duty of a master and sensor play the key rule for slave devices. Now controller board processes the data and upload it to the channels of an IoT live data Streaming server named as ThingSpeak.

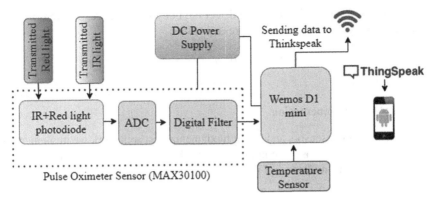

Fig. 1. Block diagram of IoT based wearable health assistant

From the live Streaming Server allocated channel data will retrieve to the Android App after every 10 ms by reading and write the API key.

At last, the Android app data will be analyzed based on the data ranges are shown in Table 1. For normal range, it visualizes as normal, if the value is lower or higher than the normal range a pop-up notification will send to the Android app users by which a user can take the necessary step for ensuring life-saving First Aid.

Table 1. Data ranges for the notifications from the App.

Data	Normal	Low	High
Spo2	95–100%	<95%	–
Pulse rate	60–90 BPM	<60 BPM	>90 BPM
Body temperature	97–99.5 °F	<97 °F	>99.5 °F

3.1 Sensing System

Pulse Oximeter sensor is capable of sensing Oxygen saturation (SpO2) which is an indispensable component of the health care approach. Normal oxygen saturation levels in humans are 95–100.

SpO2 percentage can be expressed below:

$$\% SpO2 = 110 - 25 \times R \tag{1}$$

where $R = (AC\ RMS\ of\ Red/DC\ of\ Red)/(AC\ RMS\ of\ IR/DC\ of\ IR)$

Body Temperature is considered one of the prominent signs indicating infection in the human body. It differs based on age, person, activity, and time on the day. The Normal human body temperature is 97 °F. The Infant and children may have a little higher temperature than usual. Temperature above 100.4 °F is considered as fever or infection. We used the LM35 sensor to detect the body temperature. The temperature measurement procedure of LM35 is expressed below:

$$Vout = 10 \, mv/°C \times T \tag{2}$$

3.2 Hardware Implementation

After collecting all the sensors and doing fundamental research work we implement all the sensors with the WemosD1 mini micro-controller board and attached a wrist band. Our final setup has been shown in Fig. 2.

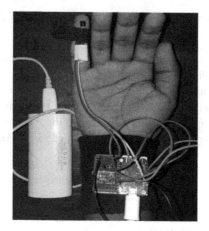

Fig. 2. IoT-based wearable health assistant Hardware setup.

3.3 Android App

To visualize the Pulse rate, Oxygen Saturation, and Body Temperature data we develop an Android App, which is named "TeleKit", as shown in Fig. 3. We used Android Studio to design the graphical user interface (GUI). It displays the numeric value of data as well as whether the data is low or high. If the health data goes to the abnormal range a notification will pop up on the user's mobile screen to get notified about upcoming dangerous health conditions.

3.4 Interfacing and Communication

Our device starts working when the DC power source is applied. Then system proceeded to initialize the I2C communication between sensors and micro-controller. The micro-controller board processes the sensor's data and uploads it to the ThingSpeak server. Depending on the wi-Fi status our Telekit app is connected to the Hardware as well as the Thinkspeak server. ThingSpeak server has been used to store data for a future healthcare perspective. This IoT server data sync to the Android app after 10mili seconds. Then

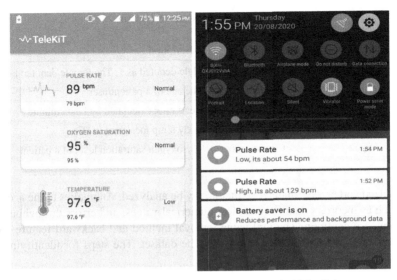

Fig. 3. Telekit android app (Developed in Android Studio)

the android app will classify the data based on the Table1 data range. If the data is high a pop-up notification will visualize in the mobile window and terminate the process and in the case of the normal data range, it displays as normal in the app screen and end the full process.

4 Machine Learning Approach

Numerous machine learning approaches are available, which helps to train and test the dataset. This function takes a data input, executes a task, and then returns the result. In the case of assisting train and testing the dataset, numerous ML algorithms are available. These algorithms complete their task by taking input values to perform the associated function and results in the output. To train up our model 70% of data has been used and the rest 30% for testing. Classifiers take into account the elements like the temperature, heart rate, SpO2 type of health parameter, and correspondingly classify the patient concerning the illness.

4.1 Data Description

Our dataset has 75 rows with five independent variables shown in Table 2. The health condition value is dependant on these independent features.

4.2 Data Preprocessing

It is plausible that the dataset used during training and validation contains errors and redundant data. The data screening technique is essential for creating a trustworthy dataset and enhancing data accuracy. Data cleaning is the process of cleansing data in

Table 2. Data types and description

Sl No	Feature name	Feature type	Description
1	Gender	Discrete	Male denoted as 1, The female denoted as 0
2	Age	Discrete	The age of a patient/user
3	Heart rate	Continuous	Heart rate; calculated by beats/minute
4	Temperature	Continuous	Body temp measured in °F
5	Spo2	Continuous	The oxygen saturation level of a patient

an organized and precise manner so that it may be analyzed. Anomalies in the acquired data, such as incorrect data formats, lost numerical values, and errors throughout data collection, are common. The null value removal method and backward feature elimination methods were being used to cleanse the dataset. The steps for identifying and classifying errors are as follows.

- The very first step in data cleaning is to look for missing data or void values to cope with them just to enhance the precision. There are 9 missing data out of 75 rows, corresponding to around 12% of the total data.
- In this scenario, the best method is to delete any rows with null values.

4.3 Data Splitting

Data should be divided into two segments for algorithm training and testing. The classifier is constructed on the training dataset, which comprises well-known classified output, before getting applied to others. The test set data is then used to evaluate the model's performance using trained data. Two situations would happen during data splitting: the model could be overfitting or underfitting. Both are terrible for the output of the system. In our system, we split the data in the proportion of 70–30%

4.4 Model Training and Testing

Our proposed system can detect the illness of a patient based on provided basic health data. One dependent variable and four independent variables exist in the dataset. The logistic Regression is originated from statistics and it is proved to be the most effective than any other Algorithm. An LR classifier with a single-degree hypothesis has been followed by Eq. 3.

$$H(x) = sigmoid\,(\theta_0 + \theta_1 \times x_1 + \theta_2 \times x_2) \tag{3}$$

H(x) is the proposition in Eq. (3). θ_0, θ_1, θ_2 are SpO2, Heartrate, and body temperature values respectively, x1 and x2 are the mean values of age and health condition. Sigmoid is a function that is defined in Eq. 4 as follows.

$$sigmoid\,(z) = \frac{1}{1 + e^{-z}} \tag{4}$$

5   Result Analysis

5.1   Data Accuracy

We collect 75 different people's Pulse, Oxygen saturation, and body temperature data with our device. At the same time, we also crosscheck the health data through a standard Pulse-oximeter and a medical Thermometer for comparing our device efficiency. After about three months of continuous data checking, we calculated the percentage error of received data. Finally get our device efficiency for Oxygen saturation, Pulse rate, and Body temperature sequentially in the percentage of 96.25%, 94.75%, 98.875%. Survey data and graph of the survey data compared with standard data is demonstrated below sequentially with bearing Fig. 4. The data comparison with the standard medical device has been shown in Fig. 5.

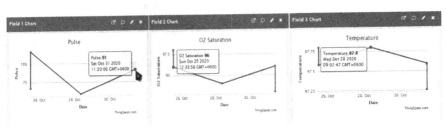

Fig. 4. Pulse, oxygen saturation and body temp data in IoT server (From thinkspeak channel)

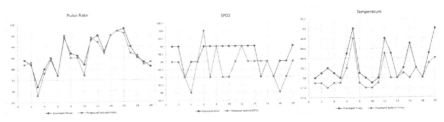

Fig. 5. Device efficiency compared with standard data (Pulse Rate, SPO2, and Temperature)

The average error in Oxygen saturation (SpO2) is 0.75 and the percentage error is 3.75%. After subtracting the average error we found the efficiency is 96.25%. For the Pulse rate, we found the average error of 1.05, and the percentage error is 5.25%, which results in an efficiency of 94.75%. For temperature sensor LM35, the average error is 0.225 and the percentage error is 1.125%. And its efficiency came out 98.875%. Analyzing the price and availability the comparison result among professional medical devices delineates that, our low-cost device would be efficient than other kits available in the market.

5.2   Scatter Plot and Correlation Matrix

We have taken an approach to machine learning using received data from the Thinkspeak server. We used the 'Google Colab' platform to depict and predict the data output. We used Numpy, pandas, and Matplot library at the beginning of the computation. The scatter plot and correlation matrix between a label and its parameters are shown in Fig. 6, which is established during model training. This is a representation of the model with a series of dataset examples. Model training takes place when each representation emphasizes how each feature affects the label.

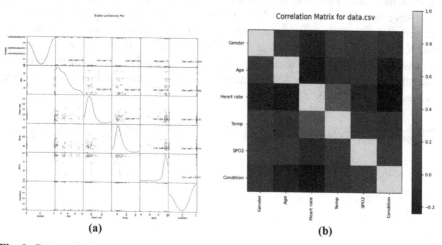

Fig. 6. Data analysis applying ML **a.** Scatter and the density plot of health data **b.** Correlation matrix

5.3 Illness Prediction

Applying logistic regression, binary classification has been done. The core of logistic regression is the sigmoid function and applying these 440 times of the iteration regression result graph shown in Fig. 7. We found the test accuracy 0.6 and train accuracy 0.67.

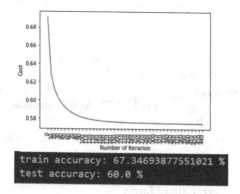

Fig. 7. Logistic regression to predict the Illness.

6 Conclusion and Future Scope

The utmost intent of this study is to enhance a low-cost efficient device in association with an IoT platform for checking and monitoring some vital health parameters and Fitness issues instantly. We hope this device TeleKit will reduce the hassle of going to the hospital and save transportation costs by notifying health data a user. The ThingSpeak server also helps the user for using data from a future health care perspective. Again, our developed ML approach is also capable of predicting the illness of the user. Some vital physical parameters like pulse rate, oxygen saturation, and body temperature will be updated continuously in the server and it will increase the model accuracy.

We have found the success percentage between the actual and observed data is identical for every aspect of the developed fitness assistance device. Finally, our optimistic mind motivates us that, this device will be a door-to-door wearable health assistant kit soon.

Acknowledgments. We are blessed to the people who participated in the survey of our TeleKit. We are also thankful to Ahsan's Lab for providing some technical and logistic support.

References

1. Mohammadzadeh, N., Gholamzadeh, M., Saeedi, S., et al.: The application of wearable smart sensors for monitoring the vital signs of patients in epidemics: a systematic literature review. J. Ambient Intell. Human. Comput. 1–15 (2020). https://doi.org/10.1007/s12652-020-02656-x
2. Wan, J., et al.: Wearable IoT enabled real-time health monitoring system. EURASIP J. Wirel. Commun. Netw. **1**(1), 298 (2018). https://doi.org/10.1186/s13638-018-1308-x
3. Manas, M., Sinha, A., Sharma, S., Mahboob, M.R.: A novel approach for IoT based wearable health monitoring and messaging system. J. Ambient. Intell. Humaniz. Comput. **10**(7), 2817–2828 (2018). https://doi.org/10.1007/s12652-018-1101-z
4. Islam, M.M., Rahaman, A., Islam, M.R.: Development of smart healthcare monitoring system in IoT environment. SN Comput. Sci. **1**(3), 1–11 (2020). https://doi.org/10.1007/s42979-020-00195-y
5. Chiuchisan, I., Geman, O., Hagan, M.: Wearable sensors in intelligent clothing for human activity monitoring. In: 2019 International Conference on Sensing and Instrumentation in IoT Era (ISSI), pp. 1-4 (2019). https://doi.org/10.1109/ISSI47111.2019.9043649
6. Kassem, A., Tamazin, M., Aly, M.H.: An intelligent IoT-based wearable health monitoring system. In: Farouk, M.H., Hassanein, M.A. (eds.) Recent Advances in Engineering Mathematics and Physics, pp. 373–389. Springer, Cham (2020). https://doi.org/10.1007/978-3-030-39847-7_29
7. Savla, D.V., Parekh, S., Gupta, A.R., Agarwal, D., Shekokar, N.M.: ResQ - smart safety band automated heart rate and fall monitoring system. In: 2020 Fourth International Conference on I-SMAC (IoT in Social, Mobile, Analytics and Cloud) (I-SMAC), pp. 588–593 (2020). https://doi.org/10.1109/I-SMAC49090.2020.9243548
8. Sasidharan, P., Rajalakshmi, T., Snekhalatha, U.: Wearable cardiorespiratory monitoring device for heart attack prediction. In: 2019 International Conference on Communication and Signal Processing (ICCSP), pp. 0054-0057 (2019). https://doi.org/10.1109/ICCSP.2019.8698059

9. Natarasan, S., Sekar, P.: Design and implementation of heartbeat rate and SpO2 detector by using IoT for patients. In: 2020 International Conference on Electronics and Sustainable Communication Systems (ICESC), pp. 630-636 (2020). https://doi.org/10.1109/ICESC4 8915.2020.9155925

10. Zilani, K.A., Yeasmin, R., Zubair, K.A., Sammir, M.R., Sabrin, S.: R3HMS, an IoT based approach for patient health monitoring. In: 2018 International Conference on Computer, Communication, Chemical, Material and Electronic Engineering (IC4ME2), pp. 1–4 (2018). https://doi.org/10.1109/IC4ME2.2018.8465482

11. Hsu, C.T., Chang, Y.H., Chen, J.S., Lin, H.H., Chou, J.Y.: Implementation of IoT device on public fitness equipment for health physical fitness improvement. In: 2020 International Conference on Mathematics and Computers in Science and Engineering (MACISE), pp. 236-239 (2020).https://doi.org/10.1109/MACISE49704.2020.00050

12. Mohsen, S., Zekry, A., Youssef, K., Abouelatta, M.: A self-powered wearable wireless sensor system powered by a hybrid energy harvester for healthcare applications. Wireless Pers. Commun. 116(4), 3143–3164 (2020). https://doi.org/10.1007/s11277-020-07840-y

13. Rai, S., Raut, A., Savaliya, A., Shankarmani, R.: Darwin: convolutional neural network based intelligent health assistant. In: 2018 Second International Conference on Electronics, Communication and Aerospace Technology (ICECA), pp. 1367–1371 (2018). https://doi.org/10.1109/ICECA.2018.8474861

14. Gandhi, M., Singh, V.K., Kumar, V.: IntelliDoctor - AI based medical assistant. In: 2019 Fifth International Conference on Science Technology Engineering and Mathematics (ICONSTEM), pp. 162-168 (2019).https://doi.org/10.1109/ICONSTEM.2019.8918778

15. Sinha, A., Mathew, R.: Machine learning algorithms for early prediction of heart disease. In: Pandian, A.P., Palanisamy, R., Ntalianis, K. (eds.) ICCBI 2019. LNDECT, vol. 49, pp. 162–168. Springer, Cham (2020). https://doi.org/10.1007/978-3-030-43192-1_18

16. Shah, D., Patel, S., Bharti, S.K.: Heart disease prediction using machine learning techniques. SN Comput. Sci. 1(6), 1–6 (2020). https://doi.org/10.1007/s42979-020-00365-y

17. Merenda, M., Astrologo, M., Laurendi, D., Romeo, V., Della Corte, F.G.: A novel fitness tracker using edge machine learning. In: 2020 IEEE 20th Mediterranean Electrotechnical Conference (MELECON), pp. 212–215 (2020). https://doi.org/10.1109/MELECON48756.2020.9140602

18. Nigar, N., Chowdhury, L.: An intelligent children healthcare system by using ensemble technique. In: Uddin, M.S., Bansal, J.C. (eds.) Proceedings of International Joint Conference on Computational Intelligence. AIS, pp. 137–150. Springer, Singapore (2020). https://doi.org/10.1007/978-981-13-7564-4_12

19. Meng, Y., et al.: A machine learning approach to classifying self-reported health status in a cohort of patients with heart disease using activity tracker data. IEEE J. Biomed. Health Inform. 24(3), 878–884 (2020). https://doi.org/10.1109/JBHI.2019.2922178

20. Swain, D., Ballal, P., Dolase, V., Dash, B., Santhappan, J.: An efficient heart disease prediction system using machine learning. In: Swain, D., Pattnaik, P.K., Gupta, P.K. (eds.) Machine Learning and Information Processing. AISC, vol. 1101, pp. 39–50. Springer, Singapore (2020). https://doi.org/10.1007/978-981-15-1884-3_4

21. Jain, Y., Chowdhury, D., Chattopadhyay, M.: Machine learning based fitness tracker platform using MEMS accelerometer. In: 2017 International Conference on Computer, Electrical & Communication Engineering (ICCECE), pp. 1–5 (2017). https://doi.org/10.1109/ICCECE.2017.8526202

22. Mahajan, U., Krishnan, A., Malhotra, V., Sharma, D., Gore, S.: Predicting fitness and performance of diving using machine learning algorithms. In: 2019 IEEE Pune Section International Conference (PuneCon), pp. 1–5 (2019).https://doi.org/10.1109/PuneCon46936.2019.9105817

An Empirical Feature Selection Approach for Phishing Websites Prediction with Machine Learning

Pankaj Bhowmik[1]([⊠]) [iD], Md. Sohrawordi[1] [iD], U. A. Md. Ehsan Ali[1] [iD], and Pulak Chandra Bhowmik[2] [iD]

[1] Department of Computer Science and Engineering, Hajee Mohammad Danesh Science and Technology University (HSTU), Dinajpur 5200, Bangladesh
pankaj.cshstu@gmail.com, ehsan_cse@hstu.ac.bd
[2] Department of Computer Science and Engineering, Stamford University Bangladesh, Dhaka 1217, Bangladesh

Abstract. The proportion of phishing attacks has soared worldwide amid the Covid-19 crisis since people started using the internet more actively. Browsing phishing websites can cause immense damage to user privacy. In this article, investigating the attributes of URLs to detect the possible legitimate and phishing websites, we presented a feature selection framework that improves the efficacy of machine learning models. In feature selection, considering the filter and wrapper method, we introduced an empirical hybrid framework that comprises two phases. To derive the accumulative feature subset, in the early stage, we performed a function perturbation ensemble using four filter techniques. Finally, to select the best features, we employed the wrapper method, in which the feature subset is passed into a statistical model to perform a p-value test (conforming 95% confidence). We used two phishing datasets, and applying this proposed hybrid ensemble framework, we derived only 45.95% of the initial features from each dataset. Thereafter, the optimized (hyperparameters) models such as Artificial Neural Network, XGBoost Classifier, Random Forest Classifier are applied to conduct 10-folds cross-validation on Data-I, the XGBoost Classifier outran with the accuracy of 96.08%. Besides, the XGBoost model performed prediction on Data-II, achieved a notable accuracy of 97.29%.

Keywords: Phishing detection · Empirical feature selection · Machine learning

1 Introduction

During the COVID-19 lockdown, the Internet has become truly essential to perform everyday tasks. Several facilities and services are getting digitalized daily. Besides, people are embracing this trend because of the conveniences they get out of it. Particularly, online marketing and banking transactions achieved utmost popularity. But, hackers always try to break the security protocols of the Internet to steal confidential information of users. They attempt to seduce people and mug private data through forged websites [1]. One of the common ways to do this is the phishing attack, a well-known cybercrime. Cyber-criminals usually replicate the contents of original websites to make the users believe that they are surfing authentic information. Besides, attackers often try to install malware by forwarding spam emails or links on social media to take control over a user system. Spam links redirect the users to phishing websites while they click on them unknowingly. As a result, people disclose their private data e.g., passwords, credit card info to hackers. The phishers usually target specific organizations such as banks, govt. database centers, defense and law enforcement agencies, and people such as celebrities, govt. officials. Phishing attack has become considerably sophisticated lately and one of the routine cyber crimes these days [2].

In these circumstances, phishing attacks are becoming a burning concern for cyber-security departments all over the world. To address this cynical issue, researchers and cyber-security experts are constantly working hard—besides, they proposed different possible solutions [3]. Phishing attacks detection based on 'Blacklist' is one of the popular preventive approaches, web browsers use this list to warn users about a potential phishing website. The 'Blacklist' contains the universal resource locator (URL) of all known phishing websites. If a surfed URL is listed on the Blacklist, then it's a phishing website and legitimate otherwise, the browsers provide warnings accordingly. But the drawback is, as tons of phishing websites are developing in a daily manner, and if the 'Blacklist' is not updated, browsers will not be able to detect the newly generated phishing URLs. Besides, hackers deploy dynamic methods to crack the 'Blacklist' approach which can be a major threat, and they also develop mirror URLs to exploit the security loopholes. However, the 'Whitelist' approach works oppositely. It contains a list of legitimate websites, and the browsers allow only the listed sites to pass through the system gateway [4]. Besides, in the heuristic-based technique, which is an extended variant of the listing-based method, URLs and other features are extracted from websites and compared with ground-list to decide websites legitimacy [5, 6]. On the other hand, machine learning (ML) based phishing attacks detection is becoming more dominating lately. In ML approaches, lists of features are extracted from URLs to predict phishing sites, as a result, these methods can effectively combat the dynamic changes of phishing attacks. The traditional ML algorithms and neural networks are doing great jobs to detect phishing websites. These robust ML models perform significantly well and are much reliable [1, 7].

In URL-based phishing websites detection, many features are extracted but not all of them are equally important. Consequently, researchers have introduced several feature selection methods to rank and select the best features from the feature space. To cite an example, Chiew et al. [8] established a novel feature selection framework named hybrid ensemble feature selection which has two phases: data perturbation and function perturbation. The data perturbation cycle derived the primary and secondary feature subsets gradually, and the final features are obtained from the function perturbation ensemble cycle. The combination of both these cycles results in a hybrid ensemble feature selection. Waleed Ali [9], on the other hand, experimented with two feature selection approaches for phishing website detection. The performance of the proposed ML models revealed that wrapper-based feature selection outperformed the filter method. Barbara Pes et al. [10] established an ensemble-based substantial approach for feature selection. They experimented with the data perturbation strategy using a set of feature selection methods. In general, they found that the ensemble feature subsets provide good outcomes, particularly in terms of stability.

In this article, we propose a hybrid feature selection framework to derive the best features from phishing datasets and thus to detect phishing websites effectively and with ease. The feature selection framework has two phases—at the beginning phase, a set of filter methods are applied to select the primary feature subsets from the dataset and then obtained the secondary (accumulative) feature subset with the function perturbation ensemble. In the final phase, the wrapper method is applied where the secondary feature subset fed is in a statistical model (Bi-directional elimination) to select the best features with a 'p-value test' ensuring 95% confidence. We used two latest phishing datasets of Grega Vrbančič for the experiment, available on Mendeley. In this proposed study, we have attempted to find out answers to the following research questions:

RQ-1: How does the Hybrid Feature Selection approach boost the efficacy of ML models to perform better?

RQ-2: Can the proposed framework outrun the previous research findings?

2 Related Studies

Over the years, scholars and cyber-security experts have developed several methods to combat phishing attacks. Until now, the performance of the ML-based approaches reflects their superiority over the conventional methods. In this section, we shed some light on the contemporary ML-based solutions introduced by the researchers to fight against phishing attack.

Based on the datasets we used in this study, Vrbančič et al. presented a method to address the parameter setting issue of deep neural networks (DNN). They applied swarm intelligence meta-heuristic algorithms (bat algorithm, firefly algorithm) to optimize DNNs parameters. They used four phishing datasets for their experiment and achieved promising outcomes in classifying phishing websites—the proposed firefly method outplayed. Considering Vrbančič's small and full dataset, the firefly method showed an accuracy rate of 90.17% and 94.39% respectively, in cross-validation [11].

Detecting phishing websites based on URLs, ensemble learning models showed better performance compared to the individual traditional algorithms. Mohammed Al-Sarem et al. [2] proposed an optimized ensemble method considering the stacking approach. They experimented with six ML classifier models, and the parameters of those models were optimized using a genetic algorithm (GA). Following that, the models were ranked to select the best three classifiers to perform stacking ensemble. However, the ensemble model with SVM as meta-learner showed an accuracy of 97.39% on Vrbančič full_data. In another study, Yazan Ahmad Alsariera et al. [7] developed meta-learner models in which Extra-tree classifier is considered as the base classifier. The LogitBoost-Extra Tree model achieved the highest accuracy of 97.58% with a false-positive rate of 0.018 in cross-validation. To deal with the dynamism of phishing attacks, Adeyemo et al. [12] proposed an ensemble-based approach that combines the tree induction and logistic regression techniques. They integrated the bagging and boosting methods with the base algorithm 'Logistic Model Tree' to build more effective models. However, they used two phishing datasets and achieved a minimum accuracy of 97.18% with the proposed models.

Neural network models tend to be highly efficient for detecting phishing websites. The existing studies showed that these models can predict phishing and legitimate websites mostly with above 90% accuracy, and provide a lower false-positive rate. A deep learning approach is conducted by Somesha et al. [1] to predict the legitimacy of websites based on URLs. They applied the Information Gain feature selection method to rank the features and selected the 10 best features for their experiment. Among the three deep learning models (i.e., LSTM, DNN, CNN), the LSTM outperformed with securing an accuracy of 99.57%. In another experiment [13], to find out the best performing algorithm Vaitkevicius and Marcinkevicius used three phishing datasets and eight widely used machine learning algorithms. The findings of the study showed that multilayer perceptron (ANN) and ensemble-based algorithms performed better. Apart from Neural Networks, the tree-based ensemble algorithms performed significantly well in phishing websites prediction. In particular, the Random Forest, Extra Trees, Gradient Tree Boosting showed promising outcomes [7].

There are tons of open-source phishing datasets available for research purposes, and the datasets contain lots of features. However, all the features in a dataset are not reasonably significant, and those features can affect an ML model's performance inversely. Consequently, the feature selection methods can be applied to derive the best features from datasets [8, 14, 15]. Waleed Ali experimented with wrapper and filter-based feature selection approaches on a phishing dataset to build effective ML models. He established 7 ML models and made a comparative analysis of their performance. His study concludes that the ML models considering wrapper-based feature selection surpassed the same models with filter method, and without feature selection [9]. In a study, Chiew et al. [8] established a hybrid ensemble feature selection, in which a set of filter methods are applied to derive feature subsets. They determined the cut-off ranks for selecting features with considering the gradient changes. Besides, the proposed feature selection framework selected only 20.8% of features from the data but achieved promising outcomes from the ML models.

Since the phishing attacks are dynamic in nature, after exploring the previous researches—in general, we can reach a consensus that ML-based methods are much reliable in addressing these cynical attacks. In this article, we introduced a hybrid feature selection framework to boost the performance of proposed models. It's a two-phase hybrid feature selection approach in which filter and wrapper methods are applied accordingly. After selecting the best attributes with this hybrid ensemble approach, the study performed cross-validation and prediction on the datasets. The study experimented with three optimized machine learning models i.e., RFC, XGBC, ANN.

3 Proposed Research Methodology

In this article, we propose an empirical feature selection approach which is more like a hybrid ensemble of the best features from the dataset. In this section, we discussed the overall proposed methodology applied in this study for phishing websites detection. The structure of this methodology has three distinct layers, namely Feature Engineering, Cross-Validation, and Perform Prediction (testing). In this study, we use two phishing website datasets of Vrbančič that are publicly available in Mendeley. We tagged the Vrbančič small_dataset as 'Data-I' and Vrbančič full_dataset as 'Data-II'. The framework of the proposed methodology is illustrated in Fig. 1.

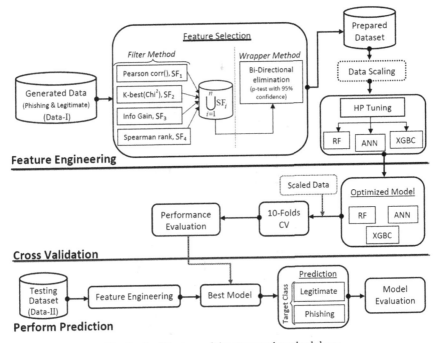

Fig. 1. Architecture of the proposed methodology

Vrbančič collected 58,645 and 88,647 website URLs for Data-I and Data-II respectively and designed a feature extraction algorithm. The algorithm extracts 111 unique features from each URL and saves them in a CSV file. The URLs were collected from Phishtank and Alexa ranking websites, and the instances were labeled (legitimate or phishing) according to the sources [16].

In the Feature Engineering layer, we propose a novel feature selection approach that showed the pathway to derive the best features from the datasets. The feature selection approach, in this study, used a hybrid framework. In this process to select the most important features from Data-I, the raw features are refined through two methods namely the filter method and the wrapper method. In the filter method, the study applied four different techniques such as Pearson correlation (PC), Chi-square (Chi^2), Information Gain (IG), and Spearman correlation rank (SR), and combined the important features with set union operation ($\cup$). Then the feature subset of the filter method is fed to a wrapper method known as Bi-directional elimination (BDE) to select the best features. In the wrapper method, the features are selected with the statistical model which runs a p-value test with 95% confidence intervals, i.e., the probability to accept the null hypothesis is only 5%. Afterward, we get the prepared dataset containing the best features, which is then scaled and fed to the ML models such as Random Forest Classifier, XGBoost Classifier, and Artificial Neural Network for hyperparameter (HP) tuning. Grid Search is applied for tuning the HP of the models, and then the optimized models are passed to the next layer 'Cross Validation'.

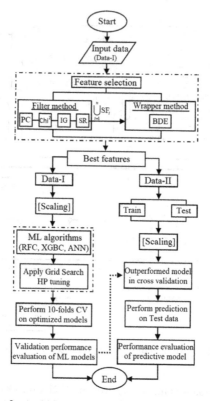

Fig. 2. Architecture of the proposed methodology

In the 'Cross Validation' phase, we performed 10-folds CV on the three optimized models and evaluated their performance. Besides, we made a comparative assessment to find out the outperformed model which is used to perform prediction on Data-II in the succeeding layer. Finally, in the Prediction phase, we split the Data-II into training and testing data then performed prediction on the testing data with the best model. We estimated the model's evaluation metrics to assess its performance in detecting phishing and legitimate websites. The flow of research methodology is shown in Fig. 2.

The experiment was conducted on Jupyter notebook environment using Python programming language. The proposed feature selection algorithm (in Algorithm 1) and ML models are implemented with different python machine learning libraries.

4 Implementation, Results Analysis and Discussion

We carried out the experiment according to the proposed methodology. In this section, we discussed and highlighted the outcomes i.e., statistical modeling and numerical simulation of this experiment.

4.1 Implementation

Dataset Description. The phishing websites dataset used in this experiment is gathered from Mendeley [17]. The dataset was found by Grega Vrbančič, and it has two variants namely, dataset_small (Data-I) and dataset_full (Data-II). He used a feature extraction algorithm to get a list of features from the input (URLs). In general, the features of the datasets can be grouped into 6 classes, such as URL properties, domain properties, URL directory properties, URL file properties, URL parameter properties, and URL resolving data and external metrics. To estimate the value of features, the website URL strings are divided into four sub-strings (domain, directory, file, parameter), besides other external services are considered. Although the number of observations in Data-I and Data-II is 58,645 (phishing-30,647, legitimate-27,998) and 88,647 (phishing-30,647, legitimate-58,000) respectively, both the datasets have an identical and equal number of features (112). The target variable defined as 'phishing', concludes whether an observation of website URL falls in legitimate or phishing class [16] (Fig. 3).

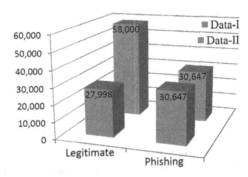

Fig. 3. Graphical representation of Vrbančič's dataset

Feature Engineering. Data-I and Data-II contain 111 features (excluding target variable) each which are one of the highest numbers among the available phishing datasets. However, all these features are not equally useful, and as the number of features increases, the dimension of the data-set also increases. Consequently, we proposed an empirical feature selection approach to select the best features. It's a hybrid approach that applies two methods namely, the filter method and the wrapper method. Filtering the most important feature subsets from the dataset is the first step of this hybrid approach, and in the final step, a wrapper method is applied to select the best features from the feature subset. However, the proposed empirical hybrid feature selection algorithm is noted in Algorithm 1.

Algorithm 1 Empirical Hybrid Feature Selection

Input: Dataset (O,F)   // O= observations, F= features

Output: Best Features

  Initialization:

1: $N \leftarrow$ FILTERMETHODS(Pearson,Chi^2,Info Gain,Spearman)

2: **for** each N **do**   // Filter method

3:   FCV$_i$ = CALCULATEFILTERSCORE(Dataset)

4: **end for**

5: $T_N \leftarrow$ INITIALIZECUTOFF(T$_k$)   // T$_k$= cut-off range of filter methods (N)

6: **for** each F **do**

7:   **if** FCV$_i \in T_N$ **then**   // Primary feature subset

8:       $SF_j = \bigcup\limits_{i-1}^{F} FCV_i$ // Set union operation

9:   **end if**

10: **end for**   // BFF = Best filtered feature

11:   $BFF = \bigcup\limits_{i-1}^{N} SF_j$ // Function perturbation

12: best_feature = []   // Empty list

13: STEPWISEELIMINATION(BFF,SL$_{in}$=0.05,SL$_{out}$=0.05)   // Wrapper method

14: **for** each feature in BFF **do**

15:   p_value = CALCULATEPVALUE(BFF)

16:   **if** p$_{min}$ < SL$_{in}$ **then**   // Forward Selection

17:     **add** to best_feature

18:     **for** each best_feature **do**

19:         **if** p$_{max}$ >= SL$_{out}$ **then**   // Backward Selection

20:           **remove** from best_feature

21:         **else break**

22:     **end for**

23:   **else break**

24: **end for**

25: **return** best_feature

Feature Selection. The filter method, in this study, used four feature selection techniques such as Pearson correlation, Chi-square, Information Gain, and Spearman correlation rank. The techniques estimate the importance score of individual features considering their frequency or correlation with other features. Each technique provides a feature subset (SF) that has the most important features in it. At the end of this method, all the feature subsets are combined with a set union operation—this process is known as 'function perturbation' [8]. Besides, from a technique to select the most correlated features, a cut-off range (Tk) is set. Each technique has an identical cut-off, determined by analyzing and ranking the feature importance scores. A cut-off range [8, 10] defines an optimal extent to select features regarding their importance score. For instance, in Table 1, the cut-off range of Spearman correlation 0.084 to 0.686 demonstrates, only the features having an importance score in this threshold point will be selected with this technique. In this study, cut-off of distinct techniques is gauged manually between the high and low feature importance score i.e., poorly correlated features are excluded. The output of the filter method is a cumulative feature subset (BFF), which is fed to the wrapper method. Subsequently, applying function perturbation ensemble on the feature subsets of four filter techniques i.e., (SF1 ∪ SF2 ∪ SF3 ∪ SF4), we obtained 89 most important features (excluding target feature) from Data-I.

Table 1. Cut-off ranges of feature selection methods

Feature selection method		Cut-off range (Tk)	Selected feature
Filter	Pearson correlation (SF1)	0.087 to 0.627	68
	Chi-square (SF2)	0.00015 to 0.688	61
	Information gain (SF3)	0.0001 to 0.336	59
	Spearman correlation (SF4)	0.084 to 0.686	67
	BFF = (SF1 ∪ SF2 ∪ SF3 ∪ SF4)	–	89
Wrapper	Stepwise elimination	p-test (95% confidence)	**51**

In the wrapper method, the bi-directional elimination (aka, stepwise elimination) technique is applied to finally get the best features set. Bi-directional elimination is a combination of the forward and backward elimination techniques, which aims to find out the features' best correlation. In this technique, a statistical model is built where a p-value test is carried out to select features with peak confidence intervals. Although the computational time required to perform the wrapper method is considerably high compared to the filter method, it selects features with maximum prediction accuracy [18]. Hence, from the filtered features, the best 51 features were selected with the wrapper method conforming 95% confidence intervals. Interestingly, the features from 'URL resolving data and external metrics' are found out to be more important compared to the other groups (in Table 2).

The output feature set of the wrapper method is used as the final features of Data-I and Data-II to perform CV and prediction. As we mentioned, features of the datasets are grouped into 6 classes, in Table 2 the number of features selected from each group is listed respectively. The shape of Data-I and Data-II before feature selection was (58645,112) and (88647,112) respectively. But after applying the proposed feature selection method, the shape reduced significantly to (58645,52) and (88647,52).

Table 2. Number of features selected from each group with feature selection methods

Feature selection	Features in each group of Data-I considering URL properties						Total feature
	URL	Domain	Directory	File	Parameter	External data	
Base data	20	21	18	18	20	14	111
Filter	15	7	17	17	20	13	89
Wrapper	7	6	10	10	5	13	**51**

Afterward, the datasets are scaled with the Min-Max feature scaling method, since data in the real world does not available in a fixed range. Thus, scaling will control the bias of the features having higher weight. Besides, the scaled data allow each feature to pay a uniform contribution in optimizing the target function. In the Min-Max feature scaling method, the data are scaled in a range of 0 to 1.

Hyperparameter Optimization. In this study, we used three machine learning models i.e., Random Forest classifier, XGBoost Classifier, and Artificial Neural Networks to detect phishing websites from the datasets. Machine learning algorithms with default parameters are less likely to perform their best than algorithms with tuned parameters. Therefore, the Grid Search hyperparameter tuning technique is applied to tune the parameters of the three models. This technique used Data-I (train-80%, test-20%) to perform parameter tuning and provides optimized learning models as output. These optimized models are employed to perform cross-validation in layer-2 of the experiment. The optimized hyperparameters of the models are listed in Table 3.

Table 3. Optimized hyperparameters of the ML models

Model	Tuned parameter selected with Grid Search CV
ANN	Optimizer = Adam, learning_rate = 0.0012, epochs = 95, batch_size = 64
RFC	n_estimators = 800, criterion = 'entropy', max_depth = 75, min_samples_leaf = 1, min_samples_split = 2
XGBC	n_estimators = 1000, learning_rate = 0.1, max_depth = 5, min_child_weight = 4, subsample = 0.7, colsample_bytree = 0.8

4.2 Experimental Results Analysis and Discussions

Cross Validation. The study performed 10-folds CV using three optimized models (RFC, XGBC, ANN) on Data-I and estimated their performance evaluation metrics. The study also calculated the Mean Square Error (MSE) rate, and area under curve (AUC) score of each fold in cross-validation. Besides, the mean Receiver Operating Curve (ROC) of each model is estimated. The study made a comparative assessment considering the cross-validation performance of the models, shown in Table 4.

Table 4. Performance comparison of ML models on Data-I in CV

Fold	ANN			RFC			XGBC		
	ACC	*F1*	*MSE*	*ACC*	*F1*	*MSE*	*ACC*	*F1*	*MSE*
1	94.04	94.31	0.0449	96.01	95.98	0.0398	**96.26**	96.24	0.0374
2	93.90	94.25	0.0456	**95.72**	95.71	0.0428	95.62	95.61	0.0438

(continued)

Table 4. (*continued*)

Fold	ANN			RFC			XGBC		
	ACC	*F1*	*MSE*	*ACC*	*F1*	*MSE*	*ACC*	*F1*	*MSE*
3	93.89	94.18	0.0455	95.83	95.82	0.0416	**96.30**	96.29	0.0370
4	93.99	94.32	0.0449	95.87	95.86	0.0412	**96.23**	96.22	0.0377
5	94.09	94.35	0.0441	**95.95**	95.95	0.0404	95.89	95.87	0.0411
6	94.12	94.40	0.0437	95.85	95.83	0.0414	**95.92**	95.91	0.0408
7	94.15	94.43	0.0438	**96.00**	96.00	0.0399	95.72	95.71	0.0428
8	93.74	94.08	0.0455	96.16	96.14	0.0384	**96.54**	96.52	0.0346
9	93.92	94.24	0.0450	95.80	95.80	0.0419	**96.11**	96.10	0.0389
10	94.16	94.40	0.0439	95.94	95.93	0.0405	**96.25**	96.22	0.0375
Avg.	94.00	94.27	0.0447	95.91	95.90	0.0408	**96.08**	96.07	0.0392

In cross-validation, the XGBC model surpassed ANN and RFC in all possible performance evaluation metrics considered in this experiment—accuracy (ACC), for example, is 96.08%, followed by F1-score of 96.07% and the MSE of 0.039. Besides, the RFC model showed a notable performance with an accuracy of 95.91% which is close to XGBC. ANN model, on the other hand, provided a decent outcome securing an accuracy of 94% and F1-score of 94.27%. The average AUC score of XGBC, RFC and ANN is 0.9855, 0.9921, and 0.9923 respectively. Considering the true-positive and false-positive rates, ROC curves of the classifier models are illustrated in Fig. 4.

Perform Prediction. The study performed prediction on Data-II with the best model XGBC. In this circumstance, Data-II is randomly split into 'train data' (80%) and 'test data' (20%). The 'train data' is used to train the predictive model XGBC, and then it performed prediction on 'test data'. Similarly, we used the selected top 51 features for Data-II. The model XGBC concludes whether an unknown instance is legitimate or phishing. Based on that, the study evaluated the model's performance on test data by calculating the evaluation metrics, root mean square error (RMSE), kappa score, error rate, AUC score, and also estimated the ROC curve and precision-recall (PR) curve.

The XGBC model performed prediction prominently good on Data-II. The model secured significant accuracy of 97.29%, F1-score of 97.01. Besides, the model show-ed a kappa score of 94.01%, around 97% of precision and recall score, and a high AUC score of 0.996. It also gained a favorable RMSE rate of 0.1645.

In Fig. 5, the performance assessment metrics of the predictive model XGBC are illustrated with a bar graph. Besides, the confusion matrix gives the information that only 480 observations out of 17,730 testing samples are misclassified where the rest of the samples were truly classified. The true-positive rate is about 0.981, and the false-positive rate of about 0.041. The ROC curve and PR curve of the XGBC classifier model is illustrated in Fig. 6. The ROC curve is based on the true-positive and false-positive rates, where the PR curve is derived from precision and recall rates.

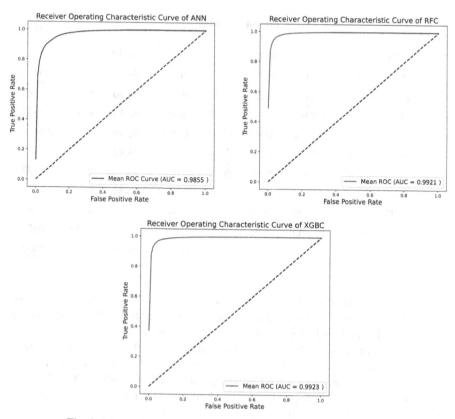

Fig. 4. Mean ROC curve of the ANN, RFC and XGBC model in CV

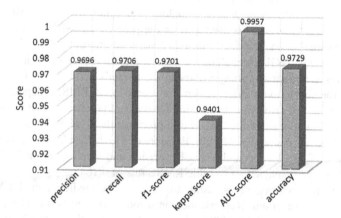

Fig. 5. Prediction performance of XGBC model on Data-II

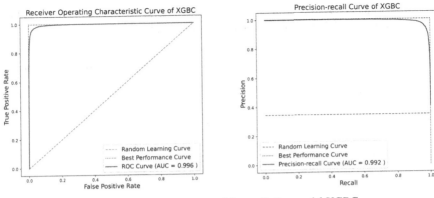

Fig. 6. ROC and PR curve of the predictive model XGBC

With this proposed study, we have achieved a considerable performance in detecting phishing and legitimate websites. As we used the latest phishing datasets for this experiment, only a few pieces of research have been conducted previously on these data. The highlighted outcome of this study is that we used only about 46% of the original features of the data. Cross-validation is performed on Data-I using three optimized machine learning models namely, Random Forest Classifier, XGBoost Classifier, and Artificial Neural Network. The XGBoost classifier model outperformed in CV, and the model is applied to perform prediction on Data-II. Now, let's compare the performance metrics of this proposed study with the existing research works.

Table 5. Performance comparison between the previous and proposed research studies

Dataset	Research reference	Best method	Features	Performance
Data-I	Grega Vrbančič et al. [11]	DNN, optimized with firefly algorithm	111	Accuracy 90.17%, F1-score 90.11%
	Pankaj Bhowmik et al. [proposed method]	XGBoost, with hybrid feature selection	**51**	Accuracy 96.08%, F1-score 96.07%
Data-II	Grega Vrbančič et al. [11]	DNN, optimized with firefly algorithm	111	Accuracy 94.39%, F1-score 93.83%
	Mohammed Al-Sarem et al. [2]	Stacking ensemble, GA-based optimization	111	Accuracy 97.39%
	Pankaj Bhowmik et al. [proposed method]	XGBoost, with hybrid feature selection	**51**	Accuracy 97.29%, F1-score 97.01%

Discussion. On Data-II, the stacking model by Al-Sarem et al. performed slightly better compared to our model since their model used all the 111 features of the dataset, but our proposed model used only 51 of the original features. Besides, the stacking model ensemble the strength of the four different ML models—on the other hand, we developed an individual model. Overall, from the comparative analysis in Table 5, we can see that the proposed model XGBC outperformed using only 45.95% features.

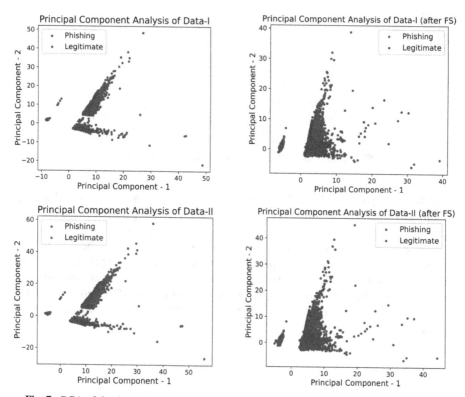

Fig. 7. PCA of the datasets before (left) and after (right) applying hybrid feature selection

Responding to **RQ-1**, the study performed principal component analysis (PCA) on the datasets (Data-I, Data-II) before and after feature selection (FS), illustrated in Fig. 7. The findings of PCA showed that hybrid feature selection reduced the overlapping of phishing and legitimate class cases in the datasets. Hence, it has facilitated the learning algorithms in decision-making and fit decision boundaries more accurately in the feature space. Besides, since the dimension of datasets is reduced, the complexity and degree of computations of models are also minimized. In response to **RQ-2**, considering the feature size of Data-I and Data-II, the proposed framework comparatively outplayed the existing studies. The outcomes of this study revealed that the hybrid framework had supported the ML models in improving the overall performance.

In this study, we endeavored to improve the outcomes of ML models utilizing a minimal number of features (only the best features) from the dataset. However, the well-organized empirical framework facilitated this experiment to achieve a notable performance—essentially, the proposed hybrid feature selection approach and the ML models with optimized hyperparameters are the fundamental factors.

5   Conclusion and Future Works

In this article, we introduced an empirical hybrid feature selection approach to leverage the performance of machine learning models in phishing websites detection. We used the two latest URL-based phishing datasets in the study. The proposed methodology of this experiment has three layers, including Feature Engineering, Cross Validation, and Perform Prediction. In the Feature Engineering layer, applying the hybrid feature selection method we derived only 51 features (out of 111) from the dataset. In this method, the raw features are refined through the filter method and the wrapper method accordingly. The hybrid approach used five distinct (4 filters and 1 wrapper) feature selection techniques in total. Following that, we optimized the proposed models (ANN, RFC and XGBC) with Grid Search based hyperparameter tuning. During the Cross Validation layer, we performed 10-folds cross-validation using the optimized models on Data-I. The result showed XGBC came up with the maximum prediction accuracy of 96.08%, F1-score of 96.07% and with MSE rate of 0.392. Finally, we performed prediction on Data-II using the best model XGBC. The model showed a significant performance with securing the accuracy of 97.29%, F1-score of 97.01%, kappa score of 94.02%, and RMSE of 0.1645 on the test data. Although the number of features of the datasets is cut down to about 46%, the proposed method outperformed the previous studies [2, 11].

Considering the proposed hybrid feature selection method, since the dimension of the datasets is reduced, the models performed notably well. Besides, their complexity and degree of computations are also minimized. We will endeavor to apply the proposed framework on different available phishing datasets and experiment with state-of-art deep neural networks in the future. In Table 1, the ad-hoc mounting of the cut-off ranges of feature selection techniques revealed promising remarks on the model's performance. Besides, we will resume the study to design an automatic assignment method of the best cut-off ranges for the feature selection techniques.

References

1. Somesha, M., Pais, A.R., Rao, R.S., Rathour, V.S.: Efficient deep learning techniques for the detection of phishing websites. Sādhanā **45**(1), 1–18 (2020). https://doi.org/10.1007/s12046-020-01392-4
2. Al-Sarem, M., et al.: An optimized stacking ensemble model for phishing websites detection. Electronics **10**(11), 1285 (2021). https://doi.org/10.3390/electronics10111285
3. Kalaharsha, P., Mehtre, B.M.: Detecting Phishing Sites – An Overview. arXiv:2103.12739v2 (2021)
4. Sarma, D., et al.: Comparative analysis of machine learning algorithms for phishing website detection. In: Smys, S., Balas, V.E., Kamel, K.A.., Lafata, P. (eds.) Inventive Computation and Information Technologies. LNNS, vol. 173. Springer, Singapore (2021). https://doi.org/10.1007/978-981-33-4305-4
5. da Silva, C.M.R., Feitosa, E.L., Garcia, V.C.: Heuristic-based strategy for phishing prediction: a survey of URL-based approach. Comput. Secur. **88**, 101613 (2020)
6. Zuraiq, A.A., Alkasassbeh, M.: Review: phishing detection Approaches. In: 2nd International Conference on new Trends in Computing Sciences (ICTCS), pp. 1–6 (2019)

7. Alsariera, Y.A., Adeyemo, V.E., Balogun, A.O., Alazzawi, A.K.: AI meta-learners and extra-trees algorithm for the detection of phishing websites. IEEE Access **8**, 142532–142542 (2020). https://doi.org/10.1109/ACCESS.2020.3013699

8. Chiew, K.L., et al.: A new hybrid ensemble feature selection framework for machine learning-based phishing detection system. Inf. Sci. **484**, 153–166 (2019). https://doi.org/10.1016/j.ins.2019.01.064

9. Ali, W.: Phishing website detection based on supervised machine learning with wrapper features selection. Int. J. Adv. Comput. Sci. Appl. **8**(9) (2017). https://doi.org/10.14569/IJACSA.2017.080910

10. Pes, B., Dessì, N., Angioni, M.: Exploiting the ensemble paradigm for stable feature selection: a case study on high-dimensional genomic data. Inform. Fus. **35**, 132–147 (2017). https://doi.org/10.1016/j.inffus.2016.10.001

11. Vrbančič, G., Fister, I., Jr., Podgorelec, V.: Parameter setting for deep neural networks using swarm intelligence on phishing websites classification. Int. J. Artif. Intell. Tools **28**(06), 1960008 (2019). https://doi.org/10.1142/S021821301960008X

12. Adeyemo, V.E., Balogun, A.O., Mojeed, H.A., Akande, N.O., Adewole, K.S.: Ensemble-based logistic model trees for website phishing detection. In: Anbar, M., Abdullah, N., Manickam, S. (eds.) ACeS 2020. CCIS, vol. 1347, pp. 627–641. Springer, Singapore (2021). https://doi.org/10.1007/978-981-33-6835-4_41

13. Vaitkevicius, P., Marcinkevicius, V.: Comparison of classification algorithms for detection of phishing websites. Informatica **31**(1), 143–160 (2020). https://doi.org/10.15388/20-INFOR404

14. Korkmaz, M., Sahingoz, O.K., Diri, B.: Feature selections for the classification of webpages to detect phishing attacks: a survey. In: 2020 International Congress on Human-Computer Interaction, Optimization and Robotic Applications (HORA), pp. 1–9 (2020)

15. Hannousse, A., Yahiouche, S.: Towards benchmark datasets for machine learning based website phishing detection: an experimental study. Eng. Appl. Artif. Intell. **104**, 104347 (2021). https://doi.org/10.1016/j.engappai.2021.104347

16. Vrbančič, G., Fister, I., Jr., Podgorelec, V.: Datasets for phishing websites detection. Data Brief **33**, 106438 (2020). https://doi.org/10.1016/j.dib.2020.106438

17. Vrbančič, G.: Phishing websites dataset. Mendeley Data. **V1**,(2020). https://doi.org/10.17632/72ptz43s9v.1

18. Mochammad, S., et al.: Stable hybrid feature selection method for compressor fault diagnosis. IEEE Access **9**, 97415–97429 (2021). https://doi.org/10.1109/ACCESS.2021.3092884

New Model to Store and Manage Private Healthcare Records Securely Using Block Chain Technologies

Ramesh Cheripelli[1]([⊠]) [ID], Swathi Ch[2] [ID], and Dileep Kumar Appana[3] [ID]

[1] Department of IT, G. Narayanamma Institute of Technology and Science,
Hyderabad, India
chramesh23@gmail.com
[2] Department of CSE, G. Narayanamma Institute of Technology and Science,
Hyderabad, India
[3] Computer Science Department, University of Ulsan, Ulsan, South Korea

Abstract. Electronic health records and data maintained require innovation. With help of various innovative advancements in technology the records of patients we can store in more secured and effective way. Till the day most of the hospitals are using the older data management schemes to store and retrieve the patients' health records. It's because of the strict medical data privacy and security rules. Which have prevented the use of the latest and innovative techniques in managing the health care data. With the use of new techniques, we can bring more transparency and security in the health care records management which will be much useful to the patients and to the doctors. To overcome this problem, we developed new model using block chain technology

Keywords: Electronic health records · Blockchain · Decentralization · Health records · Scalability · Block chain technology

1 Introduction

Blockchain innovation can change medical care by putting patients at the central point of medical care framework and working on security, protection, and interoperability of medical care data. This innovation can address another model for trading wellbeing data and make wellbeing records more effective and secure.

In Electronic Health Record (EHR) frameworks [1] are increasingly more utilized as a decent method to divide patients' records between totally various medical clinics. Notwithstanding, it's yet a test to get to dissipated patient information through various EHRs because of existing EHRs region unit territorially limited or have a place with joined medical clinics. upheld the report uncovered by the working environment of the National coordinator for Health information Technology [2], the most obstruction to get to patient records exists in the issue to search out supplier's locations. Up until now, there are many comes to beat these issues, yet the arrangements they need made region unit extreme and include updating or redesigning of existing EHR frameworks, which may require generous costs. Among them, one among the principal effectively in progress programs is go past Common Well Health Alliance [3] inside the u. s., a non-benefit making affiliation. They support EHRs, care providers, and consideration data innovation (HIT) merchants to append to their cross-country capacity network by means of confirmed reconciliation stages and go-betweens. They utilize a concentrated framework that empowers patients and specialists to search for a patient's dispersed clinical records [4]. Such a unified plan has a few downsides that it should confront the risk of weak link and bottleneck of information stream once the framework expands. In Associate in Nursing EHR framework, when patient records region unit got to for a couple of reason, the historical backdrop of all such occasions ought to be recorded in a very log document for later review on access accounts. The log record is utilized for reproducing the previous condition of clinical records, and it are normal diagrammatical as an authority archive [5–7]. Hence, we ought to in every case solidly guard the log document from filthy access and fabricate it unchanging if achievable. In this paper, we tend to propose a suburbanised framework to manage issues in dividing patient records between EHRs while not wishing on a very good quality concentrated framework. Our framework has 3 significant elements: (1) a trusty registry of patient information in EHRs that ensures access yet on the grounds that the respectability of the actual data, (2) built up security in overseeing patient information by using a chose cryptography subject Associate in Nursing giving a make and plain review way upheld an invariable access log, and (3) giving quantifiability to shroud different existing EHRs of territorial or centre clinics with the littlest sum adjustment and accessibility of the framework while not wishing on a concentrated superordinate framework.

With the blockchain arrangements in medical services area and in particularly EHRS the advantages are regularly recorded as follows:

Security: a blockchain is secure purposefully. Truth be told, under specific conditions, the data put away on the record are sealed.

Resiliency: a blockchain network can prevail in agreement and work effectively likewise if there should be an occurrence of Byzantine disappointments.

EHR communicating through encoding and computerized signature, it's feasible to safely distribute data.

Prevent dissipated data: the information is put away or referred to on the blockchain, that turns into a wellspring of truth.

This paper is structured as follows, Sect. 2 of this paper discusses literature survey and work done in this domain, Sect. 3. presents basics of blockchain technology and its dependencies. The Sect. 4 explains proposed frameworks architecture and design, Sect. 5 explains the framework performance.

2   Literature Review

In this paper we investigate a specific spotlight on the strategies and exhibitions of Electronic Health Record (EHR) Management Systems during the occasions of cataclysmic and its ensuing mass emergencies [23,25].

EMR availability, distribution and how it is working in the cloud is been proposed in [25, 27]. Patra et al. [22] majorly discussed about how regularly distributed computing is working so that with that the medical records are administration is performing. In this they majorly focused on regions which are rustic. The model which is built it must be meet the stock of essentials including availability, compliance, security, transmission of data, stockpiling and the techniques of assortment. They proposed that they can store the information pertain to the patients can be stored in cloud. This data could be distributed securely which could be used bye the clinical experts and the specialists. But they not clearly elaborated there idea, methodology, and there is no execution models or test cases are not available.

Clinical chain [32] is a case taken from the business with characteristics to various suggestion. The customer transforms into the holder of its prosperity data and gains complete access and authority over the data it manages. It furthermore provides to give straightforwardness between different social occasions related with someone's clinical consideration, explicitly clinical centres, offices, and medical care inclusions. The whitepaper is a procedure, with a couple specific subtleties. It hasn't specified any specific notification on properties flexibility. It merits referring to system it going to use to attain the prosperity of the patient, it's a support disclosure structure for crisis conditions. The support might be useful particularly in cases of failures when patient is unaware and unfit to give consent. The structure contains an emergency arm band that customer watchmen be capable of yield to procure significant material [19, 25, 33].

Beginning from the ideas in [15], Yue et al. [33] introduced the design of supposed information door application for medical services information upheld the blockchain. They guarantee to be the essential to propose a framework upheld the conveyed record innovation and focus on necessities like EHR communicating and patient command over information. The engineering presumes an individual blockchain to run on cloud, however neither they determine how it ought to be carried out nor give implementation tests.

Dubovitskaya Xu et al. [12] has proposed a new model, it seeming several circumstances, in this model they will share the records so that comparing with EMR data it has more security, assurance, and openness. This model is based on the arrangement of an oncology-unequivocal medical structure to share clinical prosperity documents for fundamental patient thought. The responses is expected to work with approval the chiefs and improve the trading of information between crisis facilities just as work on organization of trustworthy therapy and lifetime checking for patients impacted by harmful development. The patient data is mixed and taken care of off-chain in a cloud vault while passageway assents and on-chain the metadata of EHR. The model runs on understanding the PBFT and depends on top of Hyperledger Fabric. Regardless, versatility of model was not attempted in authentic a use case. The makers battle that PBFT understanding has astonishing flexibility properties attempted up to numerous centre points and simply sign the work of size as square. They determine examination of shows as further work.

One more side of the writing zeroed in on arrangements upheld permissioned blockchains [12,23,32], a network not neighbourly everybody with components to spot the clients that connect with it. Since the members are realized it is conceivable to exploit different agreement conventions while guaranteeing accuracy, protection, security and subsequently the general exhibitions. Also, it isn't really associated with digital currencies and any impetus models including instalments for execution.

3   Blockchain Technology and Its Functionality

A blockchain is essentially a spread data base of records or freely available report, in light of everything, or mechanized cases which are executed and split between various gatherings. Each exchange in the freely accessible information is acknowledged by understanding of a significant portion of the entities in the organization. Furthermore, once information is entered it not possible to wipe out. The blockchain comprises a specific and clear record of each trade anytime has been carried out. Blockchain as an idea would appear to be confounded, however it is very easy to comprehend. It is only a kind of information base. A blockchain is a cycle paced series of unchangeable data of information that is supervised by a group of PCs not claimed by any substance. This load of squares of data are gotten and bound to one another with the assistance of cryptographic standards (i.e., chain) [9,15,18,23].

Advantages with Blockchain Technology are Blockchain data is taken care of in a spread association of centre points which makes the structure and data impenetrable to dangerous attacks and concentrated frustrations. Every centre copy and stores a copy of the informational index, so there is definitely not a singular sign of frustration. Whenever data is taken care of in a blockchain, it is basically hard to upset it. Consequently, blockchain advancement is great for taking care of financial data as each change is followed and recorded on an openly available report. Exchanges do exclude a centre individual party in blockchain development as the trades are affirmed through a cooperation known as mining. This diminishes the overall costs and trade charges [7,12,19,28,37].

Albeit the computation of blockchain is secure there are some potential attacks that can occur against this association. Conceivably the most examined probability of attack is the 51% attack which could occur in case one substance sorts out some way to command over portion of the association hashing power. While such an attack has never happened till date, its probability can't be invalidated. It is difficult to change any data after it is entered in a blockchain. One more detriment of blockchain is that it uses public keys to give customers obligation regarding cryptographic cash units. The blockchain address has a private key, anyway it ought to be kept secret; in case the customer loses their private key, they will end up losing their money and not a ton ought to be conceivable with regards to it later. Blockchain records can get colossal as time goes on. A bitcoin chain requires 200 GB of limit. This could incite an insufficiency of centre points if the record ends up being unreasonably colossal

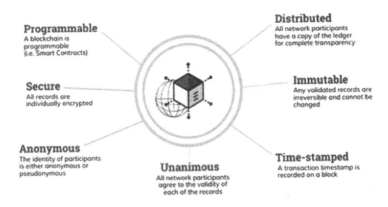

Fig. 1. Distributed ledger technology

3.1 Types of Blockchain

There are four classes exist they are Public, Private, Consortium, Hybrid.

Public Blockchain is a non-restrictive coursed record system. Anyone with web access can sign into the association of blockchain and transform into an endorsed centre. A public blockchain is principally used for mining and exchanging computerized types of cash. Bitcoin, Ethereum, and Litecoin are the most generally perceived cases of a public blockchain. If you are using this kind of blockchain, it is central to follow the security shows [2, 7, 13, 20, 28].

Private Blockchain is a restrictive record structure which is usable in a closed association. A private blockchain is routinely used in relationship with restricted permission. Generally speaking, just picked people are fundamental for the blockchain, and the affiliation has limitless oversight over the security, approvals, and accessibility. Private blockchains are used for projecting a polling form, electronic character, asset ownership, etc.

Consortium is a semi-decentralized kind of association which is administered by more than one affiliation. Various affiliations can get to the association or exchange information this sort of blockchain. Banks, government affiliations, and near components ordinarily use a consortium blockchain.

Cross breed is a blend of a private and a public blockchain. A creamer blockchain uses features of both the private and public blockchain. It is a totally versatile kind of centre wherein information can be kept open or careful as per the individual's choice.

3.2 Functionality of Block Chain

In the figure simply given the blockchain usefulness a solicitation is dispatched by a customer, blockchain setup recommends that another square is made. A square in blockchain is utilized for maintaining trades in them and these squares are circled to the aggregate of related centre points in association. That trade put inside a square is imparted to the aggregate of the centre points in association. All of the centre points in the association have a version of the full blockchain that improves them under control measure. Right when a square containing the customer trade is conveyed to the sum of the related centres, they affirm that the square isn't adjusted utilizing any means. Accepting this affirmation achieves progress, the centres add that square in their version of blockchain.

All this association of square being included on the blockchain is made by the centres coming to upon an understanding where they pick which squares are authentic to be included in blockchain are not. This endorsement is completed by the related centre points applying some acknowledged computations to genuinely look at the trade and to ensure that sender is an affirmed piece of the association. Right when a centre win concerning playing out the endorsement that centre is remunerated with advanced cash. This pattern of supporting the trade is named as mining and centre playing out this endorsement is recognized as digger. Later endorsement is done, that square is added to blockchain. After whole pattern of endorsement is played out the trade is done.

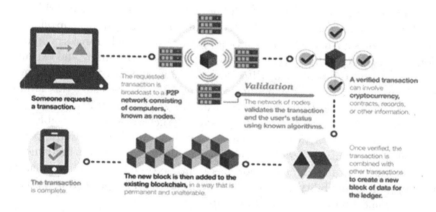

Fig. 2. BlockChain architecture

4   Design and Architecture of The Proposed Framework

The proposed work has principally has four partners they are Global administrator, Hospital administrator, Doctor and the Patient.

- The Global administrator is the administrator of an enterprise of medical clinics, and it has the full and absolute access levels in the chain of command. With these advantages they can add another association (medical clinic) to the company and on their dashboard, they can undoubtedly appoint/derelegate emergency clinic administrators.
- The Hospital (organization) administrator has not many advantages which are specific to that medical clinic which is essential for the organization/arrangement, they can't have every one of the advantages like worldwide administrator their authorization are confined to that emergency clinic.

In that clinic they can add, update, or eliminate clients with a job of patient or specialist.

- The specialist is a customer in the relationship with the appropriate work and can move records of patients and transfer/see reports of those patients to which they have been permitted induction.
- Patient is a customer in the relationship with the fitting position and can move reports in isolation, see them, see the record access logs, and moreover direct permission to their archives on their console.

The formation of this code is to engineers, to the people who willing to work in the Block Chain Platform, Document Store, and Solution Manager. Once the formation is over we will get an complete how these components are interconnected. A web application developed with VueJs it has different sorts of components on one page, those are interlinked with each other. With help of NodeJS it will be deployed on to Kubernetes on IBM Cloud. The Redis data base will be attached to it. from the Redis datastore information will be recuperate and stored through NodeJS. To keep the customer we need to use JWT.

4.1 Architecture Flow

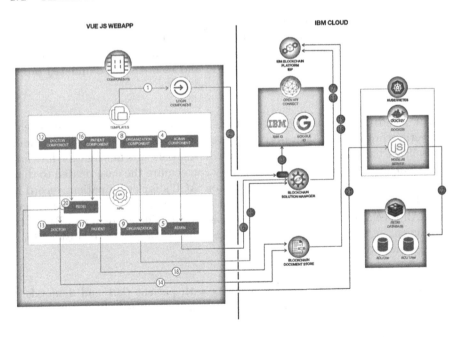

Fig. 3. Architecture flow

Login Module. Every one of the partners of the application (Global administrator, clinic administrator, specialist, and patient) start the client stream by signing their individual home page. Tapping login button prompts login entrance of Blockchain Solution Manager, facilitated on IBM cloud. login entrance utilizes OpenAPI Link and permits client login all the way through any onboarded personality supplier (in this model, we have on-boarded IBMID advertisement GoogleID). Effective confirmation prompts the JWT certifications for the client

Admin Module. The Global administrator stream starts at the administrator part and requires the client to confirm themselves through the login stream portrayed previously. After effective confirmation, the client can get to the arrangement administrator dashboard. They can see the arrangement and add/eliminate clinics from the arrangement utilizing Admin Api's. To handle Client inquiries which are assisted by Block chain Solution manager used by all APIs of administrator. It will update the records in the platform and associates with solution manger.

Organization Module. Medical clinic administrator stream starts at the association part and requires the client to confirm themselves through the login stream portrayed previously. After fruitful confirmation, the client can get to the medical clinic administrator dashboard. They can add/eliminate any client in their separate clinic with the on-boarded jobs (patient/specialist for our situation) utilizing the association Api's. All association API's interface with Blockchain Solution Manager with help of REST to handle client questions. It will interface with IBM Blockchain Platform and record will be updated properly.

Doctor Module. In this section it starts at specialist part and needs client must verify through the login portrayed previously. After fruitful confirmation, client will get to specialist page. With that transfer patient's information for clinical examination and for further study. They can acquire the data related to that particular patient through the API of doctor. ACL's for every patient record is application level ,which is kept up with over Record ACL stream depicted underneath. All specialist API's associate with Blockchain File Store across REST to handle client inquiries. The Blockchain File Store interfaces with IBM Blockchain Platform and updates record suitably.

Patient Module. In this section it starts with patient part and demands a client to confirm in login page themselves which portrayed previously. After effective confirmation, client will get to patient home page. Patient can transfer a clinical document to self or anyone, see the entrance logs of their testimonies, with help of Patient Api's oversee consents to their archives. Every one of patient API's interface with Blockchain Document Store with REST to handle client questions. It will Store with IBM Blockchain Platform and updates record suitably. To Get into the Documents patient and doctor part identify with Redis API's which summon techniques to deal with record level access control around emergency clinics. In IBM Cloud, Kubernetes group Redis API's discussion to a NodeJS worker conveyed in a Docker holder.

5   Performance Analysis

The essential undertaking to explore the displays of the model and the fundamental blockchain network model developed with JMeter, its testing API gadget kept up by Apache and expected stack test. It determines applications of web execution with the help of HTTP requests. Node.js is used for the execution of REST API which receives inputs from the instruments which are under testing. API separates interest with help of HL Fabric SDK it will confirm after it forward the SDK to association. Nevertheless, REST API fails to authentic the blockchain model when it is bottleneck. To overcome this problem blockchain is superseded with JMeter is known as Hyperledger Calliper, using this we can be able to experiment various use cases. The proposed model is evaluated based on the throughput, idleness, and execution time. Execution Time calculated in seconds as execution in between the trade insistences. Throughput insinuates the proportion of data that could be moved beginning with one region then onto the following in a unit proportion of time. Inactivity will occur when one action is going on ,so that process may not able to respond to other action .With respect to it might be suggested as the qualification of plan and satisfaction period of trade. The figure shows how the send rate expands, as indicated by both average and throughput latencies increment until the through put arrives at 500 exchanges each second. The average latency, that addresses an opportunity to execute an exchange, develops straight. Specifically, the normal inertness

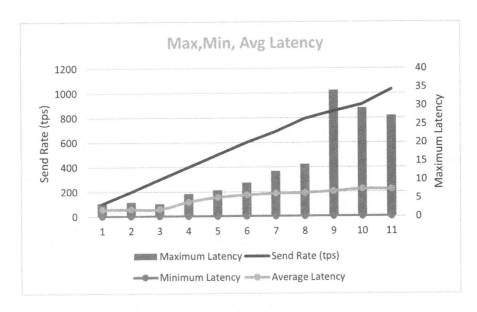

Fig. 4. Max, Min, Avg Latency

communicates the general time an exchange takes to send the solicitation to at least one companions, execute the keen agreement, supports, verify them, make the exchange, send it to request administration, structure hinder and focus on record. In the worst it may noteworthy send rate a large portion of the activities are finished. It's feasible to see read activities are more as compared to the required. For this data is available from the peers no need of any interaction is required.

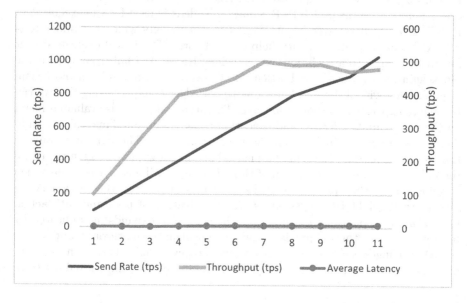

Fig. 5. Send Rate, Throughput, Average Latency.

6   Conclusion

The proposed model gives a clear blockchain-based application for EHRs and satisfies a few necessities. Regardless, to be used by an association of clinical facilities, it needs more functionalities and works similarly as extra expansive tests on cloud establishments. The experiments on cloud will spread out to local outcomes also. It will generate comprehensive assessment of how a more consideration moreover, natural apportionment impact introduction of a blockchain. This kind of examinations is suggested as a trademark characteristic of the proposition job. The future developments is like manner consolidates the extension of the current work and development of others to work on difficulties, moreover, maintain further features required by an EHRs.

References

1. Jetley, G., Zhang, H.: Electronic health records in IS research: quality issues, essential thresholds and remedial actions. Decis. Support Syst. **126**, 113–137 (2019)

2. Wisner, K., Lyndon, A., Chesla, C.A.: The electronic health record's impact on nurses' cognitive work: an integrative review. Int. J. Nurs. Stud. **94**, 74–84 (2019)
3. Hochman, M.: Electronic health records: a "Quadruple Win," a "Quadruple Failure," or simply time for a reboot? J. Gen. Intern. Med. **33**(4), 397–399 (2018)
4. Gan, Q.: Adoption of electronic health record system: multiple theoretical perspectives. In: 2014 47th Hawaii International Conference on System Science, pp. 2716–2724 (2014)
5. Vehko, T., et al.: Experienced time pressure and stress: electronic health records usability and information technology competence play a role. BMC Med. Inform. Decis. Mak. **19**(1), 160 (2019)
6. Reisman, M.: EHRs: the Challenge of Making Electronic Data Usable and Interoperable. P T **42**(9), 572–575 (2017)
7. Koczkodaj, W.W., Mazurek, M., Strzałka, D., Wolny-Dominiak, A., Woodbury-Smith, M.: Electronic health record breaches as social indicators. Soc. Indic. Res. **141**(2), 861–871 (2018). https://doi.org/10.1007/s11205-018-1837-z
8. Argaw, S.T., Bempong, N.E., Eshaya-Chauvin, B., Flahault, A.: The state of research on cyberattacks against hospitals and available best practice recommendations: a scoping review. BMC Med. Inform. Decis. Mak. **19**(1), 1–11 (2019)
9. McLeod, A., Dolezel, D.: Cyber-analytics: modeling factors associated with healthcare data breaches. Decis. Support Syst. **108**, 57–68 (2018)
10. Coventry, L., Branley, D.: Cybersecurity in healthcare: a narrative review of trends, threats and ways forward. Maturitas **113**, 48–52 (2018)
11. The future of health care cybersecurity. J. Nurs. Regul. **8**(4 Supplement), S29–S31 (2018)
12. Spatar, D., Kok, G., Basoglu, N., Daim, T.: Adoption factors of electronic health record system. Technol. Soc. **58**(February), 101144 (2019)
13. Nakamoto, S.: Bitcoin: a peer-to-peer electronic cash system. Modern Econ. **6**, 1–9 (2008)
14. Gordon, W.J., Catalini, C.: Blockchain technology for healthcare?: facilitating the transition to patient-driven interoperability. Comput. Struct. Biotechnol. J. **16**, 224–230 (2018)
15. Boonstra, A., Versluis, A., Vos, J.F.J.: Implementing electronic health records in hospitals: a systematic literature review. BMC Health Serv. Res. **14**(1), 370 (2014)
16. Aguilera, M., Toueg. S.: Failure detection and randomization: A Hybrid approach to solve consensus. SIAM J. Comput. **28**(3), 890–903 (1998). ISSN: 0097-5397. https://doi.org/10.1137/S0097539796312915
17. Androulaki, E., et al.: Hyperledger fabric: a distributed operating system for permissioned blockchains. In: Proceedings of the Thirteenth EuroSys Conference, EuroSys 2018, pp. 1–15. ACM Press (2018). ISBN: 978-1-4503-5584-1. https://doi.org/10.1145/3190508.3190538
18. Azaria, A., et al.: MedRec: using blockchain for medical data access and permission management. In: 2016 2nd International Conference on Open and Big Data (OBD), pp. 25–30. IEEE, August 2016. ISBN: 978-1-5090-4054-4. https://doi.org/10.1109/OBD.2016.11
19. Bessani, A., Sousa, J., Alchieri, E.E.P.: State machine replication for the masses with BFT-SMART. In: 2014 44th Annual IEEE/IFIP International Conference on Dependable Systems and Networks, pp. 355–362, IEEE, June 2014. ISBN:978-1-4799-2233-8. https://doi.org/10.1109/DSN.2014.43
20. Buterin, V.: Proof of Stake FAQ. 2016. https://github.com/ethereum/wiki/wiki/Proof-of-Stake-FAQ

21. Cachin, C., Vukolic, M.: Blockchain consensus protocols in the wild. In: CoRR abs/1707.01873 (2017). arXiv: 1707.01873

22. Patra, M.R., Das, R.K., Prasad Padhy, R.: CRHIS: cloud based rural healthcare information system. In: ICEGOV '12: Proceedings of the 6th International Conference on Theory and Practice of Electronic Governance, p. 402, ACM Press (2012). ISBN: 978-1-4503-1200-4. https://doi.org/10.1145/2463728.2463805

23. Maddox, P.: Testing a distributed System: testing a distributed system can be trying even under the best of circumstances. Queue **13** (2015)

24. Rolim, C.O., et al.: A cloud computing solution for patient's data collection in health care institutions. In: 2010 Second International Conference on eHealth, Telemedicine, and Social Medicine, pp. 95–99. IEEE, February 2010. ISBN: 978-1-4244-5803-5. https://doi.org/10.1109/eTELEMED.2010.19

25. Sarcevic, A., et al.: "Beacons of hope" in decentralized coordination: learning from on-the-ground medical twitterers during the 2010 Haiti earthquake. In: CSCW 2012 Computer Supported Cooperative Work, p. 47. ACM Press, 2012, ISBN: 978-1-4503-1086-4

26. Ramesh, Ch., Venugopal Rao, K., Vasumathi, D.: Comparative analysis of applications of identity-based cryptosystem in IOT. Electr. Govt, Int. **13**, ISSNonline 740-7508, ISSNprint:1740-314–323 (2017)

27. Kovvuri, R.S., Cheripelli, R.: Credit risk valuation using an efficient machine learning algorithm. In: Satapathy, S.C., Raju, K.S., Shyamala, K., Krishna, D.R., Favorskaya, M.N. (eds.) ICETE 2019. LAIS, vol. 4, pp. 648–657. Springer, Cham (2020). https://doi.org/10.1007/978-3-030-24318-0_74

28. Kim, M.G., Lee, A.R., Kwon, H.J., Kim, J.W., Kim, I.K.: Sharing medical questionnaries based on blockchain. In: Proceedings - 2018 IEEE International Conference on Bioinformatics and Biomedical Science, BIBM 2018, pp. 2767–2769 (2019)

29. Gupta, S., Sadoghi, M.: Blockchain Transaction Processing. In: Sakr, S., Zomaya, A.Y. (eds.) Encyclopedia of Big Data Technologies. Springer, Cham (2019). https://doi.org/10.1007/978-3-319-77525-8_333

30. Chohan, U.W.: Cryptocurrencies: a brief thematic review. SSRN Electron. J. (2017)

31. Wood, G.:Ethereum: a secure decentralised generalised transaction ledger. EIP-150 Revision, p. 33, 1 August 2017

32. Ramesh, Ch., Venu Gopal, R.K., Vasumathi, D.: Evaluation of key management scheme based on identity. In: 2016 IEEE 6th International Conference on Advanced Computing (IACC), pp. 545–550, IEEE (2016)

33. Atzei, N., Bartoletti, M., Cimoli, T., Lande, S., Zunino, R.: SoK: unraveling bitcoin smart contracts. In: 7th International Conference, POST: Held as Part of European Joint Conferences on Theory and Practice of Software, ETAPS 2018 Thessaloniki. Greece, pp. 217–242 (2018)

34. Ramesh, Ch., Venugopal Rao, K., Vasumathi, D.: Identity-based crypto system based on TATE pairing. Glob. J. Comput. Sci. Technol. **16** (2016)

35. Grishchenko, I., Maffei, M., Schneidewind, C.: A semantic framework for the security analysis of ethereum smart contracts. In: Bauer, L., Küsters, R. (eds.) POST 2018. LNCS, vol. 10804, pp. 243–269. Springer, Cham (2018). https://doi.org/10.1007/978-3-319-89722-6_10

36. Dey, T., Jaiswal, S., Sunderkrishnan, S., Katre, N.: A medical use case of Internet of Things and blockchain. In: The International Conference on Intelligent Systems (ICISS), pp. 486–491 (2017)
37. Yue, X., Wang, H., Jin, D., Li, M., Jiang, W.: Healthcare Data Gateways: found healthcare intelligence on Blockchain with Novel Privacy Risk Control. J. Med. Syst. **40**(10), 1–8 (2016). https://doi.org/10.1007/s10916-016-0574-6

Secure and Transparent Supply Chain Management to Prevent Counterfeit Drugs

Md. Muhtasim Fuad Fahim[1]([✉])([iD]) and Mohammad Shahriar Rahman[2]([✉])([iD])

[1] Department of Computer Science and Engineering, University of Liberal Arts Bangladesh, Dhaka, Bangladesh
muhtasim.fuad.cse@ulab.edu.bd
[2] Department of Computer Science and Engineering, United International University Bangladesh, Dhaka, Bangladesh
mshahriar@cse.uiu.ac.bd

Abstract. The production and distribution of counterfeit drugs are critical and progressively becoming a major issue in the world. One of the main reasons behind drug counterfeiting is the imperfect supply chain. It is difficult to track over the drugs from manufacturing to distribution. The major requirement of the drug supply chain is the assurance of drug quality, together with efficacy and safety. In this paper, we propose a blockchain-based platform of drug supply chain management from manufacturer to pharmacist. We provide tracking over drugs as well as visibility and the safety of sensitive drug information. The existing drug supply chain manufacturers don't know what happens with their drugs or which pharmacy is taking their drugs. But our proposed model ensures traceability so that manufacturers will be able to know which pharmacy is taking their drugs through the distributed network provided by blockchain. Our platform will provide a secure network where all participants can see all the transactions between other participants. All transactions between participants are recorded in the blockchain and other participants will be able to view the transactions history of participants. All blockchain transactions information is kept in encrypted form in a database. Also, encrypted QR code will ensure that illegitimate participants will not be able to make a copy of the information given by the manufacturer, and will not be able to produce fake drugs by using the copied information. So, it will ensure security of drug information. We have built a prototype of the platform over the Ethereum network.

Keywords: Counterfeit drug · Blockchain · Security · Encrypted QR code · Traceability · Transparency

1 Introduction

The counterfeiting of drugs has become a serious issue as people consuming such drugs face severe health risks. Fake drugs are those which may contain no

Active Pharmaceutical Ingredient (API) at all, inadequate APIs, sole or in mixes, API within the right amount but with counterfeit or fake packing, labeling and patient information leaflet (PIL). The spurious/false labeled/falsified/counterfeit (SFFC) is the comparable terms utilized by diverse administrative specialists to demonstrate the poor quality of drugs which can cause patient dissatisfaction, severe health risk, and financial loss for individuals as well the industry.

Counterfeit drugs can be introduced into the market through various channels. A chemist or owner of a pharmacy can purchase fake drugs at cheaper rates from unauthorized parties or frauds and can make a bountiful sum. Essentially, a nearby depot in-charge or territorial wholesaler channel can be a source of fake drugs, deliberately or incidentally. The fake drug market is flourishing at the cost of the patient's life, and the state machinery or government is incapable of preventing this immoral business of counterfeit drugs. The profit- making is enormous in comparison to investment in the business of fake drugs, which is a potent source of motivation to the phony medicine mafias. Counterfeiting of various drugs causes serious threat to public health or who consumes drugs and also it causes revenue loss to the legitimate manufacturing companies [3]. The lack of a solid and proficient watchfulness framework helps advancing this wrongful trade. The showcase value of fake drugs is additionally expanding due to the awkwardness in supply and demand.

In the current SCM system pharmacists have no access to such systems through which they can check if the purchased drugs are genuine or not. In this way, organizations across the country are required to record the drug-related data right from its fabricating through wholesalers or depot in-charges and retailers. Such a ledger will help to track the authenticity of the drug and will keep an overall inventory check on the produced drugs until the life cycle of the drug is ended. One essential concern while actualizing such a broad framework emerges out of the trust. A centralized server or system cannot be trusted to manage such transactions of drugs via SCM. The issue with such a centralized framework is that it offers a single point of failure, which is undesirable when actualizing such a large-scale information-intensive organization. The arrangement lies in realizing the importance of a decentralized framework utilizing adequate cryptographic measures to guarantee the security and unchanging nature of the information records. Luckily, blockchain innovation exists to offer decentralized storage and secure the record kept up on different computer hubs or nodes. In this composition, a dependable pharmaceutical verification framework based on blockchain innovation is proposed. Different partners within the medicine or drug supply chain can confirm the authenticity of the drugs they get by utilizing the proposed framework.

1.1 Existing Drug Supply Chain

This section represents the description of the participants who are involved with the drug supply chain.

- Manufacturer: The entity which produces drugs from raw materials by using various tools, equipment and processes, and then delivers those drugs to depot in-charge through a distributor.

- Distributor: Takes drugs from manufacturer and delivers those drugs to depot where a depot in-charge takes the manufactured drugs.
- Depot In-charge: The person who takes orders from a Medical Representative (MR) or Medical Promotion Officer (MPO), and places the order to the manufacturer.
- MR or MPO: The person who takes orders from a pharmacy or chemist shop where pharmacists place orders according to the need of drugs.
- Pharmacist: The person who places orders to MR or MPO according to the requirement of drugs.

1.2 Problems of Existing System

- Supply chain management (SCM) of the pharmaceutical industry does not provide visibility [1]. Manufacturers cannot keep track of their drugs.
- It is difficult for any pharmacist to know the origin of drugs.
- Existing drug supply chain does not provide the security of sensitive data about drugs and there is a lack of confidentiality as well as integrity.
- Drug information can be duplicated easily by the existing supply chain because raw data are given on drug boxes.
- Fraudulent activities and unauthorized manipulation become easy to carry out [2].

1.3 Blockchain as a Building Tool

Blockchain is a new technique for the anti-counterfeiting of products. Blockchain is a reorganized record because of its mathematical nature, and its records can not be modified. It can only be achieved by utilizing the underlying cryptographic algorithms. Its structure is immutable and in strict order. Immutability is implemented by using a hash. So, every block has reference to a previous hence it gives strict order. Since blockchain is timestamped and immutable, it can't be forged by intruders. Blockchain has two main types – Public blockchain and Permissioned (or private) blockchain. In a permissioned blockchain not everyone can write into the blockchain, as it were those members who have got permission or who have access, can write information on the blockchain. Within the setting of pharmaceutical - the superior alternative is to utilize a permissioned blockchain.

By using blockchain, we can ensure these major three things of the drug supply chain: Product authentication, Product verification and Improve shelf-life management. The following advantages can be leveraged by using blockchain in combating counterfeit drugs: all participants are involved in the pharmaceutical supply chain, blockchain is unchangeable and time-stamped, all products can register in blockchain for authenticity, it cannot be counterfeited by drug traffickers, all data can be kept secure and transparent.

1.4   Our Contribution

Keeping in mind the problems of the existing drug supply chain management system, which has been discussed earlier, we realized that the pharmaceutical industry needs an updated and secured supply chain system. The new system is to secure the drugs supply chain, to provide visibility to manufacturers and drugs regulatory authority, incorporate the features of blockchain technology and add traceability in the SCM system. In such scenarios where we need data privacy and data accessibility both at the same time, blockchain technology is the best choice. Every time a product changes hands, the transaction can be documented to create a permanent history of a product- from manufacture to sale. Also we have implemented an encrypted QR code system for the safety of drug information of drug boxes. This will dramatically reduce time delays, costs, and human error that occurs in transactions today. We have discussed our proposed model as well as we show the results of prototype implementation.

2   Related Work

There are various techniques which have already been used for tracing counterfeit drugs. The authors in [1], proposed a permissioned blockchain to store transactions and only trusted Parties are allowed to join. Also, participants have key pairs which are used to assign each participant a specific activity and they proposed a user friendly mobile app for doctors. Similarly, in Global Governance of the Blockchain (Gcoin Blockchain) double spending mechanism is proposed to alleviate the counterfeit-drug problem [4]. They proposed a QR code based identification of drugs and digital signatures for verification. Also blocks are generated every 15 s and it could handle 1.51 million transactions in one day. Also in [5] a RFID is used for each shipment of products and parties can check where or not the products have passed a legitimate supply chain. The Author of [6] proposed model assures an electronic pedigree (2D barcode verification) for every produced single unit medicine and helps to trace all distribution chains from the manufacturer to the patient. Also, the author of [3] proposed a model where illegitimate participants cannot get access because of the public key and an encrypted QR code technique is introduced which will be accessed only by authorized bodies. None of this literature introduces member revocation, but in [7] where the author proposed a member revocation without changing the key pairs of unrevoked members. In [8], the authors talked about serialization. Serialization is a unique anti-forgery method, where a unique identification number is effectively put on a pack and can be verified by the customer's phone and internet links. The authors in [9], proposed a highly scalable and enhanced trace and track system for the pharma supply chain using an IoT framework known as GDP (Global Data Plane) integrated with blockchain that helps in communication and management of data between untrusted parties. In [10], the authors proposed a blockchain-driven tool that can be used to record and time-stamp the transfer of goods at each point in the pharmaceutical supply chain. As the drug travels through the supply chain, every transaction of goods will be noted and time-stamped by scanning the barcode and the ledger will be used to ensure the security and safety of the product. In paper [11], an Internet of Things (IoT) sensor-based blockchain framework is proposed that tracks and traces drugs as they pass slowly through the entire supply chain. The authors focused on improving classic blockchain systems to make it suitable for IoT based supply chain management, and applying these new promising technologies to enable a viable smart healthcare ecosystem through a drug supply chain. In the paper [5], the authors proposed a novel POMS (Product Ownership Management System) of RFID-attached products for anti-counterfeits that can be used in the post supply chain. For this purpose, they leveraged the idea of Bitcoin's blockchain that anyone can check the proof of possession of balance. With the proposed POMS, a customer can reject the purchase of counterfeits even with genuine RFID tag information, if the seller does not possess their ownership and a proof-of-concept experimental system employing a blockchain-based decentralized application platform has been implemented.

3 Methodology

In this section we discussed the methodology we followed to develop our platform. We have considered the following specifications for our architecture.

- We have three participants in this network. They are: manufacturer, depot in-charge and pharmacist. We have created web apps for manufacturer and depot in-charge, and mobile app for pharmacists. All participants must be registered with this network. Manufacturer is registered with this network by the system that means he has an account given by the system.
- All participants must be logged in to operate with the system. First of all, if anyone wants to get access to the system he has to fill-up a registration form. This request goes to the manufacturer. Then the manufacturer will create an account for him (account information will be saved into the database) and give him the password. Then that user can login and do orders according to his role.
- When any drug will be manufactured at the manufacturer's end the manufacturer will add the drug information into the database, and depot in-charge and pharmacist can view the manufactured drug information.
- Then manufacturer will add some secret information about the drugs into another database which is connected with the previous database. Manufacturer will generate encrypted QR code (using secret key) where the Drug Accountability Record (DAR) number is encrypted. This encrypted QR code will be attached on drug boxes. All information about encrypted QR code will also be stored in the database in encrypted form.
- Pharmacists can place orders to depot in-charges using his mobile app. After receiving all orders from the pharmacists of an area, depot in-charge places orders to the manufacturer for drugs. Order databases are connected with the user (where all information of users are stored) database to get easy access with the user information. Both the transactions are recorded in blockchain

and block data are also saved into a database where we merge off-chain and on-chain data. All data is encrypted in the database.

- Manufacturer controls the order status of depot in-charge and depot in-charge can view this as a real time update. When the manufacturer completes an order status, this transaction is recorded in the blockchain and also saved in the database as encrypted data. Here we also merged the off-chain and on-chain data.
- Depot in-charge confirmation is also saved in the blockchain and block data is saved into the database. This database is also encrypted.
- Depot in-charge controls the order status of pharmacists by following the same process of manufacturer.
- Pharmacists scan the QR code and get encrypted information. Then he can see the decrypted data from his mobile app.

4 System Architecture

4.1 Generic Design

Manufacturer will generate an encrypted QR code $(Sk(QR))$ when any drug is manufactured. This secret key will be changed on each production of drugs. After getting the drugs in hand, the depot in-charge will update the chain status. When a depot in-charge receives drugs without any payment this is called primary sale according to the medical supply chain. All the transactions will be recorded in blockchain and blockchain data are saved into databases where we store encrypted data. After that, the depot in-charge will send those drugs to the pharmacy or chemist shop and the same process will be followed like the manufacturer and depot in-charge. When a pharmacist or chemist gets ordered drugs and pays money this is called secondary sale.

Figure 1 shows the generic architecture of our proposed platform.

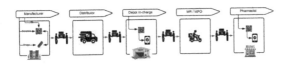

Fig. 1. Platform architecture

4.2 Activity Diagrams

Here, the activity diagrams are presented which are essentially flowcharts showing activities performed by different components of the system.

By our system, a pharmacist can: 1) place order, 2) view own orders history, 3) scan QR code and get decrypted value, 4) give transaction or receive confirmation.

Figure 2 shows the activities of pharmacists in the system.

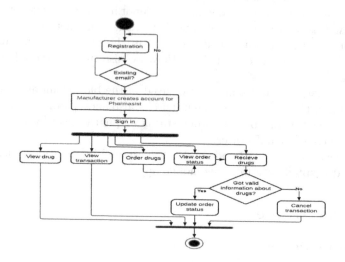

Fig. 2. Activity diagram for pharmacist

Figure 3 shows the activities of depot in-charges in the system.

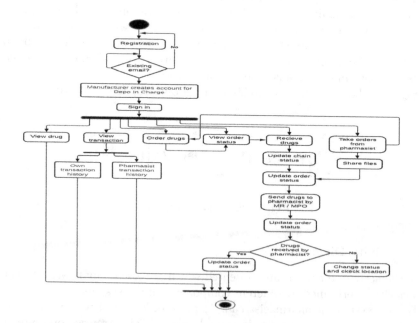

Fig. 3. Activity diagram for depot in-charge

By our system, a depot in-charge can: 1) place order, 2) search for the history of blockchain transactions, 3) update order status, 4) give transaction or receive confirmation, 5) share invoice, 6) view- personal and pharmacist blockchain transactions, user or depot in-charges information, order status, and order histories of pharmacists.

Figure 4 shows the activities of the manufacturer.

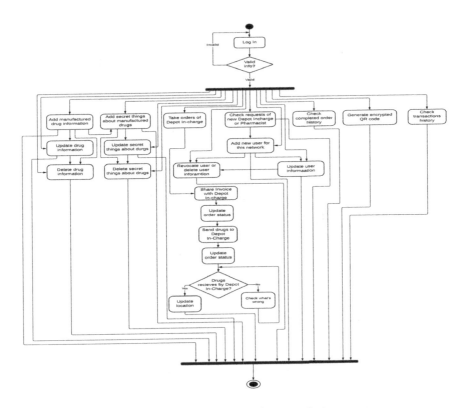

Fig. 4. Activity diagram for manufacturer

By our system, a manufacturer can: 1) add, update and delete manufactured drugs information, 2) add, update and delete secret information about drugs, 3) add user account/user, update data, remove user, 4) generate QR code and share invoice, 5) update order status, 6) view- user requests, transactions or receive confirmation history of depot in-charge, QR code information, blockchain transactions.

Figure 5 shows the whole process of our system involving all three participants.

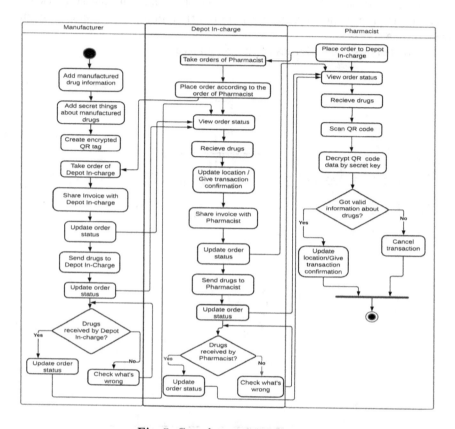

Fig. 5. Complete activity diagram

4.3 Process Description

When a new drug is produced, the manufacturer adds the description (information) of that drug in the drug storage database and secret information of production in another database connected with this database. Then the manufacturer generates encrypted QR codes and tag them on drug boxes.

For a particular number of pharmacists, there will be a selected depot in-charge for each area. When a pharmacist orders drugs to the depot in-charge, the order information is stored in a database where some fields are by default, like: role (depot in-charge), DAR (not selected) etc. Also this database has two fields- sender and receiver. These fields are connected with the user database to get all the information of the user and this transaction is saved in blockchain with three information: unique order id, email address of pharmacist and order status. When a pharmacist places an order, the role field is "Depot In-charge" by default and the order status is "order placed" by default. Then the block data has been encrypted and saved in another database, and this database is connected with the specific order information of the order database.

In a similar way, when depot in-charge orders drugs to the manufacturer, the transaction is saved in blockchain with three information: unique order id, email of depot in-charge and order status. As we discussed before, here the role is manufacturer by default and other default things are the same, i.e.: status (order placed), DAR (not selected). The returned json from blockchain is stored into the databases as encrypted data. This specific database is connected with the specific order database of depot in-charge. Then the manufacturer checks the drug inventory and updates the inventory by delivering the ordered amount to depot in-charge (the production amount reduces). Then it checks the required secret key for this order or transaction, selects the DAR field as single or multiple DAR for this order, and shares the invoice with the depot in-charge.

Then Manufacturer confirms the order from depot in-charge as a part of order status update. When the order status is completed a transaction is stored in blockchain like the previous way where we passed order status (completed) and order id into block. This information is encrypted and stored into another database connected with that order database. After that, when the depot in-charge receives the ordered drugs from the manufacturer and checks the authentication of drugs, he gives a confirmation that he has received the drug and blockchain transaction happens and the default role is changed to depot in-charge in the database. This transaction is saved in Blockchain with five information: order id, buyer name (depot in-charge name), seller name (manufacturer name), from address (blockchain account address of depot manufacturer) and to address (blockchain account address of depot in-charge). Then the returned json has been encrypted again and saved into another database connected with that specific order database collection (off-chain and on-chain data are merged here).

Then in the same way depot in-charge controls the order status of pharmacists after receiving the drugs sent by the manufacturer and completed order status has a blockchain transaction again. Then returned json has been encrypted and saved into a database connected with the specific order database collection of the pharmacist. After the pharmacist receives the drugs from the depot in- charge he confirms he scans the QR code tagged on the drug boxes and sees the decrypted information (DAR). Then he confirmed that he received the drugs and a transaction happened in blockchain where five information is stored in block: order id (pharmacist order id), buyer name (pharmacist name), seller name (depot in-charge name), from address (blockchain account address of depot in-charge) and to address (blockchain account address of pharmacist).

5   Implementation and Analysis

5.1   Implementation

In this proposed system, we used the Ethereum based blockchain network. So, this system is based on Ethereum architecture with smart contract functionality. Originally, Ethereum is a public permission less blockchain platform implementing a Proof-of-Work (PoW) based consensus protocol. The system is based on a private blockchain network and we have used Proof-of-Work (PoW) based protocol. Here we have used it as a private platform (configurable feature). All blocks are then sealed by approved signers. We have used geth which is a tool used to run a full Ethereum node on the framework. We have written smarts contracts in the Solidity object-oriented language for running Dapps (decentralized apps). Ethereum also introduces the Ethereum Virtual Machine (EVM) that enables any node to run any program regardless of the programming language.

We set up an environment to evaluate our protocol by writing programs using Solidity 0.8.3 with a computer Intel(R) Core(TM) i5, CPU 2.50 GHz, 4.00 GB of RAM, HP SSD S700 Pro 500 GB, Windows 10, 64-bit OS. We used VS Code (v: 1.56.2), geth (v: 1.10.1-stable) to run blockchain server (port: 8000) and web3 (v: 1.3.5), node (v: 14.11.0) to run our local server on port 3040 and yarn (v: 1.22.5) and mongo-dB compass (v: 4.4.1-stable) database. Some other important dependencies are crypto (v: 1.0.1), qrcode (v: 1.4.4), connect-mongo (v: 4.4.0), ethereumjs-tx (v: 2.1.2), express (v: 4.17.1), express-ejs-layouts (v: 0.0.2), node-mailer (v: 6.5.0) etc. and development dependencies are laravel-mix (v: 6.0.13), nodemon (v: 2.0.7), sass (v: 1.32.8) etc.

Figure 6 shows a transaction has been submitted into blockchain when Depot In-charge places order to Manufacturer.

Fig. 6. Submitted transaction when order placed

Figure 7 shows encrypted Blockchain JSON stored into the database when Depot In-charge places order. Here, both off-chain and on-chain data are merged. We have merged the order database data for a specific order with the blockchain data for that specific order and we have saved these data into the local database or another database collection.

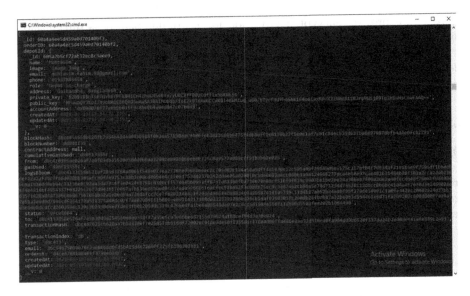

Fig. 7. Encrypted block data and order database data

5.2   Security Analysis

In our system, transaction information of every point of the supply chain is stored in the blockchain. Each new block connects with the previous block before it gets mined and also connects with the next block after mining. It provides a tamper proof network. All transactions inside the blocks are approved and concurred upon by a component or mechanism, guaranteeing that each transaction is genuine.

We have set up a secured and trusted network, where only the trusted parties are permitted to join the network. By registration policy, the trusted people will get access to the network. At the back-end, there is a permissioned blockchain to store all the specified transactions. Due to its immutability property, the stored data can never be changed. Besides this, we have built a web app named "Drug Guard" and a user-friendly mobile app to make transactions to the blockchain. By using this web app and mobile app, the participants will be able to buy authentic drugs by checking whether the transaction is valid or not. Our system can ensure that the drugs will be safe from the fraud attack and it is not possible to have any counterfeit drug in the supply chain as every transaction is stored in blockchain.

We stored encrypted data into the database where block information and order database information are merged. If any malicious user gets the database, he cannot do anything with the data as it is encrypted. For encryption of the database the aes-256 algorithm has been used.

Also, we provide encrypted QR code for DAR number. It is difficult for any illegitimate person to make a duplicate QR code and sell their counterfeit drugs. This is mainly due to the fact that a duplicate encrypted QR code can be identified during the order confirmation process, and can also be verified later through the manufacturer's order management database.

5.3   Performance Analysis

Figure 8 shows the transaction cost in GAS (wei) for depot in-charge orders. Here we tested our server using 6 depot in-charge at a time. For placing the order we passed three strings. Those are order ID, depot in-charge email, and order status into the block and these are the results in total GAS (wei). For the first order the cost in GAS is 23008 wei and for second order the cost in gas is 22972 wei and total is 45980 wei and goes on [1 ether = 1018 wei (smallest denomination of ether)].

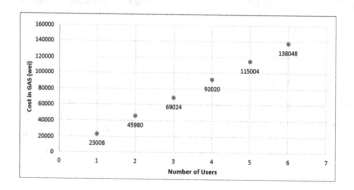

Fig. 8. Transaction cost for placing orders

When manufacturer or depot in-charge completes any order status transaction cost is fixed, that is 22276 wei. Here we passed two strings (order ID, order status) in the block. The order ID is the same ID which was created when users placed their order and for each order, order ID is unique.

Figure 9 shows the transaction confirmation table which is done by depot in-charge when he received ordered drugs and gave confirmation. We also tested it using 6 users (depot in-charge). Where the cost of first transaction is 24956 wei and cost of second and third transactions in wei are 24896 and 24908 and goes on. Total is 149664 GAS (wei).

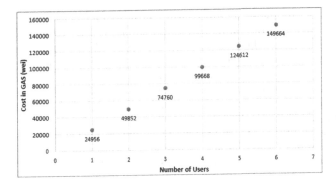

Fig. 9. Transaction cost for transaction or receive confirmation

6 Conclusion

In this paper, we have proposed a blockchain-enabled secure and transparent counterfeit drug detection platform. The platform enables tracing of drug delivery in the supply chain. By the decentralized network product authenticity is insured. This supply chain will build the trust between parties because only trusted parties can join the network and only trusted parties can interact with the system. Also, encrypted QR code reduces the chance of duplication of information and selling fake drugs thus guaranteeing drug safety. In future work, we aim to integrate end-to-end encryption for the decryption requests of QR codes from pharmacists. Moreover our platform can easily be expanded into a global drug supply chain framework.

References

1. Haq, I., Esuka, O.M.: Blockchain technology in pharmaceutical industry to prevent counterfeit drugs. Int. J. Comput. Appl. **180**(25), 8–12 (2018)
2. Ferdous, M.S., Sultana, J., Reza, M.S., Ahmed, S.: National Blockchain Strategy. Bangladesh (2020)
3. Kumar, R., Tripathi, R.: Traceability of counterfeit medicine supply chain through Blockchain. In: 2019 11th International Conference on Communication Systems and Networks (COMSNETS), pp. 568–570. IEEE, January 2019
4. Tseng, J.H., Liao, Y.C., Chong, B., Liao, S.W.: Governance on the drug supply chain via Gcoin blockchain. Int. J. Environ. Res. Public Health **15**(6), 1055 (2018)
5. Toyoda, K., Mathiopoulos, P.T., Sasase, I., Ohtsuki, T.: A novel blockchain-based product ownership management system (POMS) for anti-counterfeits in the post supply chain. IEEE Access **5**, 17465–17477 (2017)
6. Pascu, G.A., Hancu, G., Rusu, A.: Pharmaceutical serialization, a global effort to combat counterfeit medicines. Acta Marisiensis-Seria Medica **66**(4), 132–139 (2020)
7. Libert, B., Peters, T., Yung, M.: Group signatures with almost-for-free revocation. In: Safavi-Naini, R., Canetti, R. (eds.) CRYPTO 2012. LNCS, vol. 7417, pp. 571–589. Springer, Heidelberg (2012). https://doi.org/10.1007/978-3-642-32009-5_34

8. Mamtashanti, M., Rahul, J., Kashyap, T.: A review on regulatory requirements to prevent counterfeit drugs in India. Int. J. Pharm. Investig. **10**(3), 257–262 (2020)
9. Archa, Alangot, B., Achuthan, K.: Trace and track: enhanced pharma supply chain infrastructure to prevent fraud. In: International Conference on Ubiquitous Communications and Network Computing, pp. 189–195 (2019)
10. Saxena, N., Thomas, I., Gope, P., Burnap, P., Kumar, N.: PharmaCrypt: blockchain for critical pharmaceutical industry to counterfeit drugs. Computer **53**(7), pp. 29–44. IEEE (2020)
11. Singh, R., Dwivedi, A.D., Srivastava, G.: Internet of Things based blockchain for temperature monitoring and counterfeit pharmaceutical prevention. Sensors **20**(14), 3951 (2020). https://doi.org/10.3390/s20143951

Author Index

Printed in the United States
by Baker & Taylor Publisher Services